Teaching Middle School Writers

Other Books by Laura Robb . . .

Reading Strategy Lessons for Science and Social Studies (5–8)

Assessments for Differentiating Instruction

Differentiating Reading Instruction: How to Teach Reading to Meet the Needs of Each Student

Reading Strategies Toolkit: Nonfiction

Teaching Reading: A Differentiated Approach

Poems for Teaching in the Content Areas

Teaching Reading with Think Aloud Lessons

Nonfiction Writing: From the Inside Out

Brighten Up Boring Beginnings and Other Quick Writing Lessons

Literacy Links

Teaching Reading in Science, Social Studies, and Math

35 Must-Have Assessments and Record-Keeping Forms for Reading and Writing

Grammar Lessons and Strategies for Strengthening Student Writing

Redefining Staff Development

Teaching Reading in Middle School, Second Edition

Easy Mini-Lessons for Building Vocabulary

Reading Strategies That Work

Laura Robb

FOREWORD BY JIM BURKE

Teaching Middle School Writers

What Every English Teacher Needs to Know

HEINEMANN
Portsmouth, NH

Heinemann
361 Hanover Street
Portsmouth, NH 03801–3912
www.heinemann.com

Offices and agents throughout the world

The author and publisher wish to thank those who have generously given permission to reprint borrowed material:

"She Sweeps with Many-Colored Brooms"; "The Morns Are Weaker Than They Were"; and "His Bill An Auger Is" from *The Poems of Emily Dickinson* edited by Thomas H. Johnson. Copyright © 1951, 1955, 1979, 1983 by the President and Fellows of Harvard College. Published by Harvard University Press. Reprinted by permission of the publisher.

"Merry-Go-Round" from *The Collected Poems of Langston Hughes* by Langston Hughes, edited by Arnold Rampersad and David Roessel, Associate Editor. Copyright © 1995. Published by Random House, Inc. Reprinted by permission of the publisher.

"Jigs" and "Hoop Lessons" from *Connecting Dots: Poems of My Journey* by David L. Harrison. Text copyright © 2004 by David L. Harrison. Published by Wordsong, an imprint of Boyds Mills Press, Inc. Reprinted by permission of Boyds Mills Press, Inc.

"Funeral" from *Marshfield Dreams: When I Was a Kid* by Ralph Fletcher. Copyright © 2005 by Ralph Fletcher. Published by Henry Holt and Company, LLC. Reprinted by permission of the publisher and Marian Reiner.

Library of Congress Cataloging-in-Publication Data
Robb, Laura.
    Teaching middle school writers : what every English teacher needs to know / Laura Robb.
        p. cm.
    Includes bibliographical references and index.
    ISBN-13: 978-0-325-02657-2
    ISBN-10: 0-325-02657-2
    1. English language—Composition and exercises—Study and teaching (Middle school).   I. Title.
    LB1631.R539 2010
        808'.0420712—dc22   2009052338

Editor: Wendy Murray
Production: Elizabeth Valway
Cover and interior designs: Night & Day Design
Inside cover photography: Bonnie Jacobs
DVD production/direction: Kevin Carlson
Composition and interior design: House of Equations, Inc.
Manufacturing: Steve Bernier

Printed in the United States of America on acid-free paper
14 13 12 11 10   ML   1 2 3 4 5

*With deep appreciation and thanks to all the
students and teachers who made this book possible.*

*With love to Wendy Murray and Ann Tobias,
who were powerful forces behind this book.*

Contents

Foreword...ix

Acknowledgments..xi

Introduction...xiii

Chapter 1: Narrowing the Gulf Between Writing for School and Writing for Self ... 1

Chapter 2: Improving Students' Creative and Analytic Writing...................... 34

Chapter 3: Using Mentor Texts to Arrive at Compelling Reasons to Write 62

Chapter 4: Making Powerful Writing Happen Day to Day: Routines that Work ...103

Chapter 5: Making Powerful Writing Happen Day to Day: Lessons that Work 124

Chapter 6: Setting Criteria, Revising, and Editing...................................157

Chapter 7: Conferring: Answering Middle Schoolers' Need to Collaborate 198

Chapter 8: Writing Conferences in Action 220

Chapter 9: Analytical Exchanges Online: Blogs and Beyond........................253

Conclusion: Making It Your Own 285

A Statistical Analysis of the National Survey.....................................291

Appendices

A. Katherine Paterson's Writing Plans for *Bridge to Terabithia*......................301

B. Jean Van Leeuwen's Writing Plans for *Cabin on Trouble Creek*..................306

Works Cited 313

Index 321

On the DVD

Footage of student interviews about their out-of-school writing, two mentor text lessons, and editable reproducible form files.

Classroom Resources

- Interview Questions About Writing

- Ten Questions About Writing

- The Survey

- Sample Letter to Parents About the Writing Curriculum

- Ideas for Web-Based Collaborative Writing

- Some Criteria for Editing and Evaluating Nonfiction, Fiction, and Poetry

- Letter to Parents About Blogging

- Sample Blogger's Contract

- Using a Wiki

- Picture Books for Exploring Compelling Issues

- Content and Style Questions that Support Revising

- Questions that Help Students Edit for Writing Conventions

- Editing Symbols

- Status of the Class Form

- Peer Evaluation

- Self-Evaluation

- Writing Conference Form

- Write and Perform a Readers Theater Script

Teaching Take-Aways: Tips for Success

- Ten Tips for Interviewing Students About Their Writing Lives

- Tips for Dynamic Mentor Text Lessons

- Tips for Conferring with Writers

Foreword

This is a remarkable book you hold in your hands. By the time I finished reading it I had already become a better writing teacher, for this book not only told me things I didn't know about adolescent writers but gave me permission, thanks to one of our country's great teachers, to think differently about what I should be doing with those writers. Laura Robb's book has the feeling of a classified document smuggled out of the teen nation about their writing lives both in and, most importantly, outside of school. And this top-secret information, this remarkable intelligence she has gathered comes not a minute too soon, for we are in the midst of a great crisis when it comes to writing instruction.

As Arthur Applebee and Judith Langer have reported, their national survey of writing instruction reveals several trends that Laura Robb's book addresses in very substantial ways. Two trends in particular are of great concern: the place and purpose of writing in the classroom in an environment that is increasingly focused on reading instruction to the exclusion of all else; and the emphasis on those forms of writing most appropriate to state tests. While Applebee and Langer have been conducting their major study, Laura Robb has been running her own, asking over 1500 kids from all backgrounds throughout the country just what type of writing they have been doing. Her findings are fascinating—and important, for she translates these findings into practice for us under the recurring header that reads "How This Information Affects Our Teaching."

I am also grateful for the example Laura provides: She's still learning, refining, questioning. She attacks this book with the passionate curiosity of the middle school kids she has taught these many years. This is not a book that looks backward and laments; rather, it is a book that looks forward and laughs and leaps at what she discovers: nine in ten students surveyed here do some sort of writing outside of school, and about subjects that matter to them! As Laura says, many teachers complain they have no time to have kids write at school, or to take the time to teach it given all the other demands these days. Well, Laura Robb is here to help you find that time, to show you what you can do to bring writing back into the heart of the language arts class where it belongs. She gives you lessons on using mentor texts, style, grammar, revision, and editing so you can see how harmoniously giving students choice and responsibility sits within familiar classroom structures.

Laura has listened to teachers as intently as she has listened to adolescents, because she answers so many questions middle school teachers have about minilessons, scaffolding student practice, what works for struggling writers—she makes it clear how it all fits day to day, week to week. As if this weren't all enough, we find her humor and humanity on every page, cheering us all on, undaunted by the reforms from above, giving us all the courage we need to be the teachers she will, through this book, help us become.

—Jim Burke

Acknowledgments

My deepest thanks to my editor, Wendy Murray, and my agent, Ann Tobias, for believing in this book and for their ongoing encouragement. I have loved every moment of this project, mainly because it connected me with amazing teachers and students in schools throughout the United States.

I want to thank those teachers and supervisors who helped me reach the diverse classrooms of the students who completed the writing survey that I discuss in Chapter 1. Several other teachers gave me so much of their time. Some, like Cheri Kesler, Gwen Malone, Ann Robb, Katie Schain, and Jenny Smith, invited me in to teach their students. They also made themselves available to chat on the telephone and via email.

In addition, I met teachers through workshops who willingly shared their expertise and their students' work. Teachers such as Andrew Frye, Leslee Cassel-Bonilla, Liza Medina, and Carolyn Tedesco allowed me to correspond by email until I had clarified my thoughts. To all these dedicated classroom teachers, you have my respect and my admiration for your work, forever. This book wouldn't be what it is without you.

To the amazing administrators who support my work in your schools—what a privilege to work with you. Special thanks to John Lathrop, head of Powhatan School; Diana Jabis, principal of Suffern Middle School; Evan Robb, principal of Johnson Williams Middle School; and Dori Walk, Assistant Superintendent of Staunton City Public Schools.

My aim for this book was to approach teaching writing from the angle that matters most: the students' perspective. Their advice, thoughts, and writing create the beat throughout these pages. They taught me what I needed to know to make this book live up to their passion for writing. Thank you for confiding in me about your personal writing lives and your writing lives at school.

My sincere thanks go to Dr. Larry Hembroff, who spearheaded the analysis of the national survey (see pages 291–300) and researcher Dr. Nell K. Duke, who provided excellent feedback on my first chapter.

When the poet John Donne wrote, "No man is an island," I believe that he was pointing out the social nature and needs of humankind. Those five words, however, apply to those of us who write books about teaching and learning. Besides the multiple contributions of students, teachers, and researchers, others inch a book toward its publishable form. First, the feedback from my editor, Wendy Murray, propelled the manuscript to a level that I could never reach on my own. Wendy, my thanks for always being there for me and for caring so much about this book. Three writing teachers also read the book and provided me with notes that enabled me to make passages clearer and to add information they thought would benefit teachers. My thanks to Barry Gilmore, Gretchen Bernabai, and Ben Kovacs for taking hours of their time to read and provide thoughtful and insightful comments and suggestions. To Kevin Carlson, a talented and dedicated videographer, my thanks for capturing lessons, conferences, and interviews with students with such a fine instinct for the richest, right moments in a classroom.

And finally, special thanks to my husband, Lloyd, who has always supported my writing by understanding the long hours it takes to write a book.

Introduction

Like you, I teach adolescents. Middle school is my true love as a teacher. I know the pressures you're under to develop students' writing skill so that all students can pass the state tests, from those children who struggle to the ones who write with ease. In *Teaching Middle School Writers*, I show you an approach to instruction that combines your need to improve student writing with the adolescents' pull to express themselves and discover, "Who am I?" I tapped into middle schoolers' current concerns in several ways, including interviews, email exchanges, a questionnaire, and a national survey— giving me insight into well over a thousand students' writing lives. Getting to know the middle school students we teach and their love and knowledge of twenty-first-century technology has enabled me to create lessons, routines, and learning needs that capture their passion for communicating with others and with themselves.

At the same time, *keep it real for teachers* was my mantra. That is, keep it all classroom-centered, rooted in your curriculum. So in the chapters that follow you'll find writing research recommendations in the action of day-to-day teaching; ideas for heightening student engagement that worked in real middle school settings; and new literacy approaches for improving students' writing anchored in fundamental craft, grammar, revision, and editing lessons. Similarly, I strive to bring the spirit and benefits of a process-oriented writing workshop to your writing classes while staying mindful of the writing-to-prompts culture entrenched in middle schools. I know in my heart and in my practice we can have it all—that we teach skills while helping middle school students write about their interests and what they care about.

Teaching Middle School Writers will help you develop a writing curriculum that is both current and classic. I developed each chapter by drawing from four zones of knowledge: (1) research, (2) teachers' realities, (3) students' feedback, and (4) my own teaching experiences. As teachers, we balance information from these different zones and become better teachers by asking ourselves questions about what each zone has to offer us. We never stop learning.

In the sections that follow, I briefly describe each of the four zones, opening by sharing the questions that galvanized my thinking as I wrote this book.

1. Research

Where will this book take me if I dare to marry the work of researchers, theoreticians, and the pleas of teenagers who want to engage in school writing but can't?

The writing instruction I describe reflects the developmental needs of adolescents and the work of contemporary theorists about the human mind such as Daniel Pink and Howard Gardner, researchers on struggling writers such as Steve Graham and Dolores Perin, to name a few, as well as the findings of a national survey of students in grades 5–8.

How this information helps you: This book shows that the practices that work for struggling writers sit beautifully within the writing process, and the reasons students write at home can be used to empower writing for school. And so, in exploring ways to tap into students' real modes of writing, we're creating a win-win scenario for preparing them for their lives as adults.

2. Teachers' Realities

How might I write this book so teachers come away with the lessons on craft and technique students need as well as the "edgier" ideas on engaging adolescents?

Middle school teacher's schedules, responsibilities, and the realities of our testing culture inform my approach. I believe we can all be amazing writing teachers but too many of us give up because we aren't given the space and time and permission to take on new approaches gradually. Middle school writing instruction needn't be either prompt-driven or full-tilt workshop; we've got to define a dynamic middle ground where many teachers are comfortable or we risk shortchanging our students.

How this information helps you: This book shows how to use writing process within an approach that also works outside the writing workshop model. A lot of the heavy lifting is done with mentor texts—highly compelling picture books, novels, poetry, and nonfiction that hit adolescents' where they live in terms of themes, while providing beautiful models of craft, sentence structure, and all the ingredients that make up writing skills.

3. Adolescents' Writing Needs

How might I advance the need for student choice about writing topics by coming at it from a teen-centric angle? That is, might giving students more choice catch on in schools if enough teachers heard for themselves how make-or-break this factor is for students' writing achievement?

The feedback of thousands of middle schoolers informs and infuses this book. Listen to teens speak about their private writing lives on the DVD and read about what engages and motivates them in each chapter. The overarching goal of this book is to narrow the gulf between students' writing lives outside of school and in school.

How this information helps you: This book shows you how to discover your adolescent writers' interests and learning needs with questionnaires, routines, compelling topics, and other practical approaches. In each chapter I provide explicit ways to merge students' passions with the themes and skills we need to cover in our curriculum. Again, students and teacher alike can thrive in a middle ground between what matters in life and the demands of the curriculum.

4. My Own Teaching

How do I write a book so that teachers of all experience levels will learn from it?

My current teaching and interactions with teachers and adolescents informed these lessons and routines. For teachers who are just beginning to teach writing in a more process-oriented way, I know they need to see what it looks like at the beginning. In fact, when you watch the minilessons on the DVD, you will see that I chose to work with classes that had a broad range of students, from learning disabled and special education to gifted, and students for whom talking about writing was a new experience.

How this information helps you: This book shows teachers who may not themselves be "writerly" how to develop a rewarding, rigorous writing program. It offers choices from the lessons and routines that I have found to be most powerful so that teachers don't feel overwhelmed by trying to transform their approach all at once.

Different Ways to Use This Book

Read It On Your Own

There is nothing like learning with others but I personally like to sit in a cozy spot, highlighter in one hand, mug of tea in another, and read to learn.

Read It as a Group

Organize a professional study group in your school, or simply pair up and discuss it with a best-buddy colleague. I think some of the most powerful writing instruction occurs when we take a locally grown approach to improving writing instruction. That is, we learn how to teach writing largely by discussing our students' pieces and together, we develop insights and criteria for what makes their writing work and discover ways to support them. At the end of each chapter you'll find specific guidelines and ideas for professional study focused on students' writing. Professional study sections show you how to study the writing of students you teach to provide them with helpful feedback and to develop a specific focus for a conference. I include guidelines, questions to pose as you study student's work, and suggestions to make your meetings with colleagues meaningful and productive. You can also use the study guide on www.heinemann.com to guide chapter by chapter reflection.

Watch the DVD

The brief video segments feature writing lessons using mentor texts and teacher-student conferences with middle schoolers who were new to these processes. So many teachers tell me they often feel too intimidated to try what they see on professional videos because the teachers and students are so expert. The interviews with students about the gulf between writing at home and writing for school can make for rich conversations with colleagues about teaching writing—where you all are, where you want to go.

Try the Lessons

Throughout the book, you'll find concrete lessons with specific guidelines that you can use and adapt to your students' needs immediately.

Lessons on Grammar that Improve Writing

Lessons that address repairing run-on sentences, using prepositional phrases and subordinate clauses to vary sentence openings, and transforming passive into active voice deepen students' knowledge of grammar as they practice using their understanding to bring energy and relevance to their writing.

Routines that Set Expectations for Writing

For each piece of writing, you'll see how easy it is to negotiate criteria, or writing standards for content, style, and writing conventions, with your students. Criteria are organic and grow out of your lessons and what students can do. Using criteria, students revise and edit before you read a paper, easing your work load. With criteria, you have guidelines for commenting on students' writing and grading their work.

Conferring that Cultivates Independence

In addition to suggestions for you to hold, manage, and keep records of short, focused-on-one-topic conferences, I show you how to turn conferring over to pairs or small groups of students. When students confer, they ease your teaching, especially when you meet with four to five different classes daily.

Intensified Writing Instruction— It's Yours for the Taking

I want this book to be a living document in the sense that the fresh insights from students in a dozen states as well as my discussion reenergize you to look at your teaching of writing with a new awareness. As I said at the outset, this book is for you. You've got the power to gain insight into what motivates middle school students to write at high levels. And I know you can make this happen.

CHAPTER 1

Narrowing the Gulf Between Writing for School and Writing for Self

"You'll never know unless you ask!" my friends often say when I wonder aloud about whether or not to seek answers to something that piques my interest.

And what a curious, wonderful thing it is to have more than forty-five years of experience teaching middle school students, and yet still hunger to solve the mystery of what makes them tick, how to teach them best. For years I knew much about their outside-of-school reading lives, but their writing lives outside of school? I'd never "gone there" in a concerted way until recently.

As readers, adolescents have always happily surprised me with the strength of their opinions, genre jags, and taste in authors. I know they like series books, magazines,

Fan fiction describes stories that students write independently or in small groups using the characters of favorite books, movies, manga, TV shows, video games, and so on. You can go to www .fanfiction.net and browse a varied menu.

reading manga online, video game novels, and narrative video games. I would always know when they'd stay up late to finish a book because they'd come in groggy but proud. I've always loved to stand by and watch the word-of-mouth campaign around a series like the *Underland Chronicles* by Suzanne Collins or the *Sisterhood of the Traveling Pants* by Ann Brashares, or around the graphic novel series based on Rod Serling's *The Twilight Zone*, adapted by Mark Kneece. Over the years I've seen authors and series that flash bright as a comet for a season and then fall from view, and titles like Avi's *Nothing but the Truth,* which I knew would survive through dog-eared copies for years to come.

But the window on students' writing lives flew wide open much more recently. I was taking place in a discussion at a Midwestern middle school about informational writing, when a seventh-grade boy commented that he liked to draw race car designs. He opened his notebook and showed them to me. I marveled at all the knowledge of cars that went into those drawings, not to mention his obvious passion.

"Wow, do you do have other drawings?" I asked.

"My notebooks are filled with designs," he replied.

I spontaneously turned to others in the group and asked, "What kinds of writing do you do at home?" I discovered that the girls wrote fan fiction, kept journals, blogged, texted, and wrote stories—completely apart from school. The two boys in the group blogged and texted to stay in touch with friends. One boy designed sailboats, labeled his drawings, and wrote about the aerodynamic features.

"Do your teachers know about this?" I asked. Students confessed that none of their teachers knew about this writing. No teacher had ever asked them. When I left school that day, I felt as though the ground had shifted beneath my feet. But it wasn't until Heinemann invited me to write a book on middle school writers that the exchange with kids about their "secret" writing lives fully hit me. I couldn't get over the under-the-radar quality of their writing lives outside of school. Once I began working on the book, that seventh grader's race car drawings, the look of pride on his face, and the excited voices of his classmates sent me on a quest to understand more about what motivates middle school students to write.

My research started via email. I interviewed five seventh graders and nine eighth graders in Virginia and New York, some of whom I had taught, some of whom I had never met; their teachers introduced us on email. Out of these fourteen students, four boys and ten girls corresponded with me about their writing and answered "Ten Questions

About Writing." I invited an equal number of boys and girls to email me answers to the questions. The boys agreed to complete the questions, but even with two or three reminders, most of them did not finish the task. In contrast, all ten girls responded—a first glimmer of gender differences that I'd see even more dramatically in a later survey. From their answers, I learned that all but two of the students texted their friends and sometimes their family. Everyone wrote on a blog and emailed family outside of school. The girls loved writing fan fiction with a friend or a small group. Not surprisingly, texting was the preferred mode of communication of the seventh and eighth graders.

What I discovered, however, is that texting hasn't replaced other modes of writing, as adults often fear. All of these students still wrote stories, poems, and kept journals to vent their feelings and write about experiences with friends. Their responses demonstrated a passion for writing and an active outside-of-school writing life. For instance, here are some of their answers to my question "What kinds of things do you like to write outside of school or at home?"

> I like to write little stories. But usually I am working on my novel. When I can't think of something to write in my novel, I write a random story for practice, just to get my brain working. I also write in a diary. (AMANDA, GRADE 7)
>
> I like to write mysteries and stories about animals. (KAROLINA, GRADE 7)
>
> I write detective stories with lots of chapters. (KEVIN, GRADE 8)
>
> I like writing about my experiences and about sports. (MICHAEL, GRADE 8)
>
> I write poems every night right after I finish my homework. (ASHLEIGH, GRADE 8)
>
> I write stories and poems. I draw pictures of birds and animals. (THOMAS, GRADE 8)

Now, consider how these same students answered this question: "What do you like best about writing?" Their responses illustrate a *strong* desire to communicate feelings and ideas. They seem compelled to write not because they are required to do so for an assignment but because they want to express themselves and make sense of their lives.

> There are so many things I like! Mostly it's the way writing gets my feelings out. It makes me feel refreshed. It's a way of expressing myself, and makes me feel proud of myself. When I write something really

great, and share it with a parent, and their eyes start to tear, I can't even explain how that makes me feel. I feel like I've changed someone, like I've given someone a different perspective on life. (AMANDA, GRADE 7)

I like to express my feelings through stories. It helps me understand myself and things that happen. (KAROLINA, GRADE 7)

It gives me something fun to do at home. I love mysteries and forensics. Writing them is like entertaining myself. (KEVIN, GRADE 8)

I can show my experiences and tell others what I like to do. (MICHAEL, GRADE 8)

Writing poems is who I am. I find out more about friendships, what's happening to the earth, why I like or dislike things. I have to write every day. (ASHLEIGH, GRADE 8)

I didn't always write at home. Now it's a way for me to think about what's happening in my life, to understand it better. (THOMAS, GRADE 8)

These responses were heartening. At the risk of sounding sentimental, they gave me faith in the human spirit. These adolescents' urge to communicate, their need to show and share their emotions and perceptions with friends and family, and the natural way they seem to roam through various genres reminded me that writing is a need as much as it is a craft. And their honesty and intensity strengthened my sense that middle school is a time when writing is a more central, more steadying need of adolescents than many educators have recognized.

When I showed these initial responses to my editor, Wendy Murray, she said, "Let's run with this; let's find out more." She wanted a bigger sampling of evidence to inform this book, so we contacted literacy researcher and author Nell Duke, who recommended Dr. Larry Hembroff, a statistician at Michigan State University. He signed on to help me interpret the findings from the surveys that I would send to students in grades 5 through 8 in diverse areas of the United States.

At the same time students were completing the national survey, I also invited three hundred students in New York, Virginia, and Ohio to respond to the "Ten Questions About Writing" so that I'd have an additional pool of knowledge to inform my thinking.

The national survey brings credibility and validity to the anecdotal evidence about middle school writers that I collected more informally. It brings color and contour to this book, and it will make you smile as you recognize your own students, your own insights. It also represents a level of qualitative research we need to keep doing and promoting in order to keep education, research about education, and professional development teacher-centered and focused on proving the effectiveness of the reading, writing, and thinking practices that matter.

Designing the Survey

I quickly learned that constructing the national survey was a challenging task, especially if I hoped to collect useful data. With suggestions from Nell Duke, and a chapter called "Survey Research" (Baumann and Bason 2004) at my side, I wrote the survey so that each statement measured one behavior, one attitude. Without this distinction, it would have been impossible to know and track which idea students had in mind when they formed their response. For example, I needed to divide a statement such as "I enjoy writing about my feelings in a journal outside of school" into two statements:

> I enjoy writing in a journal outside of school.
>
> I write about my feelings in my journal.

1. I enjoy writing in a journal outside of school.
   1   2   3   4   5
2. In my journal, I write about my feelings.
   1   2   3   4   5
3. In my journal, I write about my experiences.
   1   2   3   4   5
4. Writing in my journal helps me think about my life.
   1   2   3   4   5
5. I respond to blogs outside of school.
   1   2   3   4   5
6. I write stories outside of school.
   1   2   3   4   5
7. I write poems outside of school.
   1   2   3   4   5
8. I write e-mails to friends outside of school.
   1   2   3   4   5
9. I text to friends outside of school.
   1   2   3   4   5
10. I write letters outside of school.
    1   2   3   4   5

Figure 1.1 When we harness the power of adolescents' personal writing, their writing in school takes off.

The final survey contained thirty-four statements and addressed writing in and outside of school. I sent surveys to five teachers I knew and seven I did not know. The teachers were located in twelve states. The survey packet included a letter requesting that, as much as possible, the teachers ask an equal amount of male and female students to complete the survey. In that letter I also suggested that they review with students the choices for responding to each statement before students completed the survey. Surveys were administered to mixed ability and culturally diverse groups: African American, Asian American, Hispanic American, and Anglo American. These groups consisted of struggling, grade-level, and above-grade-level students; the sample also included 175 special education students who learned in regular classrooms.

The survey included students from diverse cultural and economic backgrounds. They attended urban, suburban, and rural schools. Here are the twelve states that participated in the survey:

California	Michigan
Colorado	New York
Florida	Ohio
Kentucky	Vermont
Massachusetts	Virginia
North Carolina	New York

Table 1.1 lists the students by grade and gender.

Although 1501 students responded, not all of them checked one of the gender boxes; this accounts for the discrepancy. We discarded the data from students who did not identify their gender.

The survey gives us a great deal to reflect on. We can also draw quite accurate inferences from it—inferences that can show us how we might teach writing more effectively.

Table 1.1 Grade and Gender of Students

Grade	Male	Female	Total
5	154	147	301
6	208	179	387
7	189	187	376
8	164	148	312
Total	724	668	1392

We can make such inferences with assuredness because of the large number of survey questions and the fact that more than one thousand students answered the survey. In other words, the students' responses add up to "enough" to make them accurate, not just a matter of chance. You'll find a detailed analysis of the survey on pages 291–300.

What the Survey Unveiled

I'm a classroom teacher and not a statistician! In fact, I must confess that when I first leafed through the stack of charts, graphs, and written interpretations related to the survey that Dr. Hembroff sent, I shoved them into the envelope and buried them under a stack of young adult books in my office. The challenge was too great for me to deal with at that moment. But two days later, like the lion in *The Wonderful Wizard of Oz*, I mustered all my courage and set aside three hours to pore through the material. There were terms I had not used since I completed the statistics class that was a requirement for my master's degree. Over the next six weeks I relearned those terms, pored over the material, and chatted with Dr. Hembroff. Finally I began to understand the survey's implications for us classroom teachers.

You can see the survey's statistical results on pages 291–300. For the rest of this chapter, I'll explore the key findings the survey unveiled about middle school writers and how this information might influence your teaching. But make no mistake about it: although the survey certainly brings clout, its import will only matter if I—and in turn you—apply it to your teaching. In some curious way it needs to mesh quickly with all that we currently do and think about teaching adolescent writers in order for it to have staying power. With that in mind, as I discuss each of the seven categories from the survey, I include stories from my teaching life and comments by middle school students. These stories and comments were my beacon, they connected me to the data. My hope is that the stories will do the same for you, and that you and your colleagues will have conversations that bring your own stories to each category to deepen your understanding of teaching middle school writers.

Writing Outside of School

It's the second week of school and this is my first meeting with Mrs. Gold (a pseudonym), a ninth-grade teacher who has three sections of reading and writing for students who struggle. After school, on a library table, we spread out dozens of her students' responses to the "Ten Questions About Writing" questionnaire. Again and again, we read comments such as: "I hate to write," "I always fail, so why bother?" and "I have nothing to say."

The Seven Categories

The thirty-four questions fell into these seven categories.

1. Writing outside of school
2. Writing in journals
3. Blogging
4. Writing at school
5. Teachers' attitudes about writing
6. Writing on computers or by hand
7. Writing about books

I chose these areas because I wanted to include both home and school writing, and I wanted to find out not only about writing content but also about the vehicles for the students' written communication (email, texting, and so forth). Today more than at any other time, content and mode are enmeshed. Today's students have many more choices for communication than students who grew up during the paper and pen era, and we won't get to know them as writers unless we begin to contemplate their motivations, modes, and the implications of the digital age on writing audience, purpose, and genre.

Mrs. Gold taps my hand and points to a young man who is writing on a computer. "David's the one who wrote 'Why Bother?' and didn't respond to any question," she whispers. We watch him. He pauses periodically to read, then writes a stream of text. Fifteen minutes pass, and the writing and reading continues. When Mrs. Gold asks David what he is doing, he says, "I always blog after school." Over several days, Mrs. Gold graded papers after school in the library and observed that six other writers who struggled in class blogged on a computer after school.

Mrs. Gold's observations that week were in step with what I was discovering through my interviews and email correspondence with students in New York and Virginia. Students were doing a lot more writing outside of school than their teachers knew. Later, I would interview middle school students at Johnson Williams Middle School in

 Berryville, Virginia, about their writing lives outside of school, and what students said was astoundingly consistent (see the DVD segment entitled "Students Speak Out on Writing"). They talked about writing stories, drawing and writing, emailing, and writing on blogs. Romance, humor, mysteries—stories

Two and three asterisks mean that it's highly unlikely that chance had anything to do with the results. Three asterisks are even more unlikely than two.

Writing Outside of School
% of students who write outside of class by type of writing
(agree or strongly agree to . . .)

	% of All Students	5th	6th	7th	8th	9th		Males	Females	
Writing in a journal (Q1)	30.5%	38.5	28.9	25.6	31.0	25.4	**	16.9	46.3	***
Respond to blogs	24.1%	18.6	21.6	30.7	24.7	22.5	**	22.6	26.5	NS
Write stories	37.3%	45.2	43.0	34.4	27.9	33.8	***	29.2	46.8	***
Write poems	22.4%	19.7	23.0	22.2	23.3	27.1	NS	11.5	33.9	***
Write email to friends	62.1%	45.0	61.2	72.1	69.1	52.1	***	55.3	71.2	***
Text friends	63.2%	43.6	58.1	75.4	71.9	66.2	***	57.5	69.1	***
Write letters	36.2%	39.0	38.6	34.5	35.5	22.5	NS	25.0	49.8	***
Do at least one of the above	**89.4%**	**83.6**	**89.5**	**93.2**	**92.0**	**85.9**	***	**84.1**	**96.6**	***
Do 3 or more of the above	**47.0%**	**44.6**	**47.4**	**46.8**	**50.7**	**40.8**	NS	**29.7**	**66.9**	***

Nine out of ten students engage in some type of writing outside of class.

Figure 1.2 A large number of students write outside of school.

from an array of genres were written for an array of reasons, from B.J., who was going to give his father a funny story for his birthday, to Jorge, who says writing peels stress away because when he's deep into writing, stressful feelings leave.

Pertinent Survey Highlights

Now take a look at these results from the survey:

- Nine out of ten students do some kind of outside-of-school writing. The number drops dramatically to five out of ten for students who do three or more different kinds of writing outside of school (see Figure 1.2).
- More girls do three or more types of writing outside of school than boys.
- Seven out of ten students who write outside of school have not told their teachers about their outside-of-school writing lives.
- Students who have a teacher who encourages them to write in school are likely to write outside of school.

Kinds of Writing Surveyed
- Journals
- Blogs
- Stories
- Poems
- Emails to friends
- Texts to friends
- Letters

How This Information Affects Our Teaching

I invite you to ask your students to tell you about their writing lives. Use the "Ten Questions About Writing" form on the DVD or pose your own questions. If some students don't want to answer your questions on paper, meet with them one-on-one to explore their attitudes about writing. Give them time to think. Chances are, they may not speak up readily. If they have developed negative feelings about writing, see if you can discover why. Continue to build trust so you can develop meaningful writing opportunities for them, and find out the kind of support they need. Dare to ask them the questions that will help you know what they enjoy and are willing to do as writers.

Writing in Journals

I can still hear Kevin, Stephanie, and Brian telling me that when they have free journal writing at school, they're "loving it." Kevin explains, "*Free* means we get to choose the topics." As I read over dozens of emails and interviews, I was struck by the students' fondness for journal writing, and the almost desperate need to decide what to write about. Journals are students' sounding boards, confidants, places for them to vent anger, declare love, sort out their place in the social universe, or plan their future.

Ellie's mom is ill and she's angry at the world and scared her mom will die. She shows me an entry that she plans to turn into a letter to her mom. "My mom has cancer. She's been in the hospital three weeks," she says. Her voice is chipper, like she's just telling me her mom's on a business trip.

After I read her entry I say, "Ellie, first of all, I'm sorry. I bet you miss her and that it's really, really hard for her to be away from you now."

Ellie's face shows sadness "Why her?" she blurts out, on the verge of crying. "She's the person I turn to when I need advice. How long will I have her?"

I put a comforting arm around Ellie and say, "I'm hoping you'll have her for a long time. But I also know that if you turn these journal notes into a letter to her, your mom will feel your love and how much you miss her. That can help her fight and get well."

The next day, Ellie arrives in class early. "I wrote it," she tells me. "And mailed it last night. Dad thought Mom will love it."

"I bet she will," I say.

Scott does not write about his feelings. Instead, his journal chronicles soccer games and his yearning to be an astronaut. He jots plans to go to "space camp in the summer and visit Cape Canaveral to watch a rocket roar into space." I've seen a lot of students both like Ellie and Scott. I've noticed that many middle school students stay largely on the surface in journals—more like Scott's style—recording whom they talked to, what they ate, even the exact time they woke up and went to bed. When I look at the tonal range, from intimacy to matter-of-factness, what the responses all have in common to me is the adolescents' need to try to control, to make sense of things, to curb their anxiety.

Pertinent Survey Highlights

The survey results mirrored what I'd been seeing on my own: journal writing is important because so many kids seem to like it, and the nature of girls' and boys' journal writing differs. Here and throughout, some intriguing gender differences crop up:

- Students who write in journals write about their feelings, their experiences, and their daily lives.
- More than twice as many girls (67.3 percent) write about their feelings in journals than boys (30.3 percent). Boys tend to write about their lives.
- Both girls and boys use journals to think about their lives.
- Students who write in journals also write stories, poems, and letters.
- Students who write on blogs also write emails to friends and are more likely to text.

How This Information Affects Our Teaching

It's clear to me that there are gender differences when it comes to writing motivation, writing topics, and the genres students choose. I shy away from making any hard and fast conclusions that can be taken too literally in practice, but for me one clear takeaway is that the difference between what girls and boys tend to write about in their home journals can help us temper our expectations of what students share in the writer's notebooks where they collect ideas for writing topics, and in their home journals.

We can also ramp up the *amount* of free writing opportunities we give them because journal writing, it's fair to say, is pretty well received by students. We ought to encourage students to use this writing time in and out of school to find topics they care about, ideas they might want to transform into a story or a poem. It's useful to remember that students enjoy blogging, texting, and emailing because it emboldens us to weave these twenty-first-century literacies into our curriculum (see Chapter 9). We have to stop seeing these formats as non-school kinds of writing and instead bring their powerful social properties into our classroom writing.

Writing on Blogs

Like David, Mrs. Gold's student who wrote his blog after school in the library, many students are enthusiastic about blogging. When I consider writing on blogs, the image of Mrs. Gold observing students blog in the library pops into my mind. The students' comments demonstrated how meaningful blogging is to middle school writers.

> Blogging keeps me in touch with world issues. (CHRISTA, GRADE 8)
>
> I love to blog in school with classmates about issues and questions we ask. It's like having conversations with fifteen people at once. I have to think fast. (THOMAS, GRADE 8)

Not only does blogging invite students to post their opinions about topics, issues, local and world news, but it also demands quick processing of reading and fast thinking for responding.

Pertinent Survey Highlights

The survey showed that students in grades 7 and 8 blogged a great deal more than those in grades 5 and 6.

- About half the students surveyed write on blogs at home and/or in school.
- At school, students used blogs to write about books they read and respond to questions on diverse topics that the teacher or peers posed.

How This Information Affects Our Teaching

Writing on blogs, emailing, and texting friends are high on middle school students' writing agendas. We might easily say that because students blog so much at home, they don't need to do it in school. But I have found that establishing a class blog is an excellent way for students to find topics for journal writing, have quick conversations, and engage in writing and posting book reviews (see Chapter 9). Once your students experience enthusiasm for and success with writing on a class blog, I encourage you to confer with them and try to channel their positive experiences to other writing genres.

Writing at School

"Writing in school makes me feel better," Olivia, a sixth grader, told me during a conference. "I can try out ideas on friends and get help from them and the teacher. I love it when I can choose my topic."

    Like Olivia, eighth-grade students I emailed and interviewed spoke to the fact that writing at school was important and meaningful to them.

> My favorite kind of writing at school is when I can write a play with my group and we get to perform it. (THOMAS)
>
> Sitting by myself and writing poems in my head is the best. (NED)
>
> Getting to write my story every day—I look forward to that. Time every day for writing is the best. (HALEY)

Figure 1.3 A class blog captures the social nature of writing.

> Photo essays. I love them. I can surf the Internet for images. I spread them out on the floor and choose the ones I'll use. (SEAN)
>
> Having time to stare out the window and think and not having a teacher think I'm not doing anything. (KALEIGH)
>
> When I'm stuck, talking about my story to Haley. (ADDISON)
>
> Daydreaming about my characters—I do it in writing class and other classes. (JESSICA)

Students' comments showed me variations on what they consider writing at school. Their words also reveal how deep and diverse their feelings are, from wanting to think and write alone to preferring to work with peers. When teachers create safe and nurturing writing time and spaces, we help students find topics they believe in and want to pursue.

Pertinent Survey Highlights

The surveys support Olivia's comments. The data indicates a strong connection between how students feel about writing and the kinds of feedback they receive at school.

- Students who are allowed to choose their writing topics usually agree that writing at school is relevant to their lives.
- Students who write to prompts are not likely to feel that writing at school is a positive experience.
- One statement from the survey, "My teacher tries to find out what kind of help I need as a writer," correlated or connected positively to these statements: "I see myself as a good writer." "I have a trusting relationship with at least one teacher at school." "I find writing at school a positive experience." "Writing at school is relevant to my life."

How This Information Affects Our Teaching

The survey sends us a strong message: students want to choose their own topics. Watch the four-minute interviews with middle school students on the DVD. Better yet, play them to an administrator who doubts that student choice is all that important. We've known about the need for students to choose their own topics from the research of Donald Murray, Donald Graves, Tom Newkirk, Penny Kittle, and many others, and yet it's as though someone lifted the ship's anchor in the night and schools drifted away from honoring this truth. The students on the video are so articulate and in unison on this point, it's like hearing a Greek chorus bringing the truth home. Choice can develop a commitment to a topic because students care about it—sometimes are passionate about it. Of course, choice doesn't mean we never assign topics or never have students write in ways more deliberately in line with what they will be expected to do on the state tests.

"There's no time for my students to write at school," teachers tell me. Many have only forty-five minutes to teach both reading and writing. I empathize with their frustration. Still, it's possible to rethink scheduling reading and writing so that we can present meaningful lessons and students can have the time to complete them. It is possible to find the time at school for students to write about topics they care about.

What's heartening about the survey's data is how important you and I are to students' growth as writers and their motivation to communicate. When caring, responsive teachers connect with their middle school writers, the efforts pay off. Their students notice, and their students love writing.

Teachers' Attitudes About Writing

Based on my work with teachers around the country, I have observed two general approaches to writing. Teachers either emphasize process, using writing workshops to help students understand and move through the stages of writing, or they view writing as an assignment to be graded. To be honest, there really aren't a lot of teachers "in between" this spectrum. It's quite striking. From my observations, teachers who emphasize process show a keener interest in helping students as they move through the stages of writing.

Pertinent Survey Highlights

The survey offers some insights into teachers and teaching writing. The first point is a kicker.

- Only 8.7 percent of students surveyed report that their teachers know about their outside-of-school writing.
- More girls than boys feel that they have a trusting relationship with a teacher. This could be due to the gender differences between adolescent boys and girls or because teachers treat them differently.
- Nearly half the students surveyed agree that writing at school is a positive experience.
- Close to 10 percent more girls than boys feel writing at school is a positive experience.
- Students who agree that writing at school is a positive experience and relevant to their lives also tend to engage in more types of outside-of-school writing.

How This Information Affects Our Teaching

Students' responses raise this question: Do students enjoy writing at school because they are writing at home? Or do they enjoy writing at home because the teacher makes writing at school such a positive experience, which in turn positively influences their writing at home? The survey doesn't help us draw a conclusion, but Richard Allington's (2002) research of data from first- and fourth-grade teachers in six states might shed some light on it. In the June 2002 *Phi Delta Kappan*, Allington uses data from a study of first- and fourth-grade teachers in six states. Allington concludes that the classroom teachers' ability to offer students expert reading instruction has everything to do with students' progress. In my opinion, the same holds true for teaching writing. So from the survey we learn that teachers who try to help their students, who try to teach them how to improve writing, gain their students' trust and make writing at school relevant to students' lives.

Beyond that, and somewhat paradoxically, it bowls me over that less than 10 percent of students report that their teachers know about their writing outside of school. It reminds me of "the hidden life of" aspect of the American teenager. In all likelihood some out-of-school writing is meant to stay underground, but it is something to be aware of, something to tap into as we get to know our students. I'm not saying we intrude by woodenly insisting they write letters back and forth with us or tame the writing in any way—it's just something to be aware of, something to tap into as we get to know our students and look for ways for some of them to bring their writing talents back into the classroom.

The survey information informs our practice and the kind of writing environment we create for students. It reminds us that a nurturing teacher who gets to know the students, emphasizes the writing process, and offers students opportunities to choose their topics will stand a better chance of cultivating writing proficiency and a deep commitment to writing. Teachers who show students how to improve their work can motivate them to invest in writing that's relevant to their lives.

Writing on Computers or by Hand

According to the Pew Internet & American Life Project (2007), 59 percent of teens agree that they can write, revise, and edit better on computers than by hand. Clearly, we are fast approaching a time when composing on paper will be a rare practice. Five years from now our seemingly sleek laptops are going to look as antiquated and clunky as the giant boxy computers of the 1990s. But for now as I visit schools and reflect on my own teaching, I see we're in a betwixt and between phase. Aging school buildings, funding constraints, as well as the age of the teaching population all contribute to the ongoing practice of students writing by hand in notebooks. And I say this without judgment—I honestly don't know whether writing on paper versus on computers is better for writing quality and writing engagement. There are pros and cons to either mode.

For example, for several years, my class had two computers, and every student wanted to write on one of them. With only two, providing a fair amount of time for all students became frustrating. When our school purchased laptops, the problem diminished as long as I signed up far enough in advance to reserve them for a week or two. My eighth graders loved drafting on the computer. I'd estimate that at least half of the sixteen students brainstormed by hand; all used the laptop at school when it was available. The problem computers posed for me was that students would become so immersed in their writing that they would forget to print revised and edited drafts. Even with reminders at the start and during workshop, I'd hear "Oh, I forgot, Mrs. Robb." In a class like mine, which values process and uses students' process and progress to establish a grade, computers can be a challenge—although I believe that challenge diminishes the more we invite students to write on computers at school.

Pertinent Survey Highlights

The survey revealed a balance between writing on computers or by hand:

- Almost half the students use a computer to write at home.
- Half the students use a computer to write at school; the other half write by hand.

This data makes me wonder whether students who write by hand at school and at home do so because computers are not available to all students during writing class or in their homes. The survey did not consider students' access to computers at school.

How This Information Affects Our Teaching

Seventh and eighth graders that I teach prefer writing on computers. With fifth and sixth graders, this preference depends on their typing ability. For some, writing by hand is faster because they cannot type with ease. One fact I'm sure of: digital computing is here to stay. Before we know it, our students will have a tool that combines the cell phone, computer, e-texts, the Internet, phone, and video all in one. (They're already on the market but far from the mainstream or affordable enough for students.) What do we do for now? Take our cues from our students. But teachers must also be true to who they are. Start with your comfort level, and then find ways to integrate new media into your writing classes (see Chapter 9).

Writing About Books

In one fifth-grade classroom, I invited students to look through their reading response journals. I asked them to consider what they used to do and explain either why they still do it or why they've changed. Nina wrote: "I used to hate making inferences about characters. Why? It was tough. I felt I couldn't do it. Now, I'm liking it more because I know what to look for in a book that helps me do it [infer]. I can talk about it first with my buddy. I look at what they [characters] do and say and think."

In my classes, talking and then writing about reading happens when I read aloud, and after students read a chunk of text. In reading response journals, students can test hunches, change their minds, return to entries, and clarify them. So, in reading workshop, they are applying aspects of the writing process while sharpening their critical thinking.

Statements 29 and 30 on the survey address writing about reading.

> **29. I write about the books I read.**
>
> **30. I write about the books my teacher reads aloud.**

Question 29 could mean writing about books in a journal, a book review, or in an essay. Here's an example of the question being too open-ended so that the survey does not reveal which kinds of writing about books students do. The survey does show that students do write about their independent reading.

Pertinent Survey Highlights

- **Students write more about books they read independently than about books the teacher reads aloud.**

- More than 10 percent of middle school girls agree or strongly agree that they write about books more than boys.

How This Information Affects Our Teaching

In my classes and classes of teachers I coach in reading workshop, we leave literature response journals on students' desks the entire period, ready to receive their thinking. But the survey shows that students do only a limited amount of reading responses in journals. This finding concerns me because this type of response writing can develop students' ability to explore ideas on paper. In Chapter 3, you can see how journaling about my Read Aloud, *Bronx Masquerade*, led Madeline to write a life-altering personal essay.

I have discovered that asking students to respond to my Read Alouds, to their book discussions, and to their independent reading develops their ability to create hunches, to risk trying a bud of an idea that over time can be adjusted, changed, and clarified, and that can eventually transform into a position, an interpretation, that's satisfying to them. Responses can be as short as a list of words students associate with a character, conflict, setting, event, or information. Responses can be a series of phrases or sentences; they can be brief or long. What appeals to me and students about this kind of response is that the writing is a reflective journey that starts with a hunch and can change as the student moves deeper and deeper into the text.

Writing about books as an exploration of ideas offers students countless opportunities to try out a theory, delve into their emotional reactions, reread their first-draft thinking, try another path, or elaborate on their first hunches. These thinking journeys into diverse genres can teach students about how each genre works, how characters move and grow within a genre, how the author's words and language create its soul, its voice. Students need to have the luxury of working their way into a text by writing about it.

I find that continually inviting students to think on paper about different texts develops their ability to risk ideas they might censor because they feel the idea is far out in space. That's just what I want students to do—to be daring in their thinking, knowing they can always adjust ideas. By writing about reading, students develop a thinking and writing fluency that they connect to their own writing. Personal and reading response writing asks students to descend into the unknown; both have the steadying power to transform the unknown into a draft of ideas that the writer can keep or change. Eighth grader Elizabeth explained the benefits this way: "At first, I disliked the writing. It was hard to stop and think about my book. Now, it's easy and I have so much to say that I surprise myself."

Questions the Survey Information Raises

While making sense of the survey's results, I began to compile a list of questions that the data raised in my mind. To prepare middle school students for the heightened literacy demands of high school, college, and the workplace in the twenty-first century and beyond, teachers need to offer more intense writing instruction and use assessments to scaffold all students' needs in a safe and nurturing environment (Coker and Lewis 2008; Graham and Harris 2005; NCTE 2008, Troia et al. 2009).

I encourage you to think about and discuss the survey and the upcoming chapters in this book with colleagues. I want this book to be a living document in the sense that the fresh insights from students in a dozen states as well as my discussion reenergize you to look at your teaching of writing with a new awareness. You've got the power to gain insight into what motivates middle school students to write at high levels—it begins with daring to ask more questions of your students and their lives as writers. In the chapters of this book I take what I learned from the survey and interviews to reconfigure lessons I've taught for many years—check out the video to see some of it in action. I also used this teacher research to reconsider how we might do a better job of bringing out the talent in writers who struggle. Again, this isn't my book—it's *our* book, something we may use to generate more questions that will enliven and sharpen our teaching of middle school writers. When we pose questions, we are compelled to pursue the answers.

How to Use the "Ten Questions About Writing" Questionnaire

Questioning can take us on journeys we never anticipated. Let's turn now to the student questionnaire I mentioned earlier in this chapter, which was one of the motivating forces behind this book. I developed a draft of "Ten Questions About Writing," an informal questionnaire, and invited students in a sixth-, a seventh-, and an eighth-grade class to offer suggestions for tweaking the wording. I also encouraged them to add questions they believed would help teachers learn more about their writing lives. Student feedback drove the revision of my first draft. As a teacher myself, I knew that no survey would sway teachers as much as a tool that would allow them to ask the questions of their own students. And I hope you'll use it, because the candid answers that students provide will give you the anecdotal evidence you need to improve writing instruction—to open the doors to the diversity of literacy experiences and attitudes students bring into class.

I field-tested the form at Powhatan School in Boyce, Virginia, and at Johnson Williams Middle School in Berryville, Virginia. I then sent it to teachers, who in turn handed it out

The Survey Information Raises Questions

I've organized the questions under headings so you can focus your thinking on specific areas when you discus these with colleagues or mull over a group of questions to consider how you might teach writing differently.

Questions About Discovering Students' Writing Lives

- How can we find out more about students' outside-of-school writing?
- Why is this helpful to our teaching?
- How can we best encourage our students to write?
- Why is the correlation between writing in journals and writing stories, poems, and letters important to consider?
- How can we ensure that writing at school is a positive experience for all students?
- Why do students write about their feelings and experiences, and use journals to think about their lives? How can this tendency support their writing at school?
- How can we make writing at school relevant to students' lives?

Questions About Instruction

- Why is giving students choice of writing topics important to their development as writers?
- What are the benefits to students who have teachers who provide specific writing support for each student?
- Why is it more helpful for students to have teachers who address students' writing needs throughout the process than those who use writing to give a grade and move to the next assignment?
- Why is it crucial for students to save the writing that shows their process from start to final draft? How does writing on a computer affect keeping records of process?
- How can we integrate blogging into our class in meaningful ways?
- Why is writing about reading beneficial to students' intellectual development?
- How can we make writing about reading both authentic and relevant?

to three hundred students in grades 5 to 8. I intended for the questionnaire to augment the national survey and the informal correspondence by email I was conducting during this same period. I developed it as a tool that any classroom teacher could take on to learn about students' writing lives in and outside of school.

The teachers embraced the questionnaire, which allowed them to dig deeply into their students' writing lives. I asked them to hand it to students at the start of the year, so they

Questions the Survey Raises that Are Related to Gender Issues

- Why do middle school girls write about their feelings more than boys?
- What more can we learn about adolescent boys' writing?
- Why do more middle school girls than boys find writing at school a positive experience?
- Why do middle school girls tend to write more than boys outside of school?
- Why do middle school girls tend to communicate with their teacher and others more than boys?
- How can we (and should we) work to change this pattern of different attitudes toward writing between girls and boys outside of and inside school?
- Why do girls tend to use computers for writing at home more than boys?
- Why do girls tend to write more about their reading than boys? How can we change this?

would still have time to adapt their writing curriculum to the students' diverse responses, rethinking various aspects of their curriculum as needed. Though it is not a statistical survey, the data the questions provided supported every classroom teacher who administered and reflected upon the results—results that were specific to the students they taught.

Students' Responses to "Ten Questions About Writing"

Students in grades 5 to 8 in Suffern, New York; Boyce, Berryville, and Staunton, Virginia; and Waynesville, Ohio, answered the "Ten Questions About Writing" questionnaire the last week in September or the first week in October. Gathering the information early in the year had these benefits:

- Teachers gained insights into students' writing attitudes and needs;
- Teachers could discuss students' answers in a short conference to deepen their understanding of what students wrote;
- Teachers could use the data to plan whole-class, small-group, and individual student lessons;
- Teachers had information to build self-confidence among students whose responses reflected negative attitudes toward and difficulties with writing; and
- Students had the opportunity to reflect on their writing beliefs, strengths, and needs.

Whenever I invite students to respond to the questionnaire, I first demonstrate how I answer the questions myself, jotting ideas on large chart paper. This step provides students with insights into my writing life. They are always incredulous when they realize that I struggle with organizing ideas, getting started, and punctuating plural possessives. The box below shows a sampling of my responses, in italics, to questions.

This modeling, which I recommend you complete over two to three days, also shows students how to jot down a few ideas for each query prior to answering the question, as well as what a thorough answer looks like (Graham and Harris 2005). If you eliminate teacher modeling, students' responses can be inconsistent, and some might skip questions that require additional time and thought.

Spread students' own note-taking and response processes over a portion of two to three consecutive classes. Completing a few each day can prevent students from rushing to finish all ten, and it offers them briefer bursts of time to think and reflect. The directions tell students to "Write your responses on separate paper." Give students scratch paper for jotting down notes.

---

1. What kinds of writing do you enjoy?

The personal writing I love best is writing letters because I enjoy receiving answers in the mail, feeling the texture of the envelope, and having it to hold and read again and again. I also enjoy emailing, responding to blogs, writing for my website, and of course, working on books for teachers. When traveling, I keep detailed diaries.

2. What do you enjoy most about it?

Writing makes me think carefully and organize my ideas so others get them. Writing also helps me figure out what I do understand and areas I need to work on. My travel diaries help me relive trips and because of the details, transport me back to cities and countries I've visited.

5. How do get your ideas for writing?

The writing ideas for books about reading and writing come from my students and teachers I coach. Letters and emails are from my life experiences, the daily events I live through. Travel diaries recount, in great detail, each day of my trip; sometimes I even include a fantastic dinner from appetizers to dessert.

Summaries of Students' Responses to Questions 1 Through 8

1. What kinds of writing do you enjoy (letters, emails, blogging, notes, stories, articles, poems, fan fiction)? Explain why you enjoy these.

   All students wrote to communicate with friends, to express feelings, or just to have fun writing fantasy or stories. Forty-six students said there was no kind of writing they enjoyed.

   Here are the kinds of writing students enjoy. The first four had the highest number of responses: emails, texts, stories, blogging, journals, poems, letters, fan fiction, notes.

2. What do you enjoy most about it?

   The highest number of responses (185) was choosing topics. Other reasons included deciding what happens in a story, making their own stories, writing poems, writing about sports events, emails, and texting to communicate with friends.

3. What do you like least about writing?

   Here are the most common student responses: "being forced to write when you don't feel like it," "writing from prompts and story starters," "writing nonfiction and articles," "taking notes for classes," "writing about books," "my hand getting tired," "it takes longer than speaking," "running out of ideas," "a story that doesn't work," "brainstorming because it takes a lot of work," "planning."

4. What is the hardest part of writing for you? Explain.

   Spelling and using correct grammar topped the list. Here are other aspects students found difficult: finding ideas, concentrating instead of daydreaming, revising, staying on topic, beginnings, forgetting an idea, showing feelings, finding the right word, running out of ideas, thinking of a title, and having to write.

5. How do get your ideas for writing?

   Students found writing ideas in diverse places: a book; titles of books, songs, and movies; life experiences; talking to a classmate; drawing; objects in the classroom and at home; journals; other people's writing; thinking about what they love and dream of.

6. What would you like to know about how to improve your writing?

   Here 232 students wrote a version of this answer: "more about spelling, grammar, punctuation, and increasing my vocabulary." The remaining group listed some of these elements: how to make a story better, how to write good dialogue, how

Under Questions 1 to 8 that follow, I've summarized students' answers in italics. I discuss Questions 9 and 10, which ask about reading-writing connections, where I introduce mentor texts. You'll find all ten questions, which you can reproduce and use with your classes, on the DVD.

> "Writers improve their craft when they have a real purpose, have a real audience, and invest in their writing."
> Ann Kiernan-Robb, eighth-grade teacher, Powhatan School

to add excitement to a story, how to fill space because I don't write much, where to add details, and where to start when brainstorming.

7. When you think of the writing you do for school, what words come to mind? Explain your thoughts.

   The most common words were boring *and* confusing. *Other words and phrases students noted were* long, hard, too much time, getting a grade, thinking about state tests, fun when I choose the topic, scared, long essays, easy, exciting. *Out of 300 responses, 103 were positive and 197 were negative.*

8. When you think of the writing you do on your own time, by choice, what words come to mind? Explain your thoughts.

   Students who wrote at home used words such as free, no grade, no stress, I choose, have time, can choose topics, write in any genre, write fan fiction with friends, email, blog, *and* love it. *Of those who answered this question, 242 students did one or more of the following kinds of writing: stories, blogging, emails, journaling, poems, drawing, texting.*

How This Book Addresses the Needs of Writers Who Struggle

"I have nothing to write about." "I always get stuck and run out of ideas fast." "I can't write stuff that's long." These are some of the comments made on the questionnaire by middle school writers who struggle. Struggling writers can include students with learning disabilities, special education students, students with limited literacy experiences, and English language learners.

These three comments illustrate what causes students to struggle, to develop a hopelessness and helplessness regarding their ability to write. They lack a mental model of how to find topics, what a rich brainstorm looks like, how to create a writing plan, how different genres work, and what a draft might look like in different genres (Boscolo and Gelati 2007; Graham and Harris 2005, 2007).

Researchers Graham and Harris point out that we can help writers who struggle—students who believe they have little to communicate on paper—by teaching them how to generate rich lists of ideas, how to plan writing, and the benefits planning brings to drafting (2005, 2007). These teaching practices benefit all writers (Coker and Lewis 2008). In my classes, learning to plan and brainstorm are key parts of writing instruction. It's what I have to do every time I propose a book. It's what professional writers

Two Books to Read on Teaching Struggling Writers

- *Writing Better: Effective Strategies for Teaching Students with Learning Difficulties* by Steve Graham and Karen R. Harris. New York: Brookes, 2005.
- *Best Practices in Writing Instruction*, edited by Steve Graham, Charles A. MacArthur, and Jill Fitzgerald. New York: Guilford, 2007.

do all the time. (See the writing plans of Katherine Paterson and Jean Van Leeuwen, in Appendices A and B).

 You'll also observe on the DVD, as well as in Chapter 3, how teaching writing with mentor texts and how conferring with students enlarges their mental models of what writing in different genres looks like. You see, struggling writers can also be students who don't read enough to build a mental model of good writing or students who have a limited knowledge of how narrative and nonfiction texts work. We can motivate and engage them with reading by giving them choice and showing them how to choose books they can read and enjoy (Allison 2009; Robb 2008).

Supporting Writers Who Struggle

Throughout the book, I offer suggestions for helping students for whom writing is difficult. At the end of Chapter 7, which discusses conferring with students, you'll find a chart that lists the stages of the writing process, students' behaviors that require your attention during the various stages, and suggestions for offering extra support to those who need it. As I visit classes in my area and around the country, I find that by middle school, writers who struggle have lost self-confidence and the feeling of "I can do that." They struggle because they don't know how to disrupt and transform the cycle of poor writing and low grades. My hope is that some of the scaffolds will help you break through students' negative attitudes and transform those attitudes into hard work, success, and self-efficacy.

"Hey, I know I'll get a D or an F on every writing assignment. I don't know how to do better so why bother."
James, eighth grader

Choice Brings Relevance to Middle School Writing Instruction

"At home, I write for me. I write to figure out why I'm angry, upset. I work things out when I write." Thomas mumbled theses comment during our interview. His words

> "Be still when you have nothing to say; when genuine passion moves you, say what you've got to say, and say it hot." *D. H. Lawrence*

haunted me for weeks; they still creep into my dreams. At workshops with teachers who felt bound to deliver a restrictive district writing curriculum, Thomas' words came to mind. In classes where students wrote two to three sentences because they had nothing to say about the topic, Thomas' soft-spoken voice echoed in my consciousness. Survey results, students' responses to the "Ten Questions About Writing," and my emails and interviews with middle school writers persuaded me to shape this book and its content by considering what I have learned about the needs, voices, wishes, and writing habits of middle school students.

Author Katherine Anne Porter said, "You do not create a style. You work and develop yourself; your style is an emanation from your own being." That's what Thomas was trying to explain when he said, "At home, I write for me." As you read on, you'll hear the voices of students who write at home for themselves. Like two mighty rivers flowing into one, the book aims to merge students' at-home and in-school writing lives so that writing becomes "an emanation" of each student's self.

Snapshots of Middle School Students Who Write Outside of School

Pulitzer Prize–winning author James Michener (1993) wrote, "The process of becoming a writer neither begins nor culminates with the publication of a book; instead it begins in early childhood and persists as long as the writer continues to peck out words on a typewriter, or more likely today, to inject words into a processor" (vii). Michener's words shed insight into what I've discovered about the writing attitudes of middle school students. While many express concerns about a lack of choice in writing topics at school and dislike "school writing," a large group have writing lives outside of school that their teachers know little about. This desire to communicate with writing and pictures starts at an early age (Dyson 1989) and often continues into and through adolescence.

When I interviewed Amanda, who attends Suffern Middle School, she emailed a passionate journal entry to me (Figure 1.4). When I asked what prompted it, she replied, "I wrote this after my mom talked to me about being more like my sister. My sister's perfect. She gets straight As. Her hair is long and curly; she eats healthy food; she wants to

From: [redacted]
Subject: **Re: Ms.Medina's class**
Date: September 10
To: [redacted]

I do have a journal entry.. one from my diary, but it should work.. but let me know if it doesnt work, and if you need something else:

Date: Monday, January 9
Subject: Doing Barbie a favor?

I have always hated Barbie. Every holiday, the relatives that didn't even know me would give me these Barbie dolls. I would cute their hair off, and break their legs off. Barbie was a little doll sized slut, she was perfect in every way. She had a hot husband, she knew her place in the kitchen, she was fashionable. She had everything going for her, and that's what made me break her legs off. She deserved a little sadness in her life. The way I see it, I was doing Barbie a favor.

There are the people who are different, but they fake it to be like everyone else. They follow the others. They blend in, but at least they don't feel alone. I call these people the "potentially unique" or "followers."

There are the people who have nothing different about them so they pick off of other people like vultures, these people are the ones who have more friends, and people want to be like them. In my school these are the "populars." Yes, popular does just mean you have a lot of friends; it comes off the word population.

Then there are the people like me, the ones who find their own way of being different, but it doesn't really catch on. These people don't have many followers, but at least they know that they are individuals.

I call my friends, the potentially popular. They have the material to be popular; but they are just too weird. I could never be popular. I just don't like to change.

Wannabes are creepy, pathetic little pests who follow the popular girls like they were extraordinary humans. That's why you never see popular girls holding books. The wannabes hold the books for them. Kelly was a wannabe, and the popular girls just decided one day, she was worthy.

When people say, "It's what's one the inside that counts." You don't always believe them. But when you think about it, that's true. Even if you are pretty, you could be really awful, and most of the time, people don't want to be with someone who is awful.

But at the end of the day when no one else is around, that is who you truly are because you aren't trying to impress anyone.

It's the perfect people who make me upset. It's a good thing there are only a few of them. Yeah, people may say "No body's perfect." But it isn't true. Some think perfect people are just myths. But I know they are real, I know someone whos perfect.

Her name is Kelly. We were best friends for five years, until three weeks ago, the popular girls were at her locker, and I waited for her there. The popular girls were snickering, and they were asking her why I was waiting there for her. They asked if she was friends with me, I heard her say very clearly, "EW no! I would never be friends with some one like her." They laughed and walked away. The next day she acted like nothing happened, and I told her I never wanted to see or talk to her again. Since that day, I hate Kelly Sampson, and my hatred is like quicksand, it pulls me in further and further.

When I hear her name, I cringe. Everyday in the hallway, I give her the stare of death.

The worst part about Kelly is that everyone thinks she is so great. Everyone loves Kelly. Whenever I tell people she's evil, they don't believe me. Only Jen, Kelsey, Jessica, and Haley believe me. All the people that used to be friends with Kelly, are still friends with her, except me. The geeks still follow her around.

There is also this appeal to her, even when you hate her, you still hope she wants to be your friend because you miss talking too her and laughing with her. You hope maybe one day she will just apologize, she will come up to you and say, "I don't want any of this popularity. I just want us to be friends again because you mean so much to me. I miss you."

Figure 1.4 On her own, Amanda freely expresses her feelings.

be an actress. *I want to be me*." (Italics for the emphasis Amanda placed on these words.) This journal entry exhibits Amanda's individuality and her reasons for staying outside of the "in group." Her outpouring reflects the ongoing search for identity and for developing individuality while wrestling with the values that dominate the "in"-peer group that's characteristic of middle school students.

Kayla, a sixth grader at Manorville Junior High School, writes at home for different purposes. In an email, Kayla told me that she loves to draw and write about experiences she's had. "Sometimes," Kayla wrote, "I draw pictures and tell stories about the pictures to my younger sister; then I write them." Kayla sent me an example of her illustrated story-telling (Figures 1.5 and 1.6). The words *scream* and *yes* in Figure 1.5 show the reaction of Kayla's mom and sisters when they won free tickets to a Disney channel concert. "I love to talk, write, and draw about everyday stuff," Kayla emails.

I met Ashleigh, an eighth grader at Suffern Middle School, when I worked on reading and writing with her teacher, Jenny Smith, and taught ten classes during the 2007–2008 school year. On my fourth visit, Ashleigh handed me a brown envelope. "Read these when you have time," she said, then disappeared into the crowd of students in the hall.

Figure 1.5 "Scream" and "yes!" advertise Kayla's pure joy!

Kayla   August 1
        Just the other day, my mom, my
two sisters, my bestfriend Brooke, a family friend
and myself were driving and listening to a
local radio station, BLI, we hear that if you
are the 106th caller you win 4 tickets to
a Disney Channel concert. So right away
who ever had a cellphone started dialing.
We were calling for about 5 minutes when
we all hear, "hello?" My moms cellphone was
on speaker because she was driving. My
mom answers, "Are we the winners?" The
lady responds, "Yes!" Once that word came
out of her mouth the car went crazy!
We were screaming so loud I think the
car next to us heard us!
         That night, we were all outside
talking on the patio, except my older sister
was on the computer inside. All of a
sudden, my older sister said, "You will never
believe this, I just looked up that concert
and it is for babies, like baby singing
groups." All of our jaws dropped.
I went inside looked at the computer
it was like "the wheels on the bus."
The radio station probably thought
we were crazy, screaming for a baby concert.

Figure 1.6 Motivation to Write: An Out-of-the-Ordinary Joyous Event

Invisible Me

I am an invisible Person
When I'm there no one notices
It's impossible to be noticeable
When nobody cares
I am an invisible person
Don't you taunt me
I am an invisible person
Who can haunt you and taunt
you back
I am an invisible person
With no feelings nor friends
An outcast
No heart
I am no invisible person . . .
　　　　　—Ashleigh

The Last Leaf on the Tree

The last leaf on the willow tree
Oh how he felt quite lonely
As he wriggled and wobbled
and strained to break free
Waiting for the wind to blow
Pleading for his chance
"LETS GO!"
As he thought,
"Why not me?"
　　　　　—Thomas

As I waited for my flight home, I opened the envelope, which contained dozens of poems. That night I emailed Ashleigh to tell her how much I enjoyed reading her poems. I asked her to tell me why she writes poetry outside of school. Her email explains how reading poetry in elementary school led to writing poetry (Figure 1.7). By sixth grade, Ashleigh wrote poems to help herself deal with friendship problems and to document important events. For Ashleigh, writing poetry is a way to make sense of her life: past, present, and future. The titles reveal the diversity of topics Ashleigh writes about: "Confessions of a Broken Soul," "Rebel Angels," "What has happened to my beloved earth?" "Moonlight Sonata," and "Music of the Night." Her poems discuss friendship, lost love, concern for the survival of the earth and its inhabitants, and the sounds of nature. Ashleigh can step deeply inside her personal feelings through conversations with herself, as in her search for identity in "Invisible Me."

As mentioned, I found that girls wrote more journal entries, stories, and poems than boys. The girls' emails to me were also longer. The exception was Thomas Northrup, who, in his own words, "struggled with writing poems and stories until fifth grade, then started to love it." He explained, "I wrote 'The Last Leaf on the Tree' in fifth grade because my favorite cousin was writing poetry. I wanted to do everything she did."

Subject: **Re: Writing**
Date: March 24

When I was in elementary school we used to have this event called **Poem in a Pocket Week** that we did each year. The rules were that you had to write a poem by a famous poem (or write one yourself), put your poems in your pocket and then read them to a teacher. The teacher would then give you a ticket for every different poem you read to them. The student with the most tickets in their grade would win. In 5th grade, I decided to do something I never did before—write my own poems on anything I wanted to write about. My favorite season was fall so I decided to write a poem about it. **Fall** was the 1st poem I ever wrote without using a book, just my five senses. After I wrote **Fall**, I decided to write a few more poems. I thought it was a little bit fun, but not as much as I enjoyed quoting other poet's work. Even though writing poetry wasn't my favorite thing to do at the time, I wrote poems every once in a while, usually in cards I made for people. Then one day, I sadly lost my poem book! I was so angry but hey, I didn't really enjoy writing poems then either. In 6th grade, after I entered the Holocaust contest with one of my poems, my little brother Allan found it for me. I was overpowered by joy and I started writing. Later on in the 6th grade, I faced my own kinds of problems with friends and writing down poems about what I was angry about seemed to calm me down whenever I was having a bad day. In 7th grade, I finally realized why I wrote poems at home. It was like a diary, **MY** diary where I kept count of important events in my life and to sometimes teach the reader a lesson. Writing poetry sometimes in a way lets me foreshadow my future the minute pen touches paper. Every poem that I ever wrote tells a story, **MY** life story of good times and bad times and the more and more I write, the more I remember my past when I get older.

Figure 1.7 Ashleigh reflects on the roots of her love for poetry.

Now, in eighth grade, Thomas draws and writes stories and poems. In fifth grade, Thomas developed an interest in bird watching. With his dad's help, he built birdhouses for the family's backyard. Thomas began the illustration in Figure 1.8 at the end of seventh grade. "When I'm bored and have nothing to do," he told me, "I draw birds."

Figure 1.8 Drawing is a vital part of composing for some students.

Jared Chin, an eighth-grade boy at Suffern Middle School, never wrote at home until his parents divorced. In a letter attached to an email Jared explained, "After my father Ting Chin, who I saw on the weekends, moved . . . I sought out a reason to write, and it wasn't because I had to . . . I was angry and miserable so I wrote in a journal. I wrote of all my feelings and thoughts that saddened me. It was a new way to express myself, to make me feel better. I felt much better after expressing my feelings on paper and now enjoyed writing."

These writing samples celebrate middle school students' desire to communicate with others as well as their need to answer that nagging question: *Who am I?* We gain insights into our students as writers when we move beyond assigning writing to give a grade to learning how to support our students in conferences and with demonstration lessons. Instead of zooming in on the lack of punctuation in Ashleigh's poems or the spelling errors in Amanda's journal entry or some punctuation errors in Kayla's writing, it's crucial to start with what students do well. Yes, writing conventions are important, but a piece of writing with perfect syntax, spelling, and usage that says nothing is unimportant. Voice, content, passion, and imagery are primary.

Choice of writing topic takes center stage in this book. I want students to ache with caring about their topics. I want them to write about their passions and feelings, and to communicate to others what's meaningful to them. In this book I build on the wisdom of what professional writers say and do. I emphasize how important it is both for middle school writers who struggle and for those who are eager writers to brainstorm ideas and plan their writing (Coker and Lewis 2008; Graham and Harris 2005). We'll explore lessons on craft, technique, grammar, revision, and editing—lessons that support students

Above All, Student Choice

- Why is choice of topic important for writers?
- How can we add choice of topic to our curriculum?
- Why is it beneficial to teachers to learn more about students' writing lives outside of school?
- Why do students emphasize spelling, punctuation, and grammar?
- What would we like students to say about ways to improve writing? How can we get to that point?
- How could using these responses in conferences benefit students? Teachers?
- How do we support writers who struggle, who do not write much, and who have negative attitudes toward writing?

as long as they choose topics they find irresistible, compelling. You'll see how conferences inch middle school writers forward, and how blogging and texting not only tap into what these writers adore but also build their writing strength. I'll also address the need to practice for state tests so students can navigate this genre well.

I believe that students' desire to revise their drafts and to study craft and technique escalates when they have something powerful and important to say. Students' voices, insights from professional writers, research, and the lessons in this book will help you develop middle school writers who revel in their writing because their purposes are meaningful to themselves and others. *But that's not enough.* To surf that middle school writing wave and successfully glide into shore, you will need to examine your writing curriculum and include reading, writing, and talking experiences that give students new, compelling reasons to write—reasons for them to connect who they are and what interests them with what you are asking of them. In the next chapter, we'll look at where to turn to for guidance in this process

> "You don't write because you want to say something; you write because you've something to say."
> *F. Scott Fitzgerald*

Discuss Students' Writing

Professional Study Invitation

Consider your current approach to teaching writing. Together with colleagues, or on your own, think about how you might increase your students' engagement in writing at school, based on the survey's findings.

CHAPTER 2

Improving Students' Creative and Analytic Writing

*f*or six weeks, I corresponded by email with an eighth-grade teacher at a school in urban Illinois. At the same time, I planned a reading-writing lesson to model for her and her colleagues, as well as the district literacy coaches. Mrs. Crider (a pseudonym) was eager to learn, and she wrote to me about her students, explaining that she once observed a demonstration at a workshop "where groups read different texts—ones they could read. I want that for my kids." She confessed she felt dissatisfied with "using class sets of books that most students can't read."

In her third year of teaching, Mrs. Crider was very open to improving her practice, and her dedication to her students was palpable in each of our exchanges. She looked forward to my upcoming visit, calling it a "crystal moment" when she and district coaches could observe how it is possible to reach and engage every student with reading and writing.

The majority of students in her classes were Hispanic Americans, still acquiring English. In addition, her classes included a small number of African American students, and a handful of Anglo Americans. Her students were reading *Anne Frank: Diary of a Young Girl* and resisted writing about Anne Frank and disliked writing in general. Several turned in blank papers or jotted only a few words on a page.

As I entered this city school, I looked forward to meeting Mrs. Crider and to match the students' faces with their names, along with the personality sketches the teacher had shared. I walked into the office to sign in, obtain a visitor's pass, and meet the principal. We shook hands. "I've looked forward to this day for the past several weeks," I said.

"You're teaching the dummies today," the principal said as he led me out of the office.

"Oh, I'm sure they'll work hard, "I stammered. "Why don't you come watch?" I was floored by his words, and angry, but felt I couldn't call him on it right then and there.

"Can't possibly do that. Don't have time," he explained.

He handed me off to a literacy coach, who led me to the room. The class of twenty-six boys and girls hadn't arrived yet. I used this time to tour the classroom, then chatted with Mrs. Crider and the literacy coaches who would observe the lesson and debrief it with me.

The bulletin board that spanned the back wall contained computer images of World War II, including photographs of Anne Frank and Auschwitz. Computer-printed captions explained each image. Mrs. Crider had told me that only two students read at grade level. The remaining twenty-four read two to four years below grade level. Yet, their required class book was *Anne Frank: Diary of a Young Girl*. Because the majority of students couldn't read that book, Mrs. Crider read it out loud, discussed parts with the students, and had them complete writing tasks related to the plot. She was at a dead end, and I was there to show her how she could turn it around. The key was not to shelve the core text of Anne Frank but to build highly engaging, readable texts around it.

The reading-writing lesson I planned met the reading levels of these students, whom I split into five groups. Materials for students included three biographical poems about Langston Hughes from *Love to Langston* by Tony Medina (2002), and two poems written by Hughes himself (see the box on page 37 for the list). For the first three minutes, I told students about Langston Hughes' life. I emphasized his early years, which were the focus of the Medina poems I had selected.

To motivate students to think and write, I introduced three high-interest questions:

1. Based on your own experiences, how would you explain justice and injustice?
2. How do justice and injustice relate to your poem? To your lives?
3. Do ideas of justice and injustice in your poem connect to historical and current events? Explain.

With my support, the students added two more:

4. Can you connect power and control to events in your lives?
5. Why do some people want power and control over others? Is this desire positive? Negative?

I instructed students to use these questions to discuss their poems and issues in their own lives. Students wrote responses to the questions before and after reading, and then used the queries to collaborate and write about their discussions.

My Demonstration Lesson for Students

Two times I read aloud "Tell Me" by Langston Hughes.

> *Why should it be* my *loneliness,*
> *Why should it be* my *song,*
> *Why should it be* my *dream*
>   *deferred*
>   *overlong?*

I conducted a Think Aloud, sharing words that spoke to me and answers to some of the five questions we had posed. I wanted to build the students' mental model of what thinking and talking about a poem might look like. Here is my Think Aloud:

> *Loneliness* is the word that spoke to me. When I moved to Virginia from New York City, I had no friends; that was loneliness. When my parents and brother died and I had only one cousin left in my family, my heart ached with loneliness.
>
> I believe that the question this poem poses deals with injustice for those who have to defer or put off dreams just because of poverty, religion, cultural background, or a fear of trying. Before Civil Rights legislation, it was tough for dreams to become a reality for African and Latino Americans. In Germany, during World War II, Anne Frank's dreams were cut off because she was Jewish.

I explained to students what I did: I chose a word and discussed my connections to it. Then, I linked the questions about injustice to the poem. Next, I asked students to select and note works in their journal that spoke to them. Students connected these to one or more of the five questions. That's the type of modeling I encourage teachers to do. I also showed students on the overhead what a written response might look like:

> Power and control over others is alive in today's world. Look at Iran, Afghanistan, Iraq, Kenya, Rwanda, China, and North Korea. Many dreams in these countries have been deferred. Women's dreams of education and equality, and dreams of ending the cycle of poverty and illness. By using the italicized pronoun *my*, Hughes moves his question beyond himself, to everyone, and brings urgency to *not* deferring dreams.

I emphasized that focusing on content, honest feelings, and reactions is far more important than worrying about spelling.

Groups read their poems several times. Each member in a group tackled one question; members supported one another. I circulated, responding to their queries and supporting their planning process. Each group had twenty minutes to prepare, and then groups taught their poem to the class.

The students' writing showed us that they had much to say about justice and injustice, power and control, and how these related to and affected their lives. One student wrote that he learned that Langston Hughes "had a dream to write poems and he did write even though his teacher and his dad tried to stop him." Another wrote, "You should never let anyone control you if it is for a bad reason like the first-grade teacher who

Poems for Students

From *Love to Langston* by Tony Medina. New York: Lee and Low, 2002:

"First Grade"

"Jim Crow Row"

"In High School"

From *Poetry for Young People: Langston Hughes* edited by David Roessel and Arnold Rampersad. New York: Scholastic, 2006:

"Merry-Go-Round"

"I, Too"

made fun of Hughes because of his skin color." Two students collaborated and shared this piece about power:

> People want power so they can feel better. Sometimes they want it because they are insecure. Sometimes it is because they want justice for themselves and are scared of getting injustice. When they have power sometimes it gets to their minds and they start treating others with injustice.

Another pair wrote a collaborative poem to share their thoughts about Hughes' poem, "Merry-Go-Round." In "Merry-Go-Round," the boy wonders where the Jim Crow section is on a carousel, since there's no obvious front and back. At the end of the poem the boy asks, "Where's the horse / For a kid that's black?"

In response, this pair wrote the following a collaborative poem:

> *the school cafeteria*
> *groups*
> *at different tables*
> *hughes*
> *a strong man*
> *put all this in his poem*
> *so we could*
> *sit together*
> *why we still sit separate*

Notice how ideas in the Langston Hughes poem connect to the students' lives. Note, too, that students closed their poem with a question, just like in "Merry-Go-Round."

What the Literacy Coaches and I Learned

At a follow-up discussion, Mrs. Crider, the literacy coaches, and I debriefed on the lesson. We agreed that students connected deeply to Langston Hughes' experiences with discrimination and racism because they could read, understand, and discuss the poems. Comprehending the texts provided students with the information they needed for collaborative discussions and for writing with heart and commitment. Collaboration, pooling their creative energy and experiences, helped students make connections and synthesize (Gardner 2007). In addition, the coaches and I believed that the compelling questions activated the students' creative thinking because these were relevant to their world and experiences, which allowed students to reclaim ideas for writing from their own lives (Gardner 2007; Pink 2005). Mrs. Crider and the coaches recognized that going forward, they would need to foreground a study of Anne Frank and World War II with short texts such as these poems, which connected students to justice, injustice, power, and control, all themes threaded through Anne Frank's story.

"There are many books about Anne Frank on diverse reading levels," I told the group. "Bring several to the study so students can do the reading and actively participate in the learning." Because of our education backgrounds, teachers want to ensure that their students are reading great canonical texts. Yet we have to be realistic about the abilities of our readers, find materials they can read, and compromise by reading aloud selected passages from books such as *Anne Frank: The Diary of a Young Girl*. Moreover, if we build students' reading skill and stamina, they might even choose to read these books later. For me, teaching reading is no longer about *the book* that all students *must read*. It's about the ideas and understandings that students can gather from multiple texts they *can read*— texts that include poetry, informational texts, the Internet, biography, and fiction (Robb 2008).

During this follow-up discussion, I posed questions that prompted Mrs. Crider and the coaches to comment on the students' writing in response to reading. I wanted them to see that students won't resist writing if they feel both connected to the text and capable of reading it. I wanted them to see as well that these students were highly engaged in the writing because it called upon their creative and their analytical capacities. The students didn't feel as though the writing was an assignment to test their comprehension, and so they jumped into it with both feet, with passion. The writing wasn't about school—it was about them, us, humanity. Here are the thoughts I shared after the group of teachers and coaches debriefed. I invited them to explore the following ideas as they joined with teachers in their districts to study and improve reading at school.

- Select texts that have high student appeal.
- Provide students with reading material they can understand independently. This way, students can respond to their reading and discover ideas to explore in writing (Tomlinson 1999; Wormeli 2007; Robb 2008).
- Find various genres that center around the person, such as Anne Frank, on a range of reading levels that match those of your students. Raid your class, school, and public library for materials if funding is problematic.
- Before writing, ask students to discuss; talk reclaims prior knowledge and clarifies new ideas. Through talk, students create oral texts that support writing (Willis 2007).
- Use compelling questions that relate to students' lives; tapping into these can produce writing that speaks to the soul (NCTE 2008).
- Bring collaboration to writing because middle school students are social, and collaboration can foster creative thinking (Pink 2005).

Improving Practice: Taking Cues from Research, Our Students, Our Colleagues

Now let's look at the reading-writing lesson in the wider context of how we can bring more immediacy and relevance to our writing instruction. One hundred of these lessons still won't create an ideal writing curriculum. We need to have a bigger vision for what it is we are trying to do for our students.

Most often we gingerly try to cross the high wire, searching for ways to help middle school students want to write, to balance what test-driven school districts and administrators legislate for teaching writing, and to keep abreast of research on developing writing proficiency among adolescents (Graham and Perin 2007b; Moje 2000; NCTE 2008; Pink 2005; Wilhelm 2007). The reality in many classrooms, however, is that teachers are in retreat mode. There's a certain comfort in teaching the way we were taught or continuing to teach as we've always done. We need to muster our energy and resist running furiously on a teaching treadmill only to discover, when we stop, that we have remained in the same place.

When I visit classrooms around the country and chat with teachers, I come away with four sobering impressions about current middle school writing instruction:

1. Teaching writing is formulaic, following scripts from prepared programs.
2. Teaching writing focuses on test prep and improving schools' scores.
3. Teaching writing is a mixture of test prep, mandatory prompts, and process writing.
4. Time spent on writing instruction and research on writing evaluation have decreased in the last ten years (NCTE 2008; Newkirk 2009).

The overarching—and heartbreaking—reality is that teaching writing has moved away from the process workshops of the 1980s and into an era of accountability and test preparation, because the tests are the force that passes judgment on schools, administrators, and teachers (Coker and Lewis 2008; Newkirk 2009).

Teachers new to the field tell me that they have little to no undergraduate preparation for teaching writing, and recent research confirms this (Coker and Lewis 2008; Newkirk 2009). The growth of PLCs—professional learning communities—may be one bright spot in this dismal picture. If teachers collaborate on reading research, join and participate in the National Writing Project's programs, *and learn how to learn from their students*, they can more than make up for gaps in their undergraduate education.

The writing curriculum I describe in this book prepares students for the tomorrows that a global society brings. It bridges the divide between student writing and school writing, and it brings current approaches to writing instruction more in concert with what the landscape of the twenty-first century looks like. To develop this curriculum, I dipped into new and old wells to deepen my thinking:

- **Research:** What can we learn from the best research-based writing practices identified by Don Murray, Don Graves, Lucy Calkins, Peter Elbow, and Steve Graham and Dolores Perin when we combine their contributions with the research and theories of Howard Gardner and Daniel Pink?
- **Students:** How might we reinvigorate our writing instruction when we truly take our cues from students, as I described in Chapter 1?
- **Colleagues:** What are the main obstacles of effective professional development? Might manageable, focused, professional study around students' writing succeed, because it's "locally grown"—harnessing the power of teachers' collective insights and expertise, and allowing them to immediately apply the ideas of outside experts to students they know?

> "We write differently—often digitally—and we write more than in the past." "Writing Now" *by National Council of Teachers of English*, Council Chronicle *18 (1), 2008*

Cues from Research

To look for cues from research, two publications I'd recommend are:

- *Writing Next: Effective Strategies to Improve the Writing of Adolescents in Middle and High Schools* (Graham and Perin 2007a); and
- "Writing Now: What Is Writing in the 21st Century?" (NCTE 2008).

These two texts helped me confirm that the content of this book is situated in a current landscape of research and still-open questions about teaching writing. And while I believe in writing workshop, I wanted to make sure this book would draw from other approaches as well, so that teachers who are not using the workshop model can still feel a part of the conversation.

Writing Next points out that in the twenty-first century and beyond, writing well is not an option for adolescents; it's a necessity if they are to eventually participate in daily community life and in a global economy (Graham and Perin 2007a). According to Persky, Daane, and Yin (2003), 70 percent of students in grades 4 through 12 are low-achieving writers, not good enough for this large population to compete for twenty-first-century jobs; solve twenty-first-century economic, political, and social problems; and participate in the democratic process.

The *Writing Next* report provides eleven elements that can improve writing achievement in grades 4 through 12. Keep in mind that one program, one way of teaching writing, cannot meet the needs of the diverse populations we teach. That eliminates scripted and prescriptive programs—a one-size-fits-all approach. The authors of *Writing Next* recommend that administrators and teachers select those strategies most appropriate for students attending their schools, making the teaching of writing student-centered and responsive to individual needs. The following list contains six elements I chose from *Writing Next* because I believe they need to be integrated in English language arts classrooms. These elements, listed in the order that Graham and Perin placed them in, can become part of a writing workshop or part of traditional English classrooms.

- **Writing Strategies:** Teachers demonstrate—and students practice and apply—craft and technique lessons for finding ideas, planning, drafting, revising, and editing.
- **Collaborative Writing:** Adolescents work together on writing projects such as Readers Theater, dramas, interviews, revising, and editing.
- **Inquiry Activities:** Teachers work with students to develop compelling questions that drive writing, discussions, thinking, research, and reading.
- **Study of Models:** Teachers provide students with models of good writing by professional and student writers, so students learn about craft, technique, style, voice, and organization.
- **Prewriting:** Teachers offer students experiences that enable them to generate and organize ideas for writing.
- **Process Writing Approach:** Teachers model writing lessons, provide students with the time to write at school, and offer students individualized instruction through conferences.

Five Other Important Skills Highlighted in *Writing Next*

- Summarization
- Specific product goals
- Word processing
- Sentence combining
- Writing for content learning

You can download a copy of *Writing Next* from www.all4ed.org/publication_material/reports/writing_next.

"Writing Now" is a policy research brief created by the National Council of Teachers of English to address issues of writing in a changing world. The brief dispels a myth that drives writing instruction in middle schools today: that the primary goal of writing tasks is to measure mastery of content and of writing skills. This myth perpetuates a view of writing that can stifle creativity, imaginative play, and the desire to share and communicate thoughts about relevant life experiences such as friendships, cliques, peer pressures, rivalries, justice and injustice, and identities.

My interviews and ongoing email conversations with middle school students in Virginia and New York, and the results of the national writing survey I conducted (see Chapter 1), support the research of *Writing Next* and "Writing Now." They invite us to take a closer look at the kinds of writing middle school students do for school and the kinds of writing they complete outside of school. In the next section, we'll look at two researchers who are not in the education field per se, but whose work has profound implications for teaching and learning in the twenty-first century.

Learning from the Work of Daniel Pink and Howard Gardner

In his introduction to *A Whole New Mind*, Daniel Pink (2005) explains how right- and left-brain differences will determine our futures:

> But the well-established differences between the two hemispheres of the brain yield a powerful metaphor for interpreting our present and guiding our future. Today, the defining skills of the previous era—the "left brain" capabilities that powered the Information Age—are necessary but no longer sufficient. And the capabilities we once disdained or thought frivolous—the "right brain" qualities of inventiveness, empathy, joyfulness, and meaning—increasingly will determine who flourishes and who flounders. (3)

Inventiveness, empathy, joyfulness, meaning, and the ability to synthesize mounds of data in order to grasp the big picture are qualities Pink believes our students need for the next age: the Conceptual Age. Why? Because this era asks them to inquire and collaborate to solve problems we face in the United States and the world. As the world moves at a breakneck pace, it creates more problems to solve, problems such as the melting of ice caps, limited water supplies, air and water pollution, shrinking food supplies, the lack of alternative fuels, and economic meltdowns. For Pink, the thinking, writing, and learning that take place at school should train students for the era of solving global and national problems.

What Does This Mean for Middle School Writers and Their Teachers?

You might consider asking students to use their writing to address problems in their community. For example, there was a plea in our local newspaper for books, paper, and paints for an area day care center. Meg, an eighth grader, brought the article to school and shared it with the class. She organized a "Social Responsibility Club," and twelve students from eighth grade met with me at lunch once each week. Students raised money by contributing a dollar a week from their allowance. They also wrote a letter to parents of children at our school and a letter to the local newspaper asking families to donate picture books, paper, and paints. They collaborated, searched for solutions, and wrote to support a worthy cause.

Schools and their surrounding communities have similar problems that need solving. When teachers invite students to do this, we provide them with the practice and personal satisfaction they can dip into when they are called upon to solve issues that move beyond their community.

Like Pink, Howard Gardner (2007) rallies readers around the kinds of minds and thinking people need for today and the future. In his introduction to *Five Minds for the Future*, he says:

> While making no claims to have a crystal ball, I concern myself here with the kinds of minds that people need if they—if *we*—are to thrive in the world during the eras to come. The larger part of my enterprise remains descriptive—I specify the operations of the mind that we will need. (1)

Gardner explains that we live in a time of vast changes, including globalization, growing quantities of information, and new and ever-changing technological advances. Such changes call for you and me to develop new ways for students to learn and think at school—ways that prepare students to deal with the expected and unexpected in the future. Gardner challenges teachers to invite students to play with and think about information, experiences, and problems using stories, debate, dialogue, humor, role play, questions, illustration, video, and drama. For Gardner and Pink, play, inquiry, creativity, and collaboration have become the thinking and problem-solving quartet for today and the future.

Gardner's goal is to develop students who can deeply understand a topic and think about it in diverse ways in a group and independently, then synthesize this diverse data and solve problems. The compelling issues and questions on pages 76–79 can lead students to this kind of thinking and writing. For example, to bring relevance to their reading, seventh graders I taught studied friendships and wondered, *What makes them work? What makes them go bust?* Groups read realistic and historical fiction, developed interview questions, and interviewed peers, teachers, and family members. Groups collaborated to make connections and synthesize their data, then prepared written notes for group presentations and findings. Groups agreed that building trust, listening and talking, stepping into their friends' shoes to understand their side, and being supportive when things get tough make a friendship work. Friendships dissolve, students pointed out, when trust disappears, when one friend gossips or passes rumors about the other, and when support during hard times is missing. The class agreed that communicating, listening, and holding honest conversations are the foundation of friendships because these build trust and can mend a friendship that is cracked by gossip and rumors.

The problem-solving nature of this project enabled these students to utilize the five capacities that Gardner believes learners will need to survive in the future. Through inquiry, collaboration, and in-depth reading, students explored the concept of friendship, using their disciplined minds. After reading and discussing, students made connections across texts and interview data, using their synthesizing minds. They thought about friendships in unique and innovative ways, using their creative minds. They stepped into the shoes of others, using their respectful minds. Finally, they moved beyond self-interest to explore innovative solutions, using their ethical minds.

Cues from Students

By now you know my bias: we can learn more by talking to our students than from any other source. To gather more information about adolescents' writing in and out of school, I selected students in Virginia and New York to interview by email, using the same set of interview questions about writing. I purposefully limited the number of students because I knew I would be corresponding with them for more than a year. From these back-and-forth emails, I collected middle school students' stories, attitudes, and insights about writing in and out of school. The data celebrates the students' honesty and how much they respond to adults who build caring and trusting relationships (Gardner 2007; Moje 2000; Pink 2005).

The interviews and emails on pages 46–47 are from eighth-grade students I taught at my school, Powhatan in Boyce, Virginia, and from eighth graders in Jenny Smith's class, at Suffern Middle School in Suffern, New York. I did email and interview students from Eastport South Manor Jr. High School in Manorville, New York, whom I have not met or taught; Carolyn Tedesco, a dedicated teacher I met while facilitating professional development on Long Island, helped me initiate communication with them. Though I

Figure 2.1 Drafting is serious work.

extended an invitation to fourteen students to email me, six of the students and I developed an email relationship that taught me about their writing lives.

These middle school boys and girls come from different religious, ethnic, and cultural backgrounds. Some are high achievers, others have average grades, and five are in special education classes. No matter what their backgrounds or socioeconomic level, all have unique voices and dreams. For example, Ashleigh wants to be a poet; Amanda, a novelist; Stephanie, an actress, because her dad inspires her every time he performs in a community play; Brian, an electrician, because he loves gadgets; Thomas, a doctor who helps people in third-world countries; and Kevin, a forensic detective, because he loves reading mysteries.

Though their dreams differ, every student agreed on one point about writing at school: more choice. More choice in topic, more choice in genre, more ways to find ideas, and enough time to write well. Many noted that they enjoyed free journal writing so much more than completing prompts and practicing for state tests. Stephanie, an eighth grader from Suffern Middle School, nailed the feelings of her peers: "My journal is who I really am. In it are secrets, passions, heartache, and joy."

Eighth grader Kevin agreed. When asked, "Is there anything else you want to tell me about writing at school?" he said, "Let us write about our lives . . . what we really are interested in."

When I asked Amanda, a seventh grader, "What kinds of writing do you enjoy doing at school?" she explained, "I enjoy creative writing. I don't like specific topics. I like writing about how I feel at the moment or something totally random and make believe." Students' words resonated with much of the writing that middle school students choose to do outside of school (see Table 2.2).

As you look at Tables 2.1 and 2.2 on the next few pages, compare the goals and purposes for writing that students have with the goals and purposes for writing that schools have. Table 2.1 highlights the writing expectations that teachers, parents, and school administrators have for students. Table 2.2 features what students want to write and what a large group of them throughout this country *do* write outside of school. Each table has three headings. Here are the headings for the first table:

- *Reasons*, which lists the reasons for writing;
- *Writing Tasks*, which lists the kinds of writing completed; and
- *Purposes*, which explains the goals or points of the writing tasks.

Note that I changed the middle heading on the second table, which highlights what students want to write, from *Writing Tasks*, which implies writing for school, to *Writing Forms They Use*, which covers writing to communicate the thoughts, feelings, and beliefs of self and others.

Study the tables. Discuss them with a colleague, with an administrator, and at team, department, and faculty meetings. Consider your school's culture and population, and the need to adjust the emphasis on test prep in middle school, because test prep devours too much of school writing time.

Table 2.1: The Reasons and Purposes for Writing at School

I've based the data in this table on the long-term teacher training I have been doing in Virginia; Long Island, New York; Ohio; and Michigan; on comments and evaluations by teachers and administrators who attend my workshops throughout the country; and from discussions I've had with teachers, administrators, and parents in my community. One parent summed up a perspective on writing that many adults hold: "I want my son to pass the tests with the best scores. You'd be better off teaching him to diagram sentences than all of this choice writing and peer work. That's what I did [in school]." Unfortunately, many adults' ideas about education come from personal experiences.

Table 2.1 The Reasons and Purposes for Writing at School

Reasons	Writing Tasks	Purposes
write to prompts	topic sentence, introduction	pass state tests
	supporting details	make AYP (Annual Yearly Progress)
	conclusion	
	narrative, informative, and persuasive essays	
write for class tests and assignments: reports and essays	topic sentence, restate a question	do well in subject
	supporting details	show content has been learned for state tests
	concluding sentence or paragraph	pass state tests
	essays (five-paragraph)	make AYP (Annual Yearly Progress)
	grammar and usage	
	spelling rules	
	paragraphing	
	content and organization; edit for mechanics	
	before, during, and after reading; use graphic organizers	learn content and determine inportant ideas
		have study guides for tests
		help students understand that brainstorming can make the writing easier
		pass state tests

With change comes the need to educate parents and school boards who don't know the research. This takes time, patience, and commitment. To support this point, I've included a sample letter to parents on the DVD that you can adapt and a timeline of suggested meetings to discuss the research-based adjustments to writing for school.

Table 2.2: The Reasons Adolescents Write Outside of School

To discover what and why middle school students write outside of school, I have synthesized data from the following: the findings from the surveys discussed in Chapter 1; the emails, interviews, and responses to the "Ten Questions About Writing"; as well as my forty-three years of teaching grades 4 through 8 and twenty years of coaching and model teaching in grades K through 12. Writing is more important to adolescents than we think. In interviews and email correspondences, students continually used versions of these words and phrases when asked about writing outside of school: *lots of time, my choice, no stress, no grades, love it because it's from me,* and *I can let go of myself.* Table 2.2 reflects the kinds of writing students choose to complete on their own.

Table 2.2 The Reasons Adolescents Write Outside of School

Reasons	Writing Forms They Use	Purposes
write to answer compelling questions, express strong opinions	jots, notes	to discover what they know, think, and feel
	journals, diaries, letters	to find where they stand on an issue and/or question
	persuasive pieces	to work alone and with a partner or group
	stories, poems, plays	to have choice, time, and an opportunity to make mistakes and focus on the content, then revise if they want to
write for class tests and assignments: reports and essays	write a podcast	
	multiple genres	
	emails, texts, blogs	to share ideas, feelings, concerns, gossip
	homemade videos	to react to the ideas of others
	social networks such as AIM, Facebook, MySpace	to connect with other media; to read about other teens
	fan fiction	to work with a group and write original stories based on the characters, plots, and settings in the work of beloved authors
	multiple genres	to discover the answer to their big questions: *Who am I? Where do I fit in this complex world?*
	diaries, journals	
	poetry	
	jot writing	
	blogs	
	social networks	
	fan fiction	

> I'm not taking the position that middle school writers should develop a school district's writing curriculum. I am extending an invitation for teachers to look at surveys, interviews, schools' needs, and what students enjoy, then reflect on this information to develop a rigorous curriculum that engages students and improves their writing.

What Can We Glean?

There is a disconnect between what motivates students to write at home and at school. Of course, students can't always just write "what they want" at school, but it's reasonable to offer them opportunities for choice writing. Moreover, I'm concerned that they don't know enough about writing craft and technique, revision, and editing. Repeatedly, their answers to the question "How can teachers help you improve your writing?" focus on improving grammar and spelling. Furthermore, emails, interviews, and students' responses to the "Ten Questions About Writing" questionnaire reveal little to no knowledge of reading-writing connections, mentor texts, and craft lessons such as "show, don't tell." My gut feeling is that prior to the pressures of high-stakes testing, such writing lessons were prevalent in some middle schools. Now, with limited time and the pressure to meet Annual Yearly Progress, test prep has taken center stage.

For me, the big takeaway from the table data is that we have to address two questions:

1. With the pressure to spend large chunks of time on test prep in order to pass high-stakes testing, how can we carve out time for the writing that motivates adolescents?
2. How can we integrate lessons on craft, technique, and genre into school writing?

When we teach craft and technique and encourage our students to study mentor texts, we advance their knowledge of how genres work, how to plan writing, how to transition from paragraph to paragraph, and how strong verbs, specific nouns, and sensory imagery can improve writing across genres. Chapters 3 through 5 offer examples of these kinds of writing lessons. As well, you can watch aspects of writing in action on the DVD, which shows students interacting and conferring with one another and with me. Throughout the book, when you see the icon on the right, pause to watch a specific section of the video.

> When students repeatedly ask for more spelling and grammar lessons to improve their writing, I worry that there might be too much emphasis on conventions and not enough on craft and technique.

Cues from Our Colleagues

So far, as we've explored what it takes to narrow the gulf between writing in and out of school, we've looked at cues from research and students. The third strand very much

Figure 2.2 Eighth Graders Collaborate

combines both: professional study. It's teacher action research and, in the kind of professional study of writing instruction I believe in most, *students'* work rather than professional texts take center stage. The most effective professional study occurs when teachers examine the writing that students have generated over the year. Sure, it's important to read, study, and discuss journal articles and professional books with colleagues but there's nothing as powerful as discussing the writing produced by students in your school so you can explore what's working, identify what's not, and figure out how you can bridge the gaps. Some tips and choices for doing this bimonthly or monthly follow:

Defining Mentor Texts

A mentor text is a text you use for teaching students about craft, technique, usage, and genre. These can be texts published by professional writers or student texts. When you use students' writing, select pieces by students who are not presently in your classes, and be sure to remove their names.

> "Whatever you can do or dream you can, begin it. Boldness has genius, power and magic in it." *Goethe*

> Graham and Perin (2007a) found that a combination of teaching process writing and engaging in professional study supported teachers' growth as writing instructors and was more effective than teaching without professional study.

> Chapters 3, 5, 6, 7, and 8 each end with a discussion of one or two pieces of student writing so you can deepen your understanding of the process and experience the benefits of this kind of professional study. The conclusion presents other topics for study.

> "Students' writing and self-evaluations of their process inform and energize my teaching because I'm responding to what they need." *Katy Schain, sixth-grade teacher, Johnson Williams Middle School*

Discuss Students' Writing

Guidelines for Effective Professional Study

When you meet with colleagues to study students' writing, bring photocopies or make an overhead transparency of a piece. If you have time, study two pieces of writing from different students and/or grades. The questions on pages 53–54 can support your use of inquiry to think about and discuss students' writing. Then I move to inquiry, posing questions to find aspects of the writing that need support. Inquiry helps me set a positive tone while I am reviewing students' writing. Questions are kind, and they point me to areas that relate to the students' strengths, so that progress includes building on what student can do. These collegial conversations help you decide what kinds of lessons you will offer students.

Guidelines for Comparing Early and Recent Pieces of A Student's Writing

Having students store all of their writing in one folder offers you and them the option of comparing early and recent writing to observe growth, identify revision and editing needs, and suggest reasonable goals. The questions that follow help you take a long look at students' writing by asking them to choose and compare a piece from early in the year and a recent piece.

- How does the earlier piece compare with the recent one?
- Why do these pieces change your thinking about the student?
- Can you show the growth (or lack of growth) in content and style?
- How does the student's application of craft lessons show progress? Needs?
- What improvements in writing conventions does the comparison show? Needs?
- How does the writer's voice differ in these pieces? Or is it the same?
- Can you suggest one or two writing goals that emerge from this comparison?

Some Questions to Pose

Powerful Topics Lead to Powerful Writing

- How does the writer demonstrate a passion for the topic?
- Does the writer choose topics he or she cares about?
- Why do you (or don't you) hear the writer's voice in this piece?
- How can you help the writer find topics he or she cares about?
- Why does the writer seem reluctant to share ideas that are meaningful to him or her?

Content and Style Grab the Reader's Attention

- How does the title prepare you to read?
- What three or four words come to mind after reading the piece?
- Why does the lead (or introduction) catch the reader's attention?
- Does the writer show an understanding of the genre he or she uses?
- How does the writer develop ideas? Are these detailed and specific? Give examples.
- How does the writer include craft and technique, such as show, don't tell; strong verbs; specific nouns; and sensory images?
- Are the ideas in logical order? Explain.
- Why is the ending convincing?
- How does the writer use figurative language?
- Why is the voice strong?
- How does the writer follow established criteria?

Writing Conventions Bring Clarity and Meaning

- Does the writer use the active voice?
- How does the writer vary sentence beginnings?
- Do you notice that the length of sentences varies? How does this contribute to the success of the piece?
- How is the writer doing with paragraphing?
- How is the writer doing with spelling?
- How is the writer doing with commas?
- Does the writer use complete sentences?
- If there are sentence fragments, are these written for a specific effect?
- Do subjects and verbs agree? Give examples.

- How does the writer use capitalization?
- Does the writer show possession correctly?

Decisions About the Student's Learning
- What positives should I share with the student on a sticky note?
- What should I ask the student to revise?
- What writing conventions does the student need support with and reteaching?
- What is the one point (two at most) I should confer on with the student?
- Would a peer conference be enough to support this student? What would the focus be?
- Have I prepared some guiding questions for a conference?
- What part of the criteria (or rubric) does the student need to work on?
- Would the student benefit from a conference with me where I support him or her with writing conventions?

Use Feedback to Confer with Students

Studying students' writing to determine strengths and needs is the first step. Next, on a sticky note, I jot down a list of areas that require my guidance. The following list includes the strengths and needs for a fifth grader's first draft of a piece on Harry Houdini, which I write on the front and back of a sticky note. The student based the informational piece on a biography that he read.

Strengths (front of sticky note)
- quote as the lead
- fascinating details
- variation in sentence openings

Needs (back of sticky note)
- confusing sentences
- weak title
- general statements that need support
- spelling errors

The list enables me to open a conference by pointing out and celebrating the strengths. Young writers' psyches are fragile, and helping them understand what they've done well enlarges their self-confidence, permitting me to address one need.

Next, I mull over the needs, consider the criteria for this piece (see pages 159–65), and decide on one issue I consider important to this student's growth. For me, clear sentences are a key writing element because content—what the writer is communicating—is crucial. To teach this, I ask the student to read the piece out loud and to put a check next to any part that seems confusing. As much as possible, I try to offer students strategies that work independently.

On the back of the sticky note, I prioritize the other needs, which I can address after I've worked with the student and released responsibility for revising confusing sentences. Here's what I was thinking.

> This student can work with a peer on writing titles and on correcting spelling. I need to think about the spelling errors and incorporate some of these in Word Sorts of specific patterns. Words that end in *-ay* and *-ful* are two we can work on during a conference. Another big topic is providing support for general statements such as "Houdini is the best magician ever." I'll present demonstration lessons, complete collaborative writing using a Read Aloud, and work on this during a conference if necessary.

Having the the two lists makes thinking about strengths and needs easy. I number the needs in the order I believe I'll address each, and then I jot some notes about whether the students will confer with me, a peer, or a peer and me.

Using inquiry to analyze students' writing through professional study with colleagues or when you confer with students has these benefits:

- It sharpens your ability to analyze students' writing on your own;
- It increases your knowledge of possible scaffolds that can support student writers;
- It encourages you to find strengths and needs; and
- It offers choices for conference topics.

Inquiry, the act of posing questions, supports your ability to provide feedback to students. Interventions depend on the student's writing expertise, previous work, and the context and purpose of the piece.

Invitations for Professional Study

Set the agenda for your next three English department or grade-level team meetings. Include an administrator. During the first meeting, discuss the results of the national survey in Chapter 1 and the questions the survey raised on pages 20–21 considering how these impact your writing curriculum.

For the second meeting, ask two teachers to volunteer to bring uncorrected students' writing to analyze with the group. Make sure that when the meeting ends, these volunteers collect the copies of their students' work and file them in a safe place if the conversation needs to continue. Otherwise, take the copies home, tear them up, and place them in recycling. You do not want marked-up copies to somehow find their way back to the students.

The third time you meet, discuss the results and questions raised by the "Ten Questions About Writing" questionnaire. Throughout the year, set aside time to discuss the survey and the ten questions, always linking ideas to your school's culture and students' needs.

Revisiting the Middle School Writing Curriculum

So we've taken our cues from research, students, and our colleagues. But just how does that help us plan our teaching? In the heading I purposefully used the word *revisiting* because I think we can plan a writing curriculum by integrating what researchers and teachers know worked in the past with some new thinking. No need to reinvent the wheel. Figure 2.3 illustrates the three elements that will shape the writing curriculum suited for the twenty-first century.

Use a Writing Process Approach

Adapting the process of professional writers for schools, Don Graves (2003) and Lucy Calkins (1994) presented case studies and literacy vignettes to show how process positively impacted the writing of children. Steve Graham and Dolores Perin (2009) included prewriting and a process writing approach as two of the "key elements of effective adolescent writing instruction" (11). The lessons in this book include the process approach to writing as well as demonstration lessons that build students' mental models of how these process stages work: collecting topics, brainstorming ideas, and planning; studying mentor texts to learn more about process; writing for a specific audience, revision, and editing (Chapter 6); and the need for extended time for writing at school.

> "In the writing process, the longer a thing cooks, the better." *Doris Lessing*

Teacher demonstrations of strategies for discovering topics, brainstorming, planning, drafting, and so forth include Think Alouds that explain why the strategy helps writers, and a written model of how the strategy works. Graham and Perin list writing strategies as their number one instructional element because strategies support writers who struggle as well as proficient writers (Coker and Lewis 2008; Graham and Harris 2005, 2007; Robb 2004; Troia and Graham 2002; Troia et al. 2009).

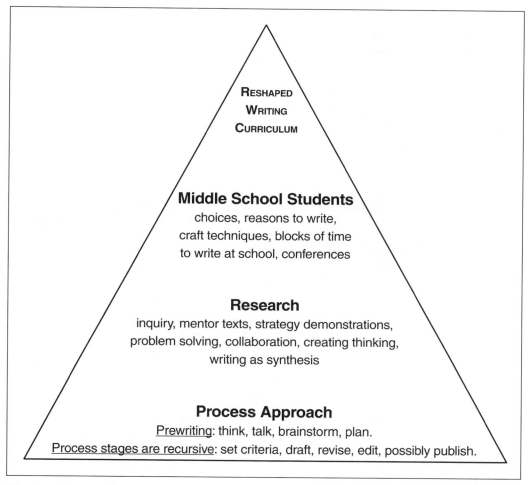

Figure 2.3 Key Elements for a 21st Century Writing Curriculum

Honor the Needs of Middle School Students

While writing this book, here's the question I had to wrestle with: *Is continual free choice enough for middle school writers?* Results of the survey in Chapter 1 led me to consider two points:

1. Students celebrate outside-of-school writing because they have the freedom to choose their favorite genres and the writing is ungraded.

2. Students register positive feelings toward in-school writing when they have teachers who care about them as writers.

Yes, the teacher makes a difference. But is test prep and writing to prompts enough to prepare students for the amount and wide range of writing that future schooling and the workplace require? Clearly, the answer is "No." Left to their own choices, students will continue to write fantasy, fan fiction, romances, blogs, and texts. That's not enough either. Let's limit time spent on test prep and fine-tune choice to involve writing about topics students care about, topics that interest them, topics that are relevant to their lives, but also topics that are relevant to world problems and issues that surround them. I want writing instruction to include genres such as memoir, short story, and the essay, but I also want writing instruction to prepare students for their future lives.

To accomplish this, we need to introduce adolescents to a broader body of ideas and genres. There are two ways to do this—ways that Graham and Perin (2007a) list as two of the big eleven in *Writing Next:* inquiry, and the study of model or mentor texts. Inquiry, asking questions, is a writerly behavior that can drive every stage of the writing process as well as move students beyond the personal writing they did for themselves to considering the issues that define a global society—the issues they'll wrestle with in their lifetime. Extending adolescents' view of the world and showing them writing that moves beyond their personal interests to passionate, political editorials; responses to books; interviews with community members; and analytical writing that invites them to synthesize data have a place in a middle school writing curriculum. The more we integrate mentor texts into the core of instruction, the clearer we make those reading-writing connections to diverse texts, which allows us to prepare students for the wide range of writing and thinking they will need and use as they mature.

Embrace a Creative, Problem-Solving Approach

Developing students who will be the problem solvers of tomorrow takes center stage in the writing of Howard Gardner and Daniel Pink, and we'd do well to contemplate their research and theories. They challenge us to include ways of learning—inquiry, collaboration, synthesis, creativity—that enable students to tackle problems and find solutions or reasons why solutions are impossible. You can divide among teams of students the compelling questions that emerge from relevant personal, community, and global issues in your reading and writing units. Teams can then explore options and solve problems by discussing, thinking, and writing. (See Chapter 3 for more about compelling questions.)

Learning From Students' Writing

During an all-day workshop I conducted in New York City in April, 2009, I invited sixty literacy coaches to analyze the piece of writing shown in Figure 2.4.

Chapter 1

Mammoth Eye is the name of the homicide detective agency in east 1. a. As for me my self and my partner, Harry Baker, are the rookies.

"So what are you and Carla doing this weekend"? Harry asked. Carly, my wife of seven years, was a waitress of 6 years at the golden fork diner just a few blocks away from the agency. "Well considering the fact that Carla's going to her parent's house so she can get her mother to stop calling me the high school hack I'm just going to scavenge threw the cold case room". I said but unfortunately I was unable to stop what happened next. "You haven't caught on yet have you?" Said Harry, his tone getting more serious. "Caught on to what"? I ask. I knew what he was talking about; I was just hoping I could his attitude back to its normal happy and dopy self. "So long as Ortise is head of assignments we've got a better chance of winning the New York lottery". He said. Ortise and his partner Lincoln are head of assigning assignments. "Oh come on I don't think they're intennicilly trying to keep us from actually doing something, things have just been a little quiet around here". I said. "I don't trust Ortise neither but I'd like to keep my job even if it means sucking up to a 4 eyed weirdo and his bold headed partner.

Figure 2.4 Kevin loves writing mysteries.

Here is the background information I shared with them.

> Kevin is an eighth-grade student in Rockland County, New York. He receives extra services in reading and has always been mainstreamed into heterogeneous classes. Detective television shows are Kevin's passion, and he writes detective stories on his own, outside of school. The year I worked with Kevin and his class, he gave me the introduction and first three chapters of *Scar*, a book that he was writing at home. Kevin wanted feedback from me; he expressed great pride in his writing and asked me to email him my thoughts, which I did, pointing out the many positive aspects I observed in his writing. My goal was to support Kevin's enthusiasm for writing, knowing that his teachers would provide lessons on how to punctuate dialogue (see Figure 2.3).
>
> Considered a reluctant writer at school, Kevin was a minimalist when he wrote to prompts or assigned topics. In an interview, he emphasized three times that he wanted to have choice in school and that was why he enjoyed free choice journal writing at school.

I organized teachers into partners and gave each pair a copy of Chapter 1 of *Scars*, explaining that the introduction begins with the murder and decapitation of Gwen Elgon, a twenty-nine-year-old woman. Next, I handed out questions relating to "Content and Style" and "Writing Conventions," which were similar to those you'll find on the DVD. I invited partners to find positives they could share with Kevin and to decide on one or two areas where teacher support could improve Kevin's writing.

Only one teacher out of the group of sixty felt that she could not find any positive elements in this piece. It was difficult for this teacher to move beyond writing convention errors. Her negative comments caused others to say that focusing on what Kevin could not do would discourage him from continuing to write on his own and in school. When composing detective stories, Kevin saw himself as a writer; he told me several times that he dreamed of publishing a book in which detectives used forensic information to solve a series of crimes. Maintaining Kevin's positive view of himself as a writer was high on my agenda; teachers at the workshop concurred. Here is the list of positive elements that fifty-nine coaches agreed upon:

- Contains excellent vocabulary: *scavenge, rookies, sarcastic, intentionally*;
- Puts reader quickly in the agency's office with "Mammoth Eye";
- Sets up conflict between rookies and Ortise;

- Uses dialogue to build background information and introduce characters;
- Contains conversations that show he has knowledge of detective-talk; and
- Sets the scene for Chapter 2 at the end with the phone call.

Though there are several writing convention needs, all teachers felt that it would benefit readers of this story if the author edited for writing dialogue, beginning a new paragraph each time the speaker changes as well as punctuating dialogue correctly. A starting

> **To Edit or Not to Edit, That's the Key Question**
>
> Throughout this book I will make the case for teachers not to edit and rewrite part of students' work. For students to improve, *they* must do the editing and rewriting. However, there will be times when you may write a sample sentence or model a technique for students so they have a point of reference. See Chapter 6 for an in-depth discussion of revision.

point might be to study dialogue in Kevin's present independent reading book during a teacher-student conference. Next, coaches suggested scheduling three or four short one-on-one conferences with Kevin to involve him in editing the dialogue. Another recommendation was to ask Kevin to read his writing out loud, listening for missing and extra words. This would also help with separating the speakers because Kevin would see and hear speaker changes.

In addition, coaches suggested that the teacher review punctuating dialogue in a lesson with the entire class, then move to working with students who continued to struggle with this writing convention by studying how professional writers set up dialogue. Most important, teachers would ask students to edit their own work.

This process, as you can see, is positive for the student and teacher, and it moves far beyond reading papers to give grades, with the teacher marking the corrections. Using the questions on pages 52–54 as guides, teachers can practice collaboration and positive feedback to nurture young writers' fragile self-concepts, and identify positive ideas for teaching that can improve students' writing.

Discuss Students' Writing

Professional Study Invitation

As you plan for your next professional study meeting, consider asking teachers to bring writing samples by special education and/or students with learning disabilities. Many, like Kevin, have a flair for narrative or informational text. Bringing their work before the group can provide teachers with beneficial feedback that can improve students' use of writing conventions and their organization.

CHAPTER 3

Using Mentor Texts to Arrive at Compelling Reasons to Write

To introduce a writing unit on the personal narrative to my eighth graders, I read aloud *Bronx Masquerade* by Nikki Grimes, a series of short fictional personal narratives and poems written from the perspective of a teacher and his ninth graders in a Bronx, New York, high school. On Fridays, when Mr. Ward, the teacher, invites his students to participate in "open mike," they share a poem they've composed, or artwork and photographs. The students in the book reveal their hopes, dreams, anger, frustrations, worries, and joys. Their words and images ring with honesty as they reveal secrets about themselves, home conflicts, stories of abuse, and feelings about being stereotyped as a jock or a nerd. I knew *Bronx Masquerade* would resonate with my eighth graders and open up avenues for their own writing.

In *Bronx Masquerade,* a boy named Tyrone responds to each narrative and poem. This commentary gives the collection even greater depth. When I asked students what they thought, one commented, "Tyrone's like their sidekick, always commenting on what's happening."

Mentor texts like *Bronx Masquerade* are at the heart of teaching writing and reading. The reading-writing connection can seem elusive to both teachers and students, and yet when you select a powerful text you know your students will love, the connection comes into focus. Students hear you read a text aloud, absorbing all the qualities that make it tick, from sound to content to structure. Then you give them an opportunity to read it on their own, and all the while you are casting the conversation so that students realize they can apply the ideas to their own writing. Here is how the teaching and learning proceeded with *Bronx Masquerade.*

Each day, for the first few weeks of this seven-week unit, I read aloud one or two narratives, the accompanying poems, and Tyrone's responses. I placed several copies of the book in the class library, since most students wanted to reread it. For the first exercise, I asked students to work in small groups to figure out questions raised by the narratives and poems in *Bronx Masquerade.*

I used this exercise as a prelude to what my students would eventually do: generate questions relating to their own lives, questions and musings that would in turn help them find a topic, brainstorm ideas, create a plan, and craft personal narratives and poems. As you will see in the pages that follow, their writing constructed meaningful bridges between them and other middle school students. Most important of all, my students' work helped them see that school is a place where they can write in ways similar to the kind of writing they do outside of school.

I started the process by asking students to tell me the questions the kids in Mr. Ward's class might have asked before writing. I recorded these questions on chart paper (see the box on page 65).

The next day, I invited students to generate a list of their wonderings in their writer's notebooks. As you read on, you'll follow Madeline's journey from questioning and responding to prompts to composing a personal essay and poem. Her work reveals the energy and authenticity of voice that compelling questions unleash in students' writing. Her questions illustrate what's on the minds of many middle school writers (see Figure 3.1). Most students will share when asked, as long as they have the choice not to share with classmates and the promise that you will not make their writing public.

A few days later I asked students to respond to a prompt in their writer's notebooks: "If only I was . . ." I wanted to help them delve into their feelings about who they are and

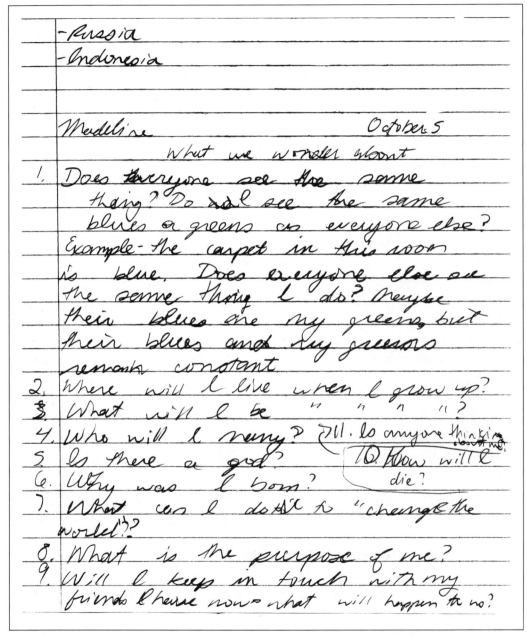

–Russia
–Indonesia

Madeline   October 5
                What we wonder about
1. Does everyone see the same
     thing? Do all see the same
     blues or greens as everyone else?
Example- the carpet in this room
is blue. Does everyone else see
the same thing I do? Maybe
their blues are my greens, but
their blues and my greens
remain constant.
2. Where will I live when I grow up?
3. What will I be   "   "   "   "?
4. Who will I marry?   ?11. Is anyone thinking about me.
5. Is there a god?   10. How will I die?
6. Why was I born?
7. What can I do tll to "change the
world"?
8. What is the purpose of me?
9. Will I keep in touch with my
     friends I have now- what will happen to us?

Figure 3.1 Madeline's wonderings led her toward a writing idea that mattered most.

- What do I want to do if I live?
- Why should we dream about the future?
- Why shouldn't we defer our dreams?
- How does it feel to want something bad enough like Tyrone wanting to be a songwriter?
- Why do we allow and then try to hide abusive behavior?
- How can teachers (other adults) help you do what you're passionate about?

- Why do we try to cover up who we are by wearing masks?
- Why do we fear sharing parts of ourselves?
- Why do we feel we have to hide being smart?
- Why do we try to please others when we really want to do something else?
- Why do our parents want to take over our lives and tell us who to be and what to do?

what they want to become. In the second paragraph of Madeline's piece, she compares herself to a tomato whose skin is fragile like hers (see Figure 3.2). Then she confesses, "The truth is I don't know myself" and closes with "no one thinks how I feel." This comparison, combined with a strong desire to find herself, led Madeline to risk revealing a secret she harbored—a secret only her parents knew.

After three weeks, students had heard a dozen short narratives and poems from *Bronx Masquerade.* It was time to examine how this mentor text could provide students with insights into the structure of personal narratives. Students and I took ten to twelve minutes at the start of three writing classes to make reading-writing connections by analyzing the content and style of a few narratives and poems. Students' noticings became the framework for their narratives:

- Ten in first person;
- Has dialogue;
- Focuses on one powerful event or moment or dream;
- They're short;
- Honest voice, like the person is talking to us; and
- Get right into the point, the happening.

Use several short Read Alouds—parts of picture books, magazine or newspaper articles—because they can enlarge the amount of questions that students raise for their writing and reading. (See Picture Books for Exploring Compelling Issues on the DVD for a list of picture books to read aloud and the issues each illustrates.)

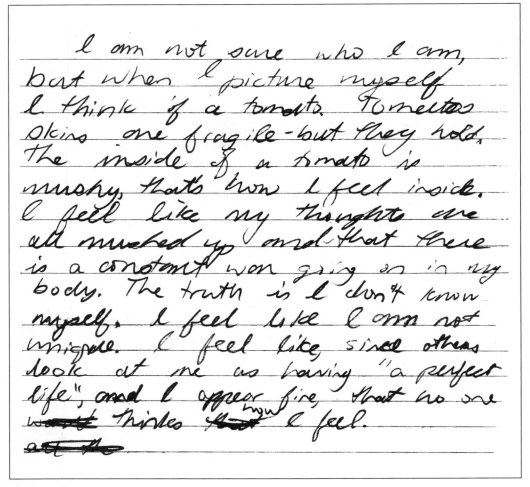

I am not sure who I am, but when I picture myself I think of a tomato. Tomatos skins are fragile—but they hold. The inside of a tomato is mushy, thats how I feel inside. I feel like my thoughts are all mushed up and that there is a constant war going on in my body. The truth is I don't know myself. I feel like I am not unique. I feel like, since others look at me as having "a perfect life", and I appear fine, that no one knows how I feel.

Figure 3.2 Madeline expresses her identity anxieties.

Inquiry and a Mentor Text Drive Students' Personal Narratives and Poems

During the seven weeks in which I immersed my eighth-grade students in *Bronx Masquerade*, I designated a quiet area where they could think about their topics and write. The quiet area contained a small table with four chairs and two oversized pillows. They could also work on a bench in the hallway outside the classroom. The box on page 67 shows how I organized the forty-five-minute periods to give students sufficient time to let

The Day-to-Day Schedule of the Unit

<u>Time Frame:</u> 7 weeks

<u>Read Aloud and Mentor Text Discussions</u>: 10 to 12 minutes

<u>Writing Time:</u> 30 minutes

<u>Wrap-Up and Homework:</u> 3 minutes

The Week-to-Week Schedule of the Unit

Week 1: Read aloud mentor text and discuss it.

Weeks 2 and 3: Brainstorm a list of questions related to the mentor text; have students brainstorm their own personal questions.

Weeks 4 and 5: Confer one-on-one; have students plan and draft their essays.

Weeks 6 and 7: Peers use criteria to confer about content and writing conventions; students revise; teacher-student conferences.

topics bubble up from the mentor texts and inspire their own short personal narratives and poems. Be flexible, however, and let the students' needs lead your instructional and curricular decisions.

Before students began to plan and draft their personal essays, I met with them individually. I asked them to bring pages from their notebook that would help them develop a question that could drive and focus a personal narrative. After Madeline showed me the entry in Figure 3.2, she said, "I'm ready to tell my classmates a part of me they don't know." The compelling question Madeline posed was, "Will telling my secret help me and others understand who I really am?" The following excerpt, which is from Madeline's self-evaluation at the end of the project, shows the degree to which a mentor text and a compelling question can motivate a student to write:

> When I first started this project I knew what to do right away. It was a problem that had been bothering me for days—my depression. I sat in my kitchen alone with music playing softly in the background, a pencil and paper in front of me. First the tears began to pour out, but when there was nothing left, I began to write notes to use in class. Pieces began to fit together and I discovered I really hadn't understood me. My narrative helped me sort out my feelings and get better. Over the next few weeks I realized it was important to tell my friends and teachers what was going on.

Negotiating and Knowing Others
In this unit, students collaborated to pool ideas, negotiated their responses to outstanding models of writing, and trusted one another with their own writing. Such collaboration taps into students' creativity and prepares them for the problem-solving challenges and writing demands they'll meet as they press on with their education or enter the workforce.

Figures 3.3 and 3.4 show close-to-publishable drafts of Madeline's narrative and poem, which she chose to read to the class. Everyone, girls and boys, gathered around her, giving hugs and whispering caring words. Sounding like Tyrone in *Bronx Masquerade*, Liz's comment reflected the initial shock: "Wow! I never expected that!" Madeline's revelation was followed by an outpouring of warmth.

As my class studied what Mr. Ward's students wrote about in *Bronx Masquerade*— abuse, broken dreams, loneliness, negative self-concepts, parental pressures—the book enabled them to pose questions that turned them inward and confront issues they had buried. As Madeline explained, "I realized that it was okay to have depression and that I could use this to help others and be more empathetic." With *Bronx Masquerade* as their mentor text, writing personal narratives and poems heightened their empathy, their ability to deal with issues, and their ability to find topics by synthesizing events, feelings, and relationships (Gardner 2007; Pink 2005).

Guidelines for Using Mentor Texts

As I've learned from the work of Louise Rosenblatt (1938, 1978), who developed reader response theory, when students encounter a new text, they first experience an aesthetic, emotional response to a text. This is followed by the analytical response that invites them to consider content, organization, style, genre, craft, and technique, which they can internalize, thus learning about writing from their reading. Unfortunately, more and more often I see teachers jumping directly into analyzing texts, which ruins the aesthetic experience for students. I find that the most effective mentor texts are those students have already read or heard and enjoyed *before* we shift into an analysis of craft and technique.

Louise Rosenblatt developed the concept of aesthetic and analytical responses in two ground-breaking books: *Literature as Exploration*, published in 1938, and *The Reader, the Text, the Poem*, published in 1978.

My Seceret

I sat in the middle of the classroom and watched. All around me my friends were laughing and having fun. Why can't I be having fun? Are they trying to exclude me? Do they know what they're doing to me? Thoughts flashed through my brain. I couldn't think straight. They hate me. They don't love me like I love them. My eyes became foggy with tears. I was in the middle of a classroom but in a corner of my mind. I was alone. "Stop!" I said to myself. Breathe. I decided that the only thing left to do was to tell my parents; this had been going on for too long. I talked to my dad that night, and bursting into tears I told him how I'd been feeling. He asked me some questions and prescribed me a medicine for my sickness.

I have depression. I try so hard to act happy around my friends and not breakdown. I guess I'm doing a good job because no one would ever think that I'm, depressed unless they pay close attention. But no, I am invisible to everyone else. They go on with their lives while I stand in place, silently, weeping. Doing this just makes me feel lonely and isolated from everyone. I wish I could tell someone other then my parents how I feel, but I can't. If I do they'll look at me and treat me differently. But by not telling people, I feel like they don't know the whole me so I can't close enough to them. I want someone who will love me unconditionally, and have no expectations. I tell myself to keep going because someday I will find that person. One day I can make something of myself. I'm good at math and I liked life science. Maybe I could be a doctor. I want to be a psychiatrist or a guidance counselor. I want to help people who have felt like I have. I want to be someone who can help them when no one else will, like the person that I

Maybe one day I will tell, but not yet. I still feel like crying when my friends joke around without me. Sometimes I even imagine what they would do if I died. Would they cry? Would they care? Would they come to my funeral? It could be any day that we die, and I want to get my secret out before they. Somehow, I know that if I told they would understand.

Figure 3.3 "My Secret" by Madeline

In Between Faces

Exhausted of hiding from me,
Near Bursting
From the burden of a secret *and truth.*
It's like racing,
With a heavy weight,
Strapped onto my back.
It forces me out of my comfort zone,
Skating on thin ice,
As I run from the truth.
Thorns catch me
Breaking the skin on my ankles
Holding me tight.
I cannot escape it,
It's there,
Like a room of mirrors
Reflecting and reminding the truth-
I am my own best friend and worst enemy
I can't escape from myself.

Figure 3.4 "Stuck with herself," Madeline reflects to understand.

In fact, familiarity with a text offers a kind of learning insurance that enables students to move deeply into analysis and make powerful reading-writing connections because they've traversed that material before. First time around with a text, readers are scrambling to get the gist. Second and third times, they're making connections, exploring meanings, enjoying figurative language, or noticing specific phrases.

The texts I use as mentor texts come from three sources:

- Material I read that captivates me and compels me to share it with students;
- Read Aloud texts I share with students; and
- Texts that students choose to share and study.

If a poem or part of a story is new for students, set aside time for them to read and/or hear it, to discuss it, and to react to it before they begin studying it for writing craft, technique, and genre. In these first readings, students get the hang of what the author is saying and bond to the text. Multiple readings target the author's craft and technique. Try learning from a mentor text by yourself and experience how multiple readings take you below the surface.

> "Provide adolescents with good models for each type of writing that is the focus of instruction. These examples should be analyzed and students encouraged to imitate the critical elements embodied in the models."
> *Dolores Perin, "Best Practices in Teaching Writing to Adolescents"*

Figure 3.5 Writing and revising needs comfortable spaces.

Mentor Text Lessons: Quickly Turn the Process Over to Students

When you demonstrate how to analyze a mentor text, beware of holding the floor for no more than two or three minutes because you'll lose middle school students in a heartbeat. Remember, active involvement, not passive listening, is the way to capture their interest. So quickly turn the process over to your students.

Also, in order to ensure that there are plenty of examples for students to discover, I only unearth a few of the text's treasures. That is, my demonstration lessons focus on just one reading-writing connection. For example, I might think aloud how I analyze a text's lead; the author's use of sensory imagery or extended metaphor; personification; how the author handles changes in time and setting; and so on.

Next, I ask kids to find a partner, read the piece several times, and share their reading-writing connections. I like to start the process with this open-ended question: What did you notice about craft? Technique? Figurative language? If this doesn't ignite discussion and thinking, I pose a question.

For instance, one day my class studied Dickinson's poem about the sunset:

> *She sweeps with many colored brooms,*
> *And leaves the shreds behind;*
> *Oh, housewife in the evening west,*
> *Come back, and dust the pond!*
>
> *You dropped a purple raveling in,*
> *You dropped am amber thread;*
> *And now you've littered all the East*
> *With duds of Emerald!*
>
> *And still she plies her spotted brooms,*
> *And still the aprons fly,*
> *Till brooms fade softly into stars*
> *And then I come away.*

I asked, "Why does Dickinson use a housewife?"

Danny marvels at the uniqueness of the metaphor: a housewife sweeps night into our lives. He says, "When the comparison is different that you kinda go, 'Yikes,' and see it; that's the best." He adds, "She is kind of a stand-in for the sun setting."

Jeannette points out the repetition in the poem and connects it to the repetition of a broom being swept. "I guess you have to really think that metaphor through to see if the link works," she adds.

Margaret points the class to the last stanza, noting that Dickinson "keeps the housewife and her broom alive 'till the end. It's a stretch for me to imagine brooms fading into stars, but the word *softly* makes it happen."

Frequently, students see things in a mentor text that we miss because their experiences differ from ours. For example, Hattie brings attention to the word *littered*: "My partner and I felt that *littered* is the opposite of what a housewife does." She explains that *littered* "startles—it creates a picture of random splashes of color in the sky." This is an *a-ha* moment for the other eighth graders, and for me. Turning over to students the act of making reading-writing connections illustrates the force behind collaboration; many minds see more than one mind at a time (Gardner 2007; Pink 2005; Willis 2007).

Partners spend about ten minutes analyzing the poem. They continue to notice specific words and the reasons for repetition, which stay true to the images a housewife and broom conjure. When the ideas spring from students, the concepts resonate and resound in their writers' minds, becoming tools to use as they brainstorm topics and ideas for metaphors.

For the final question, I ask the eighth-grade partners to explain how they can apply what they've learned from Dickinson's poem to create their own poems with extended metaphor. Here are some of their thoughts:

- Make your metaphor unique; test it to see if it works.
- Use strong verbs—they make pictures in readers' minds.
- Make sure you can see what you want others to see.
- Repetition can help your poem.

Questioning Techniques that Put Responsibility on Students

Use these suggestions to turn the study of mentor texts over to students:

- Organize students into pairs or small groups.
- Explain the purpose for studying the text. If you have multiple purposes, consider giving groups or pairs a different purpose to work on. Then have students teach one another.
- Encourage students to inquire—pose questions that support their reading-writing connections.
- Ask students to find concrete examples of craft or technique from the text.
- Call for volunteers to share their findings; jot these on chart paper.
- Invite others to comment or pose questions.
- Close by asking students how this knowledge can impact their writing.

Figure 3.6 Sharing Part of a Great Read

Mentor Text Lesson in Action

See me present a lesson using a memoir by Ralph Fletcher

Most writers agree that writing is hard work; it takes effort and lots of time to craft and shape a piece that feels just right for readers. This happens because professional writers carry a treasure in their minds and imaginations—a treasure that they mine to help them create suspense, plot a story, build character, craft energetic leads and endings, or explore metaphor. I urge you to make your students aware of professional writers' strategies and tips.

Plan Reading and Writing Units Together

Inquiry compels students to pose questions about their reading. It becomes the force behind investigating and solving problems. It also helps students understand how to cope with changes and global issues such as poverty, loss of family income or diminished income, the need to defer a dream, the death of a family member or pet, the breakup of a friendship, the need to move, and so on (Wilhelm 2007). Questions that drive students' reading can also lead students to find writing topics they're passionate about.

I can't separate reading and writing. As I plan a reading unit, I use inquiry to connect texts with writing possibilites. I'm intoxicated with ideas that the essays, stories, and poems I pore over suggest about themes, genre, and craft. I ask myself:

- What writing lessons do my students need?
- Which mentor texts will support these writing lessons?
- What issues and problems lend themselves to students' inquiry?

For me, the planning is always a balancing act. Do I simply attend to curriculum requirements, such as teaching students to write a persuasive essay, or do I also offer students options to write other kinds of persuasive pieces, such as editorials, letters to the editor, or op-ed columns? I understand that school districts require students to write in specific genres, such as a lyric poem or a short narrative, and I do attend to these requirements. Whenever possible, however, I stretch beyond the requirements to offer students that wide range of writing experience they'll need for their future lives.

In addition to required writing at a specific grade level, students need opportunities for choice of topic and genre. Choice allows students to explore and research compelling questions in meaningful ways; choice permits students to select the genre that works best for their compelling question and the topic they develop. For example, if two students in the same group explore why friendships dissolve, one might use realistic fiction while the second turns to fantasy to show the end of the last friendship on earth.

Inquiry can also bring diversity to a study and turn students' reluctance into relevance, boredom into energy, and indifference into commitment. Compelling questions that emerge from relevant issues and problems invite students to search for answers using avenues you and I might never consider. One student might use inquiry to develop a peer survey about broken friendships, while the other gathers data from song lyrics. Compelling questions that emerge from relevant issues and problems invite students to search for answers using avenues you and I might never consider. Schools might view surveys as a more acceptable tool for gathering data than song lyrics, but the second option shows creativity and can also yield worthwhile results. However, inquiry can bring this kind of diversity to a study and turn students' reluctance into relevance and boredom and indifference into energy and commitment.

Issues, Compelling Questions, and Problems Drive Writing

"Do we have to answer those questions?" a fifth-grade boy asked his teacher. I was visiting his class in a school in the Midwest. The questions were part of a novel unit of study that the teacher had purchased for her proficient readers and writers. Clearly, the questions, which had been created by an adult, did not resonate with this fifth grader. "Can't my group ask and answer our own questions?" he pleaded. His teacher looked toward me for help as she searched for an answer that would honor the boy's request, yet keep him focused on the assignment.

The only response that would satisfy the student—bringing relevance to his writing about his reading and honoring his wonderings—would be for the teacher to adopt an inquiry approach to writing and reading (McTighe, Seif, and Wiggins 2004; Wilhelm 2007). I find that the questions students pose, the ones that bombard their minds when they're engaged with their reading and writing, are more challenging and meaningful than the factual questions found in guides to books or in the teacher's editions of basal reading/writing programs.

In this section, I list ten issues that connect to students' lives, each followed by the questions my students have raised over the years that yield passionate, unique, and relevant writing. The issues and questions, along with the literary genres that students choose to express their ideas, enable them to determine their audience. Do not offer them to students as a prepared list of questions; students will not own them enough to write with commitment and voice. Instead, use them to model the kinds of queries you want students to pose. The primary purpose of wondering is for queries to grow out of your own students' experiences, passions, emotions, values, and beliefs. Invite them to create their own questions; this means that you will recreate the list of compelling questions with each section of writing you teach.

> Go to the DVD for a list of picture books that you can read aloud to address the ten issues that follow.
>
> **DVD** CLASSROOM RESOURCES

Ten Issues and Compelling Questions

I deliberated over which issues to highlight here. I selected these ten because, in my classrooms, these consistently raised questions in students' minds that led them to write from personal experiences as well as from information they collected during interviews, surveys, and research.

Encourage your students to give specific examples as they explore these issues and questions—the details, the events, and the information are what connect readers to writing.

1. CHANGE AND LOSS
- How does personal illness or a handicap change lives?

- How do families and individual members deal with a parent's job loss?
- How do I cope with the death of a parent, pet, friend, or sibling?
- Why is moving away from my friends and family so hard? So exciting?
- What do physical changes do to my feelings about myself?
- Why is it or isn't it good to suffer?

2. **CHALLENGES, CHOICES, DECISIONS**
   - Why do I feel that it's possible to overcome some challenges and not others?
   - When do goals become challenges? How do the obstacles make me feel? Act?
   - Why can challenges be positive? Negative? When are they a mixture of both?
   - How can a negative challenge become positive?
   - How do challenges present choices in life?
   - How can a decision set challenges into motion?

3. **RELATIONSHIPS: INSIGHTS INTO SELF**
   - Why do some relationships work and some fail?
   - What leads relationships to dissolve?
   - Why is having friends so important?
   - What does it take to fit into a group? A place?
   - Why have relationships with parents, teachers, friends, or siblings become adversarial?
   - Can I have a relationship with myself? Why or why not is this good? Bad?
   - Why is trusting someone part of happiness?
   - Why is my pet my lifeline these days?
   - How does approval or disapproval from parents affect my relationship with them? With others?

4. **COPING WITH FEARS**
   - What do I fear? Why do I fear it?
   - Why do fears affect my dreams? Actions?
   - Why is the future both scary and exciting?
   - Why do I fear changing schools?
   - Why do I worry about being ignored by the in-group? Or kicked out by them?
   - How do my fears affect my thoughts? Emotions? Decisions?

5. **PRESSURES: INNER AND OUTSIDE INFLUENCES**
   - Why do I need so much approval from peers?
   - Does gossiping (and/or telling lies) make me a traitor?
   - How has moving created pressure in my life?
   - Why do people pressure others?

- Why do people put pressure on themselves?
- Why is there so much pressure during a sports game? Can you describe these pressures?
- Have I ever influenced or pressured someone to do something? How did this turn out?
- How and why do popular culture and media pressure women into always looking perfect? How does this affect young girls and women? Men?
- Which gender has more pressure, and why do I think this?

6. **IDENTITY SHAPING: HOPES AND DREAMS**
   - Why do I guard my privacy at home?
   - What do I want to be? Why?
   - Why do I hope that my grades will improve?
   - Where will I be in ten years?
   - Where do I go to daydream and wonder? Why is this place special?
   - Why do I want to fit in?
   - Why don't I care about fitting in?

7. **OBSTACLES AND SELFHOOD**
   - How are language barriers obstacles in my life?
   - How can weather become an obstacle?
   - How can where I live be an obstacle in my life?
   - Why are religion and race obstacles?
   - How was my parents' divorce an obstacle in my life?
   - Why are the expectations of others [parents and teachers] obstacles for me?
   - How is the fact that I'm never included in social things at school an obstacle? Give examples.

8. **WAR AND CONFLICT**
   - Is there such a thing as a just war?
   - Why is conflict bad? Good?
   - How do I feel about a family member going to war?
   - What would life be like without conflicts?
   - Why do friends make wars?
   - How can I avoid conflict at home?
   - How can people and countries achieve peace?
   - Why do people get angry and frustrated with one another?
   - Do power and control have anything to do with conflicts?
   - Why can power and control be positive forces? Negative forces? Both?

9. RESTRICTIONS, RULES, AND REBELLIONS

- Why do I feel the need to break some rules and restrictions? In what situations are rules broken? Give examples.
- How do others view teen rebellions? Teens breaking rules?
- How do the rules I make at home affect other family members?
- Why is it okay for me to make and break rules but not others?
- What are my rebellions? How do these affect my emotions? Thoughts? Actions?

10. CONFORMITY/NONCONFORMITY

- Why do people work so hard to fit into a group?
- Will I feel better if I'm part of the in-group?
- Why do people (or I) want to conform and then not conform?
- Why are some people able to resist conforming to what groups or members dictate?
- Why do some people feel pleasure in excluding others from their in-groups?
- Is it easier to conform and go with the flow or be different?

Show Your Students How to Create Compelling Questions

If students have never created their own questions for reading and/or writing, it's beneficial for you to demonstrate the process. Start with modeling, especially for fifth and sixth graders, and then turn the process over to the students when the quality of their questions shows you they're ready for independence.

Even if students have been through the process once or a few times, it's still good practice to always start with modeling and thinking aloud. These acts refresh the students' memories of two things: (1) the nature of compelling questions; and (2) the ways they can use lists of ideas related to issues and problems to compose compelling questions for reading and writing.

Reserve about ten to fifteen minutes of three or four consecutive classes to model the process. The time will diminish as students practice and internalize the process.

The First Day

Have students pair-share on everything they think they know about the structure and elements of a genre or an issue. Follow this by asking students to jot down a list in their journal. The list can come from ideas they've discussed with a partner and any new thoughts that popped into their head.

The Second Day

Collect a list of statements from students' journals that relate to the text structure of the genre or to the issue. Write these on chart paper, leaving two lines between each statement. (You will use the space to turn the statements into questions.) Here's part of a list of statements from a sixth- grade class about fantasy.

- People go on quests.
- There's good versus evil.
- A quest can be a search for your own self.
- The hero has to deal with evil forces.
- At the end there's changes in the characters, maybe relationships.
- A quest tests the limitations of the main character.

The Third Day

Reread the list and invite students to add statements to it. In a Think Aloud, show students how you transform statements into questions. I write questions on the chart in the blank spaces with a different-colored marker. Be sure to leave two or three statements incomplete for groups to change into questions on the fourth day. In the list below, a question appears below each statement in italics.

- People go on quests.
  Why do people undertake quests?

- There's good versus evil.
  How do struggles with good and evil shape the quest?

- A quest can be a search for your own self.
  Can you show how the quest is about who the hero is and who he or she wants to become?

- The hero has to deal with evil forces.
  How does the hero deal with evil and negative forces met on the quest?

The Fourth Day

Review the statements and questions, showing how the questions relate to and grow out of the statement. Now, ask groups to change the last two statements into questions. Here's the type of work that sixth graders do:

- At the end there's changes in the characters, maybe relationships
  What and why are the changes at the end of the quest—changes in the characters, their relationships, and the places they live?

- A quest tests the limitations of the main character.
  How and why does the quest test the hero's limits of endurance, patience, and forgiveness?

You can help students generate questions with reading materials; with video, TV, and movie clips; and by surfing and reading on the Internet. Also practice generating questions together from students' life experiences, picture books, magazine and newspaper articles, or other short texts such as folktales, myths, legends, and poems.

Fifth Graders Create Compelling Questions for a Biography Unit

Cheri Kesler is a fifth-grade teacher at Powhatan School, a K–8 independent school surrounded by the Blue Ridge Mountains. Together we planned a five-week biography reading-writing unit for her fifteen students, who would each read a biography at his or her instructional level. Two students read at the fourth-grade level, two read at the sixth-grade level, and the rest read at the fifth-grade level.

The issue to bind fifteen different biographies together was "obstacles." Cheri and I agreed that we would help students understand the text structures and features of biography, but their writing would grow out of the issue of obstacles. We planned to help students develop questions to discuss their reading and drive their writing, and then ask them what genres they might choose to write a piece about obstacles.

> Compelling questions can spark meaningful discussions of diverse books, and lead students to writing topics that are highly interesting to them.

Overcome	Still Have
"fear of deep water"	"fear of snakes, which limits where I hike"

On the first day, students pair-shared on the word *obstacles* in an open exchange of ideas. I asked them to bring to the discussions any ideas that surfaced in their minds. After pairs shared, the modeling began. On chart paper, I wrote a double-entry journal that included my name, the date, and the heading *Obstacles*. My purpose was to show students what their journal entries would look like and to create a charted resource students could use (see sample above).

I wrote *Overcome*, and on the right-hand side I wrote *Still Have*. Under *Overcome*, I wrote "fear of deep water"; under *Still Have*, I wrote "fear of snakes, which limits where I hike."

Consider This

I never call for complete sentences when I ask students to think of ideas; the restriction of composing sentences gets in the way of generating ideas freely.

I explained that content and ideas count, and that students should do the best they could with spelling. I also pointed out that handwriting needed to be legible so students could reread their notes. Partners shared ideas from both columns and Cheri recorded these on chart paper. These fears were obstacles for many fifth graders: not doing well at school in spelling, reading, division, and not being able to complete their homework. Other fears that became obstacles were life-changing events such as fear of losing a grandparent or pet, or the fear of death.

On the second day, to broaden students' thinking about obstacles, I read aloud the picture book biography *Wilma Unlimited,* by Kathleen Krull. Reading picture books to enlarge students' concepts of an issue and genre has the same power as a wave that knocks you breathless at the ocean.

After I read several pages, I paused and invited pairs to discuss the obstacles Wilma and her family faced. Partners shared these with the class, and Cheri added the obstacles to the list on the chart. Next, pairs created questions about obstacles that could drive their reading, and then they selected questions they felt might lead them to discover writing topics related to obstacles (see list on page 83).

Separate Discussion from Writing

Discussions are oral texts, and we should value them by asking students to share, listen, and question one another without writing. After a discussion has ended, ask students to silently recall, connect, and reclaim new ideas, then jot these down in words and/or phrases in their writer's notebooks or journals.

Compelling Questions About Obstacles Drive Fifth Graders' Writing

As they explored topics for writing about obstacles, students adapted the list of discussion questions they had created for reading. Some students used the questions as springboards for exploring relevant, writing topics that sparked related queries; others used a question to openly brainstorm and then surprised themselves with one or more related writing ideas. For example, while exploring the question "How is fear of the dark an obstacle?" one student decided to investigate the darkness—bad feelings and thoughts—inside her mind and not the darkness of the night. Of course, the student may decide not to write about these idea-detours, but the ruminating plants seeds for future writing ideas.

Note how the following questions about obstacles, which Cheri's students created, differ from the ones on page 78. Each group of students' questions will be unique.

- How are my fears obstacles? Explain.
- How can I overcome my fears?
- What kinds of discrimination have I experienced? What caused the discrimination? How did I deal?
- What things about a person can help the person overcome obstacles?
- Why have my outbursts become obstacles? How can I overcome these?
- How and why was the death of a grandparent an obstacle? Was I able to overcome my feelings? Explain.
- How is fear of the dark an obstacle? How can you overcome this?

The students' questions reflected their problems and their search for solutions, which they later synthesized in their writing.

Making Tough Decisions About Reading-Writing Units

There are times when it makes sense to invite students to try writing in a certain genre, such as fairy tale or realistic fiction, because it links to the reading unit you're pursuing. If you want everyone to try their hand at a genre, make sure that your students have the maturity and the reading and writing background experience to deal with the complexities of these genres. Asking students to complete writing tasks that are beyond a challenge and fall into the frustration zone can discourage middle school writers and diminish their self-confidence (Schunk and Zimmermann 1997; Tomlinson 1999; Vygotsky 1978; Wormeli 2007). However, if a few students want to write in a challenging genre because they have read widely in that genre and have a keen knowledge of its text structure, then encourage and support them. This is what choice means for you and your students.

In the five-week unit, Cheri and I agreed that it wouldn't be fruitful to ask fifth-grade students to write a biography based on research or interviews. Moreover, we wanted to offer students choice by inviting them to explore one of the questions swirling around the theme of *obstacles*. Depending on their topic and audience, students would decide on the genre. To begin, we asked students to list possible genres in their journals. Then we met to discuss their ideas, which we wrote on a large chart as a resource for everyone to use. Here's what they suggested:

- Poem
- Short, short story
- Fairy tale
- Diary entries
- News article

Cheri and I gave the students two options: (1) explore *obstacles* in any genre you wish or (2) write an informational piece. We knew that some students were experts on topics that were their passion, such as swimming, oceanography, and making and flying kites. All students needed to use the stages of the writing process to craft a piece.

Compelling Questions Lead to Powerful Fifth-Grade Plans and Drafts

Daniel chose to do a series of diary entries about overcoming a challenge: "How can I overcome my fears?" Before he brainstormed and created a plan, we met to talk about his topic. "What are you planning for these diary entries?' I asked.

"I'm goint to write about the time I struggled with sprinting," said Daniel.

"Can you tell me more about this struggle?"

" Yeah. I kept needing breaks when I practiced," said Daniel. "I felt tired and thirsty, Then a fourth grader taunts me and says that I'll stink running the mile. I'm going to write how I changed that."

"Why did you choose to write diary entries?"

"Well." Daniel paused to think. "Well, I can show my feelings and how my friends helped. I can also tell why I was determined to beat this obstacle and that fourth grader's prediction. It felt more right than a story because I could give my point of view."

During our conference, Daniel indicated that he would plan for three entries. Once he started, he completed four entries (Figure 3.7). That's the way of writing plans. They start you thinking about the writing journey and take you to places you never thought you'd visit. The four diary entries illustrate how Daniel dealt with this obstacle. He includes dialogue, uses repetitions effectively—"Sprint! Sprint! Sprint!"—and shows how his peers cheered him on and supported his goals. Figure 3.8 shows a portion of his finished piece of writing.

Rikesh decided to write a narrative about an obstacle he experienced whenever he picking up his pet gerbil, Midnight: Midnight peed in Rikesh's hand. At first, Rikesh insisted that a story could just describe his gerbil. In a conference, he and I chatted, and Rikesh quickly nailed the problem for his story. When he focused on what the gerbil didn't like (see Figure 3.9), he said that the writing helped him "figure out that the gerbil peed because it feared being picked up." As Rikesh explains in his essay, he decided to pick up the gerbil every few days to get it used to being handled.

> "My plan helped me write because I didn't have to keep stopping to think of ideas. My draft changed from the plan because I found good ideas along the way."
> *Rikesh, fifth grader*

Students Weigh In on Writing About Personal Experiences

There will be times when, as students discuss questions with peers, a query will surface that doesn't exactly relate to the issue, or a student may prefer not to delve into and share personal experiences. When I asked the nineteen students in Jenny Smith's eighth-grade class at Suffern Middle School to complete a Fast Write on how they felt about sharing parts of their lives with an audience, all but two students felt it was important. Ten students agreed that sharing something tough in your life could help someone who had gone through a similar event. It could also help the writer understand and move past the tough experience. Michael Rodriguez, a sensitive young man, wrote: "I feel ok to share my life with other people. Its ok because some people don't know who I am." His classmate, Douglas Volpicella, said he would not share something "embarassing and strange because it would make me feel bad and cause it is like they are making fun of me." Michael and Douglas are honest about the plight of dozens of middle school students who tend to hide who they are from others only to experience loneliness and tinges of regret. Brian Williams also expressed reservations: "I would share when I was younger," he wrote, but he lacks "enough courage" to share anything now.

WRITING PLAN FOR DIARY ENTRIES

NAME_____DATE_____

THREE TO FOUR ENTRIES

FIRST ENTRY
• working on starts   1, 2, 3 go! I sprint for 3 seconds then
• get going fast   pace
• run mile
• kind of nervous

SECOND ENTRY   I keep a cool nice pace going.
• work on pacing
• get a good speed
• two laps
• really nervous
• one 4th grader says
  I will fail

THIRD ENTRY   Sprint! Sprint! Sprint! I sprint my legs
• work on finish   off and finish.
• get a good kick
• one lap
• super nervous
• think about what
  4th grader said

FOURTH ENTRY   into the field. We unload
• ride to race   The bus rolls
• heart clinching
• finish 8th
• get medal
• Try to forget what
  4th grader said but
  can't

Figure 3.7 Daniel's details support his writing.

Day 1:
    1, 2, 3 go! I sprinted for about 3 seconds and pace. I run four corners three times. Then I finish in a time of 7:25 seconds. "I need to break six." I tell Cameron shortly after he finished after me. "You'll do it." he laughed. We go to the water fountain and take a few sips. We walked back to the field and waited for the following to finish.

Day 2
    I keep a cool nice pace. This time a ran only ran two laps. I took my daily water fountain trip. When I was walkin back to the field a fourth grader walked up to me. "Youre going to stink at mile." he sneered. "Hey. I did good this year I'll do good again." I tell him. He walks away slowly. I watch him the go back to the field.

Day 3
    Sprint! Sprint! Sprint! I sprint my legs off. This time we only do one lap so we won't be tired. I finish I don't get tired or thirsty. I'm still thinking about what the kid said. "Don't worry. He's just messing with you." William said. "That's the problem." I said.

Figure 3.8 With ideas out there, the writing flows.

WRITING PLAN FORM FOR NARRATIVE STORY

NAME_____DATE_____

POSSIBLE TITLES: MY Gerbil Midnight

intro BEGINNING
—what My Gerbil looks like.
—When I got it
—2 months ago

black with
white under its
chin

My Gerbil is
very unique
and unlike any
animal I know.

My Gerbil is black
with white under its
chin like a the moon in the night sky,
it is because of this I named it midnight

My gerbil pees in
my hand.

I put it back in
the cage fast.

MIDDLE
—what my Gerbil likes,   —wheel
—what it does   —hut
                —used take token   —hair
                —stuffes   —ect
                  into hut   —me
                —chews hair   guests
                —goes into my
                  lap
                —plays with his sisters
                  Gerbil

END
—what it dislikes   —being picked up
how I help —what its scared of —bull (rolling ball)
it   —strange people
—ending sentence   —squares/cubes
(everyone bugs a make   —my   Something
it go in its ball or I pick it
up)   as you can see my gerbil is unique.

Figure 3.9 Rikesh tries out ideas while planning.

These Fast Writes highlight the importance of teacher flexibility when students choose topics to explore. We must make certain that all students are comfortable with an assignment or a suggestion before we ask them to proceed. We must also reserve time for students to explore and discuss questions that stir writing ideas, and to discover writing projects that emerge from reading units. When students can select topics that they care deeply about, their writing contains a strong voice and sharp details, and readers can reexperience what the writers have lived though.

Compelling Questions Lead to Powerful Poetry

The Fast Writes that the eighth graders completed in Jenny Smith's class were a prelude to a poetry lesson that used David Harrison's *Connecting the Dots* as a mentor text. We used the students' reactions to the concept of sharing parts of their lives as a springboard for discussing Harrison's poems about his life journey from age four to sixty-five. After reading aloud several of my favorites, I placed "Jigs" and "Mr. Smooth" on the overhead projector and asked groups, "What do you notice?" Here's their list:

- On top of the poem is his age and some background information about the poem.
- The poems focus on one part of an event.
- They're short.
- There's dialogue.
- There are strong verbs: *shove* and *waddles* in "Jigs."
- There are stanzas.
- They have punctuation.
- They're about events in his life. The events are ordinary like what happens to us.

Out of the last item on the list, students developed an overarching question to drive finding ideas: *What parts of our lives, past or recent, could become an autobiographical poem?* The list of what students noticed became the content criteria for their original poems.

Michael, a student in special education, often finds reading and writing tough. Because Michael chose to write about what he loved—wrestling—he was able to make use of rich brainstorming (Figure 3.10), which he observed "was easy to do." From there, he crafted an affecting poem (Figure 3.11). When readers arrive at the last line, "I won . . ." they share the excitement and pleasure Michael felt. Shaping a poem was new for Michael, but he quickly learned how to mark breaks in the lines (Figure 3.12), then play with spacing his stanzas.

Compelling Questions Lead to Powerful Fiction

Another eighth-grade teacher, Ann Kiernan-Robb, worked with me to develop a reading-writing unit around the issue of pressure. Ann led the reading workshop, and I facilitated the writing workshop. We introduced the unit by inviting students to complete Fast Writes on the word *pressure*. Groups shared their Fast Writes and developed questions that could help them find writing topics. Addison suggested the following question and quickly chose it as her topic: "How and why do popular culture and media pressure

In event in My life was a wresling tournament. I won all three maches, my first mach
I was shaking because I thougnt I was
going to lose. When the mach started
I kept moving around untill I sau
an open spase to shoot. I grabed
his neck I tryed to do pouch the migit
I got the move than I layee him on
his back and pined him in 30 seconds.

      The second mach I hade to
v.s my freind Phil. Phil was taller
then me, and biger the me. I was
afrade because my bod was shaking,
I felt so cold and I was nervus,
and I was afrade Phil might hate me.
When the mach s

Figure 3.10 Michael's love of wrestling makes it an ideal topic for him.

women into always looking perfect? How does this affect young girls and women?
Men?"

At first, Addison leapt out of her chair and shouted, "I have it! I have it!" Then she quietly relaxed on a pillow resting against the wall, thinking, finding her characters, and plotting her story. For three days, Addison wrote at the computer, so immersed in her story
that she was unaware of her classmates' chatter and the bell announcing the end of class.

On the fourth day, Addison entered class waving two and a half typed pages of a
story. "It doesn't work. I'm done. I can't picture what's going to happen next." I asked

When the match started/Phil
tried to put me on my back/& time
ran out so slow like a turtle./It was
second quarter/and I was so tired.
When the time started I was on the bottom,
Phil was on a referee position. I reversed
the move Phil was going to do. I grabbed
his neck/and put him on his back
there 15 seconds to pin him./I pinned
him in 57 seconds/I had 3 seconds
remaining. I won it all/I was thinking and
I won.

The match started
My ercing Phil
Tries to put me on my back
Time ran out
Second quarter started
I was tired
I was on the bottom
Phil was in a ~~referee~~ referee stance
I I reversed Phil army chomp
I got up fast
I grabbed his neck
Put him on his back
"15 seconds left to pin"
He kept moving around and around
"keep still"
I caught him and ~~pined~~ pinned him in 57 sec
3 seconds to spare.
I
.

Figure 3.11 From Paragraph to Shaped Poem

I'm Thirteen and I wrestle for suffern
middle School.

My Match Started. I was againts my freind Pi

Phil tries to put me on my back
time ran out

second quarter Started
I was tired
I was on the bottom
Phil was in a referee Stance

I reversed phil's arm chomp
I got up fast
I grabbed his neck
put him on his back

"15 second left to Pin"

He kept Moving around and around

"keep still"

I caught nim and Pinned him in 57 second
3 seconds to spare

I won . . .

Figure 3.12 A Victory in the Ring and with the Poem

her to let me read her draft and suggested she read or work on another piece. Reluctant at first, by the end of class she gave me a copy. The next day, we had a conference. "I'm stuck," she said. "I'm not sure how to get Allie's friend, Dawn, to find out about Allie's bulimia."

"How might she find out at school?" I asked.

"Dunno," was the first response.

"They're eating lunch together," I pointed out. "What will Allie have to do?"

"I got it!" Addison whispered. She booted up a computer and started writing. Addison put both girls in the bathroom, allowing Dawn to discover Allie's secret. (You can see this section from her narrative, "Not a Statistic," in Figure 3.13b.)

Sometimes when students get stuck, we need to allow a day or two for the writing to cool and then hold a conference to ask questions. These steps can rekindle students' commitment and passion and help them plot the middle and end of a story.

> **Students' Plans and Writing Success**
>
> I urge you to read students' plans carefully, as I do, and then confer with those who need scaffolds. A thoughtful, detailed plan provides students with the ideas and organization they require for drafting a piece (Coker and Lewis 2008; Graham and Harris 2005). For more about plans, see pages 134–38 in Chapter 5.

"Not a Statistic" was not a text for Addison to abandon. She used internal monologue and masterfully employed the technique of show, don't tell. But like many middle school writers, her frustration and momentary inability to further the plot resulted in a rash decision to drop the piece. Fortunately, I was able to help Addison by listening to her concerns, recalling her electric reaction to the compelling question she composed, and creating a safe writing environment. These actions opened the communication channels between us, and they helped Addison find her way to the end of her story. This is what writing teachers need to do for every student who passes our way.

Learning from Students' Writing

In this chapter I've begun to extol the importance of planning writing before drafting. It's what every writer does, from Newbery Award–winning author Katherine Paterson to myself, writing for teachers. Students' writing plans differ widely and often harken back to what they've learned in lower grades. Like Daniel, some use lists; others create intricate webs. Plans are and should be messy because they represent the inner conversations and ongoing adjustments of the writer.

A good example of this is the plan for *Cabin on Trouble Creek*, by children's author Jean Van Leeuwen, which is shown in Appendix B. Jean wanted to tidy up the plan, but I

Not a Statistic

The voice blares from the TV, the noise utterly cacophonous to my sensitive ears. I can't see the television from my perch on the stairs, but I know what my mom is watching. I can figure it out from the narration. Her eyes are glued to the screen, where a news feature on Eating Disorders is playing. I press my face against the banister, as if peering out from the bars of my prison cell. "The percentage of girls with this disorder has dramatically increased over the last five years…" *No. Stop it. Don't call it that! I can feel my jaw clenching, my eyes stinging as the tears I can't seem to fight brim over. That isn't what it is. It's not a 'disorder', it's not some disease! It's normal, I swear it is. I'm normal. I'm just Alicia, I'm not one of those statistics on the screen, what I do is different.* I tell myself this, and I want to believe it, but it's hard, harder than it should be.

I can't bear to listen any longer, and I retreat to my room. It's probably well past 11 by now anyway, and I'm supposed to be asleep. Once I'm safely behind my closed bedroom door, I can feel unashamed as I cry, collapsing on my bed as I let the force of my sobbing shake my entire body. *There's nothing wrong with me, there's nothing wrong with me, there's nothing wrong…* I repeat it over and over inside my head, hugging my knees to my chest in an attempt to draw comfort from the position. My stomach twists and churns, and I feel an acidic liquid rising in my throat, though it's been hours since I last purged. I jump to my feet, wiping furiously at my streaming eyes, and tear into my bathroom. As fast as I can, I yank up the toilet seat lid, and heave the contents of my stomach into it until an appalling odor wafts up from the water. I wipe at my mouth, the nauseous feeling in my stomach gone. Now I need to brush my teeth again, to rid myself of this horrible bitter taste. I close my mouth for a moment, and taste bile and stomach acid, caked on my tongue. I grab my toothbrush, ripping it from the cup I keep it in, squeeze some toothpaste onto it, and begin brushing furiously. Five minutes of continuous brushing pass before I feel the essence of it is completely gone.

"You're okay." I say out loud to myself. "I'm okay." I smooth back my bangs from my forehead, resting my weight on the sink in front of me, closing my eyes as my

Figure 3.13a The Opening of Addison's Story

breathing begins to slow. As I open my eyes, I catch my reflection in the mirror, and almost throw up all over again. I hate my face, I really do. I know most thirteen-year-old girls probably say that, but when it comes to me, I hate all things Alicia. I tend to avoid mirrors whenever I can, but sometimes, at moments like this, I happen to catch a glimpse. I hate my face, too much of an oval, not enough of a heart-shape, with no cheekbones to speak of. I hate my eyes, too close together, a disgusting grey-blue in color. My hair, so pale blonde it's almost silver, caught somewhere between wavy and curly. Most of all, I hate my nose, doughy and misshapen. No matter what I do, no matter how much makeup, I know in my heart that there is a place I can never reach. I can never be as beautiful as the celebrities on TV, or as thin as the models in the fashion magazines. This is why I avoid my reflection, because the crushing knowledge that I will never be beautiful suffocates me, until I'm drowning under an ocean current that I can never overcome.

* * * *

"I… The look in her eyes, horror and betrayal, tells me something. I've been doing something that she believes is wrong, and maybe it is. "I have to, I *had* to, okay? I have so much I need to fix, there's so much wrong with me-"

"Did you ever think this wasn't the way to fix it?" She snaps, taking a step toward me.

"No…" I shake my head, trying to stem the flow by pressing my fingertips to the area just under my eyes. "I'm sorry, Dawn, don't tell anyone." I plead, meeting her eyes again. Her arms fold around me, hesitant at first, and then, she's hugging me. My best friend, who's seen this ugly side of myself I wanted to hide from everyone. I suppose I'd started to hate her, hate everyone, for never noticing what was happening.

"I'm so, so sorry." I whisper fervently. I squeeze my eyes shut, not moving or saying anything. The moment is too fragile, like a dried flower or a butterfly's wing, and I'm afraid to shatter it. *Maybe we can stay like this for a just a little bit longer, and maybe I won't have to go through it all alone anymore.*

Figure 3.13b Through conferring, Addison discovered an effective resolution to her powerful story.

declined the offer, knowing that the original would show students how messy and filled with adjustments the process can be. I chuckle as I recall the neat outlines my teachers and professors required in high school and college. I planned using elaborate lists, wrote, then completed the required outline at the end. I don't know of any writer who thinks in headings with Roman numerals and subheadings with alphabet letters.

If the planning shows that the student understands the point of the piece and the kinds of details to include, then he or she can focus on the writing. Planning helps writers avoid those false starts, especially with narratives, when the student has a great idea that fizzles out because there's no problem or conflict. Planning enables both young and professional writers to recall, select, and weave memories, facts, stories, and observations into possibilities (the plan) that permit writers to focus on writing well and on crafting a piece that knocks out the reader before the first round ends.

For professional study, let's use the questions on pages 52–54 to find positives and one or two needs for two pieces of writing by eighth graders. We will examine the effects of students planning or not planning, and use our list of positives and needs to create suggestions for working with that student in the classroom.

The first student, Hank (a pseudonym), lives in a district near my home in Winchester. Teachers at his school and I used the piece of writing shown in Figure 3.14 to better understand Hank's needs. He wrote his essay in response to a prompt: "If you awoke one day three times smarter what would you do?" The prompt came from the state's test-prep website, and teachers assigned it so students could practice for the state test on writing. Since the teachers wanted to simulate the testing environment, students received no directions with the prompt. Though Hank's teacher had introduced writing plans at the start of the school year, Hank wrote without planning.

Sometimes, it's difficult to find positive statements for a piece of student writing, but it's important to try. Otherwise, middle school writers like Hank can become discouraged. Here are the positive statements from the teachers in grades 6, 7, and 8 who attended my workshop:

- Hank has a desire to complete good deeds: increase food growth, stop hunger, and find a cure for AIDS.
- He tried to organize the piece into three things he would do.
- He has a social conscience: Hank states that he would finish school quickly, then help the world.
- He tries to organize the essay with words like *first, second, finally.*

All present agreed that student planning would have resulted in better organization and prevented Hank from repeating "The first thing" twice as well as points made in

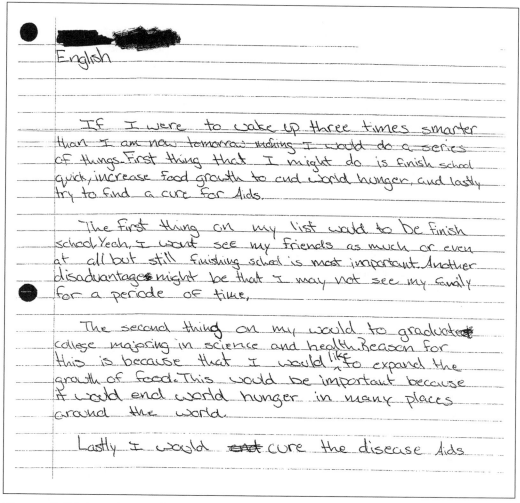

Figure 3.14 Learning to plan can move Hank's writing forward.

the first paragraph. Student planning, along with support by his teacher, could have helped Hank think through his points before drafting. Here are some needs teachers pointed out:

- A title;
- An introduction and conclusion;
- An elaboration of details with reasons and examples; and
- Time to read the piece out loud to identify missing words and awkward sentences.

Teachers felt that addressing all of these issues at once would create anxiety within Hank and negatively impact his self-esteem, so they set priorities and decided to concentrate on planning. Providing support with a writing plan could help Hank collect notes for the introduction, body, and conclusion. A conference would also raise Hank's awareness of the structure of an expository essay. During the meeting, the teacher would also have several opportunities to applaud Hank's progress and boost his self-confidence.

Because students' writing informs instruction, the discussion of this piece ended with ideas for reviewing, reteaching, or introducing a new writing lesson. Teachers made these suggestions:

- Reading a piece out loud to discover missing words, to identify editing needs, and to look for sentence meaning.
- Elaborating details.
- Developing a paragraph.
- Creating a title.
- Demonstrating different kinds of introductions.

Next, the group studied a first draft letter composed by Benoit Mathieu, an eighth grader in my class. Each year, students write a business letter to John Lathrop, the school's head, explaining the positives about their school experience, presenting some negatives, and suggesting some possible changes. John writes back to each of the thirty students in eighth grade, making the letter writing an authentic experience. Before designing plans, Ben and his classmates posed these questions: "What were my best and least favorite experiences at Powhatan?" and "What new suggestions do I have?"

A simple plan (Figure 3.15) enabled Ben to note that he needed an introduction and a conclusion. In the plan he included direction points such as "introduce yourself and establish a purpose" for his opening paragraph and noted his intention to weave "more nice things" into the conclusion. Ben's plan shows what he wanted to include in the second and third paragraphs, which enabled him to compose a detailed, organized letter. I shared with teachers the comment Ben made during a brief conference, which illustrates the benefit of planning: "Once I knew what to include in each paragraph, I concentrated on giving details."

As you read through Ben's letter (Figure 3.16) to John Lathrop, notice how closely it follows the organization in Ben's plan. A skilled writer, Ben understands that a plan is the foundation for writing well. Of course, the level of planning depends on the topic, genres, and the level of thinking the writer needs to do.

Letter structure

1st Para - Introduce yourself + establish purpose

2nd - Nice stuff/ Things you've enjoyed

3rd - Criticisms / suggestions for improvement.

4th - More nice things and move into conclusion.

Figure 3.15 Ben's plans support writing his letter.

Here are the positive comments teachers made:

- Strong voice; he believes in what he says.
- States purpose clearly at close of first paragraph.
- Explains why winter Tuesdays and the survival trip are beneficial.
- Offers specific details for improvements: electives in sports, more sports options that prepare students for high school; elective classes such as photography, drama, etc.
- Gives reasons for each recommendation.
- Ends positively and refers, gracefully, for the need to improve some areas.

Here are suggestions teachers made for following up with Ben at school:

- Praise Ben for his plan, organization, elaboration of ideas, and strong voice.
- Review or reteach the structure of a business letter before Ben and others compose their final drafts.
- Work on editing for spelling, especially the letter's closing.

Dear Mr. Lathrop:

My name is Benoît Mathieu and I am an eigth grader at Powhatan. I have had a pretty good experience at Powhatan, but there is still more for improvments. The purpose of this letter is to tell you some things I've enjoyed about Powhatan, and some suggestions for improvements.

Some things I've enjoyed are winter Tuesdays and the survival trip. Both of these trips allowed students a break from the boredom of everyday school. They have also allowed students a good change of pace, fresh air, and fun. Winter tuesdays have allowed me the oppurtunity to learn how to ski; a hoddy I will certaintly enjoy throughout my life.

Some suggestions for improvements are more sports selection, and a selection of inschool electives (such as in public schools). Added sports options/selections could include: baseball, tennis, swimming, cross country. More sports allow students the oppurtunity to pick which sport fits them best, so that students can develope thier skill in the sport to be more prepared for high school sports. The selection of inschool electives could

⌐⟶

Figure 3.16 Notice the wealth of details.

include photography, drama, creative writing, architectural design, and concert band. Each student should be required to take one elective per year. Electives allow students the oppurtunity to find out which subjects interest them, so they can pursue these interests in high and college. Electives also allow students the freedom to choose a course for them-selves and is therefore obviously a course the particular student enjoys. This will allow the student to actually have a class that they can look foreward to, have lots of fun in, and express themselves. Apart from this, electives are an excellent change of pace and experience.

   As I have previouly mentioned, I have had a pretty good experience at Powhatan, but there is still room for improvements. I hope you consider my suggestions for making Powhatan a better school. I hope you also consider the things I've enjoyed about Powhatan, and make sure that future students have the pleasure/ opportunity to ex-perience the same joyous ~~things~~ experiences that I have had!

sincerily,
Benoît Mathieu

Figure 3.16 *Continued*

Discuss Students' Writing

Professional Study Invitation

To prepare for your next professional study meeting, invite two or three teachers to volunteer to bring in a student's plans and writing, as well as a piece from a student who did not plan. At the meeting, explore what students did well, find ways students can be helped, and collect ideas for whole-class or small-group writing demonstrations. These meetings will help the group grow as writing teachers.

CHAPTER 4

Making Powerful Writing Happen Day to Day

Routines that Work

If you hang around middle school students, you'll see that it's hard not to notice their attention to appearance—and hard to remember that we had our own versions of these trends when we were that age! My neighbor's daughter, Julia, began experimenting with hair color and makeup in seventh grade. Her dad, a family physician, chatted with me about this dramatic change from Julia-in-elementary-school to Julia-in-middle-school. "My wife and I try not to look shocked, but to be understanding, as hair color and clothing choices change," he said. "We know Julia is searching for her identity."

Young adolescent girls seem to change their hair color and styles as often as their earrings. I watch girls go from brown with magenta streaks to ash blond to dark brown with blond streaks to jet black all in the space of a few weeks. Others experiment with nail polish: it's green one day, pale pink the next, and brown-and-blue stripes for the rest of the week. Boys' outward appearance, like the girls', reflects a quest to define their identity. One boy I taught recently spikes his hair with gel; another shocks adults by spraying purple streaks onto his dark brown hair. Baggy pants alternate with jeans. Think back to James Dean '50s, the Hippie look, Punk, Grunge, and Goth, and you realize that the salient look of teens is *always* evolving. The constant: high energy, bravado, and aloofness are often a cover for inner turmoil.

Listening to young adolescents in the hallways or the cafeteria, you hear their energetic talk about music and social plans, hear their strong opinions about school and home rules, and observe their passion for friendships and acceptance from their peers. Even their physical growth spurts are uneven, allowing some to fit comfortably at desks and others left with no room to park their gangly legs. Adolescence is a time of change and great insecurity—a time for a journey to figure out the big life question: "Who am I?" (Dillon and Moje 1997; Jackson and Davis 2000; Moje 2000; NMSA 2003; Schunk and Zimmerman 1997; Van Hoose and Strahan 1988).

On their odyssey of self-discovery these middle schoolers relish challenging adults and forming thick-as-thieves peer groups as a means to gain control over their lives and decisions. Despite that, middle school teachers know this is also an astoundingly opportune time for social, emotional, and intellectual growth.

The challenge is to offer classroom routines and content that don't fly in the face of what adolescents need, but that complement it. Such a learning environment meets six needs of middle school learners drawn from the survey, the answers to the "Ten Questions About Writing" questionnaire, and interviews and emails that I discussed in Chapter 1. After I discuss the six needs, I'll explore how they reside within writing workshop routines and the latest research on the most effective practices within a workshop model.

Six Needs of Teaching Middle School Writers

There is no one perfect writing curriculum that works for all teachers and students. But when we weave in the following six conditions, we stand a good chance of engaging students in writing and encouraging them to view writing as central to communication in and outside of school (Allison and Rehm 2007; Fisher and Frey 2007; Tomlinson 2008).

1. **Responsibility.** "I can do it by myself," one student in my survey said. Adolescents thrive in the atmosphere of learn-by-doing. They want to take on real responsibility and control over their learning, and we can meet this need by turning over the "doing" of our lessons to students quickly, by permitting them to make decisions about topics; to negotiate deadline dates for drafts, revisions, and publishable pieces; and to use self- and peer evaluation to support revision and editing.

> "Sometimes I spend evenings on my bed wondering about why I was born, what I'll be, and what my life will be like when I'm older."
> *Liz, seventh grader*

2. **Relationship.** Integrate this concept into your classes and celebrate the power that resides in it. Practice, camaraderie, the "given" that we're in the game together—we would do well to transport that spirit into our teaching, and exploit the benefit of many minds working together. Teams of students can collaborate throughout the writing process. Sorrel, an eighth grader, said, "Partner and group work give me confidence. When someone in my group says, 'That poem brought tears to my eyes,' I feel I can meet every writing obstacle."

3. **Relevance.** "Give me reasons to write" is the mantra middle school students repeat. How might we respond to this challenge? For me, it's a matter of meeting them halfway. I listen to their viewpoint and voices early on—and often. I have to get to know my students *over time* in order to sustain their drive to write. Relevance is a close cousin to inquiry, but for me, relevance is more powerfully connected to relationship. That is, the unwritten pact between me and my students is that they will work hard and unfurl their intellectual and creative capabilities if I work hard to discover the topics that matter to them and let them negotiate some reading and writing tasks. Relevance gives students reasons to write.

4. **Inquiry.** Infuse your writing class with opportunities for students to wonder about self, feelings, friends, school, family, relationships, and issues about justice in their community and beyond. Have students ponder their lives—*Why do friends grow apart?*—or find themes in their reading—*Can a war ever be just?* Invite them to explore their questions through reading, writing, and discussion. Just about anything you teach, when flipped upside down as a question, can rouse middle schoolers out of a passive learning stance. Ask: *If Abraham Lincoln and Franklin Delano Roosevelt were great presidents, does that mean you need a war to be considered a great leader? How might a peacetime president achieve greatness as a leader? Is it easier or harder? Why or why not? What is the theme that unites all of Gary Paulsen's novels?*

How do free verse poets create rhythm without rhyme? When students study the work of professional writers with a questioning, writerly eye, they expand their knowledge of genre, writing craft, and technique (Wilhelm 2007, 2008).

5. **Choice.** The desire to choose is as old as humankind. It was one of the strongest responses in the research in Chapter 1. Student choice can ensure that relevance, and it can drive students' motivation to hit on the right topic, genre, and audience.

6. **Hope.** At a USBBY conference in New York City, author Katherine Paterson told me, "I can't listen to that speaker. His message about nuclear disasters feels hopeless. It gives me nightmares. I need hope to survive and write." Hope breathes feelings of "I can make good decisions" or "I will work out this problem" or "I can improve my writing" into our hearts and minds. It's hope that nudges adolescents to pick themselves up and work to move beyond failure. When teachers create a hopeful, trusting writing environment that shows students the teacher is their advocate and mentor, then students' self-confidence and willingness to take risks as writers increase. They dare to write about topics they care about, they ask questions, and they develop the ability to work hard at writing and revising.

> **Scheduling Tip**
>
> The reading and writing connections can be woven into a workshop approach or a traditional forty-five- minute class period. If you have daily, forty-five-minute periods to teach reading and writing, then I suggest that you plan over two weeks:
>
> **Week 1:** Schedule reading three times and writing twice.
> **Week 2:** Schedule writing three times and reading twice.
> Following this schedule can bring depth and meaning to each discipline (Gardner 2007).

Giving the Needs a Context: A Process Approach

The six needs of young writers can take root in a range of writing approaches, but they flourish as a part of a process approach to writing. In turn, major studies show that a process approach to writing is the most effective form of writing instruction. Consider this finding from Coker and Lewis (2008, 234):

> The National Commission on Writing, in 2003, 2004, 2005 called for a writing revolution and viewed the teaching of writing as the neglected "R." Researchers Coker and Lewis support the commission's view pointing out that "According to a recent report from the National Assessment

of Educational progress (NAEP), approximately 70 percent of students in grades four, eight, and twelve were deemed "low-achieving" writers who wrote at or below the basic level (Persky, Daance, and Jon 2003) and failed to meet the NAEP proficiency goals for writing. (Graham and Perin 2007a)

Effective writing instruction and assessment are endangered. Studies of the National Commission on Writing combined with Graham and Perin's *Writing Next* (2007a) and NCTE's "Writing Now" (2008) call for teachers and administrators to transform ineffective writing instruction into effective instruction (Coker and Lewis 2008; Graham and Harris 2007; Graham and Perin 2007a, 2007b; Newkirk 2009).

Graham and Perin followed up *Writing Next* with a second study that confirmed and extended what they learned in their first study (2007b). This second study identified ten requirements or goals that pointed to the need for a process approach to writing.

From Research to Practice: Core Recommendations I'll Explore

The four themes from the 2007b Graham and Perin study that I will address in this chapter on routines and the next chapter on lessons are:

- **Promote students' writing progress with strategy instruction**. Provide students with explicit teacher modeling of strategies that help middle school writers use background knowledge to find topics and brainstorm ideas, plan, draft, revise, and edit their writing.
- **Teach grammar and improve students' knowledge of grammar skills** but know that skills in isolation do not improve the quality of students' writing.
- **Offer scaffolded instruction when students require it**.
- **Create a motivating, engaging, and nurturing workshop environment** by giving students praise for their hard work and progress with a strategy.
- **Balance test prep**.

The Elephant in the Room: Test Prep

We can't reinvent our writing curriculum unless we wrestle with the reality of standardized tests, which have taken up all the room in our writing time and made us skittish about how we teach writing. In the March/April 2008 issue of *Instructor* magazine, an interviewer asked author Lois Lowry, "If you could give a gift to teachers, what would it be?" Lowry's response charges us to make writing and reading much more than test prep: "Time to be creative and explore imagination. Time not geared toward testing." When teachers make a commitment to *reduce* the time students spend writing to prompts similar to those on state tests, they can adjust the goals of their writing curriculum and carve out time to develop students' writing skill as well as make them test-wise.

Let me share a true story along with the hard data from state testing to illustrate and support my point. In 2004, Sarah Armstrong, Assistant Superintendent of Staunton City Schools, asked me to conduct several workshops over three years with middle school teachers. I led these starting with the 2004–2005 school year. Writing scores were consistently low: 2 percent passed the state test at the advanced level, 60 percent passed at the proficient level, and 39 percent had not passed (see Figure 4.1).

The state's department of education required that students who were not passing make progress over two years. Otherwise, the state would take over teacher training.

About a ninety-minute drive from my home in Winchester, Virginia, Staunton City Schools are part of a small-town, rural community. With an enrollment of 2,761 students spread over one high school, one middle school, and four elementary schools, 40 percent of Staunton's students are economically disadvantaged, 16 percent handicapped, and 28 percent African American, Hispanic, and Asian American. To support this literacy story, I've included the graphs that reveal students' progress in writing on the state test (see Figure 4.2).

The primary purpose of my first visit was to gather information on the status of writing at Shelburne Middle School. I discovered that though teachers had a daily, ninety-minute reading-writing block, students were not writing every day. The most writing occurred about two months before students took the state writing test. During this time, students practiced writing to various prompts taken from the state's site on the Internet. Not much evaluation occurred in terms of studying students' writing to discover what they did well and areas that needed reteaching. On this first visit I also learned that teachers felt insecure about how to teach writing; most were not writers and had dipped back to the negative feelings toward writing they held while in school themselves. However, every teacher wanted to learn how to teach writing, every teacher wanted the students to learn to write well, every teacher wanted the students to enjoy writing, and every teacher expressed great concern about improving test scores.

At our second meeting we developed a plan for students and for teachers, knowing that when instruction responds to students' needs, teachers have to adjust practice to meet those needs. My goal was to negotiate changes and build consensus among the group, which included language arts, special education, and resource teachers. By the end of the day, we agreed to three changes:

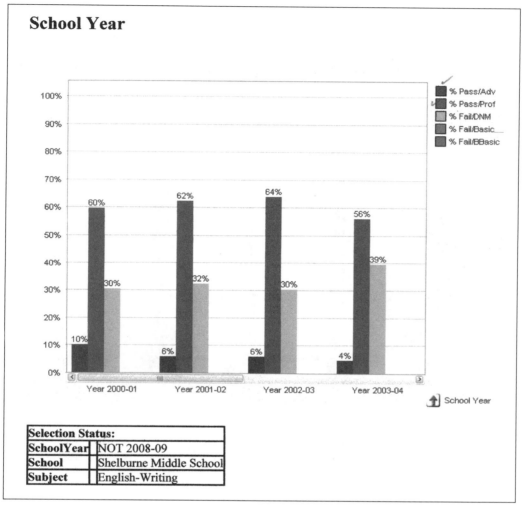

Figure 4.1 The failing rate is too high!

1. **Professional Study Among Teachers.** The plan asked teachers to form a study group and not only read professional articles and books, but also present demonstration lessons to one another at team and department meetings on genre structure, craft, technique, writing conventions, and analyzing mentor texts. Teachers felt relieved that they did not have to write in front of their students to illustrate the process.

2. **Professional Development Workshops.** Staunton scheduled six all-day workshops. Teachers wrote, observed my writing lessons, presented lessons to the group, brought issues to the group for feedback, and learned to study students' writing so they could offer demonstration lessons and conferences that supported students' needs.

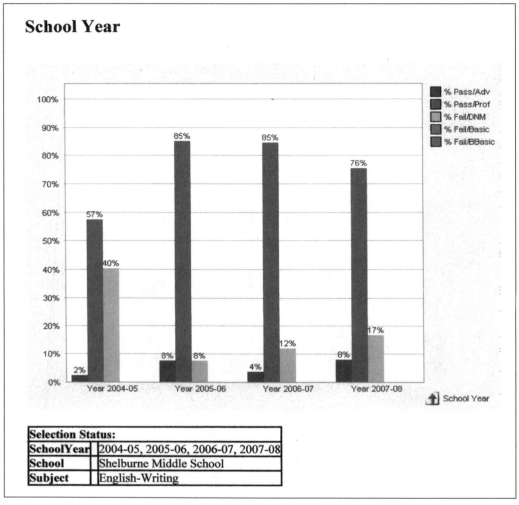

Figure 4.2 In 2007–2008, hard work shows!

3. **Increase Amount of Students' Writing.** Students wrote every day, using the writing process, on topics they chose as well as specific district writing requirements such as a short narrative in sixth grade and a persuasive essay in seventh grade. Students became test-wise by writing to a prompt every six weeks. Teachers studied the prompt writing to list what students did well and areas that required scaffolding and reteaching. The graphs of state test scores in Figure 4.2 illustrate the steady progress students made.

At that time, I did not have the supporting data I would later receive from the "Ten Questions About Writing" questionnaire. However, I still believed that students at Shelburne Middle School would work diligently on becoming test-wise if they could also develop their writing skill by drafting and revising pieces on topics and genres that they chose and felt were relevant to their lives.

A Look at the Bar Graphs

Let me begin by explaining what the three bars in Figures 4.1 and 4.2 represent. The bar at the left, always the shortest bar, shows the percentage of students who passed the state test at an advanced writing level. The middle bar shows the percentage of students who passed at the proficient level, and the bar at the right shows the percentage of students who did not pass.

No progress occurred on the testing results from the 2003–2004 and 2004–2005 school years. During this time, teachers were learning about workshop; experiencing the writing process; and preparing and presenting genre, craft, and technique lessons during our professional study days, at grade-level team meetings, and in their classrooms. Teachers also brought samples of students' writing to our sessions and learned how to analyze these for what students did well and for areas that needed reteaching and/or scaffolding. As students wrote daily, teachers created demonstration lessons to respond to where students showed they needed to progress with content, style, and writing conventions.

It took two years for the state tests to reflect students' progress. In the 2005–2006 and 2006–2007 school years, the state tests illustrated the progress students were making at school. The passing rate increased dramatically, and I left Shelburne Middle School to work on differentiating reading instruction and writing workshop at Lee High School in Staunton, Virginia. However, the 2007–2008 scores at Shelburne dipped enough to concern the principal and Jen Morris, the librarian; both believe the drop was due to three outstanding teachers moving from the area. Their replacements did not have a background in writing workshop and writing instruction. To ensure that the downward turn shifted upward, the superintendent asked me to provide two full days of professional study on writing with middle and high school English teachers. Jen Morris agreed to follow up with continued training, and we decided that it would be wise to partner newcomers with experienced teachers.

Making Writing—and Reflecting on Our Students' Writing—a Top Priority

My experiences at Shelburne Middle School, along with the responses from students on the "Ten Questions" questionnaire, led me to develop a set of truths about successful writing and writing instruction. Narrowing the gap between students' engagement in writing outside of school and their disengagement in school can seem like a vast endeavor, so it helps me to list out the most essential recommendations:

- Students need to write daily in order to learn to write well.
- Writing genres, craft, and technique need to be taught; students need to apply this knowledge to their own writing.
- Students' writing informs the demonstration lessons that teachers present to small groups and the whole class as well as during conferences with students.
- Students can become test-wise when we teach the state writing test as another genre, which creates time to offer choice writing.
- Professional study has to include analyzing students' writing at team or department meeting. Schools need a resource person who can support teachers, continue their learning process, and model teach.
- Learning about the teaching of writing is an ongoing process and can occur by working with a peer partner, by studying students' writing, and by reading professional articles and books.
- To keep writing gains permanent, all new teachers should be partnered with experienced writing teachers.

Shelburne's students developed the writing skill and positive attitudes toward writing that enabled them to score high on the state test. Teachers' experiences enabled them to understand that professional study at the building level needs to be ongoing, enabling teachers to sharpen their instructional writing skills. During the second and third years, the all-day workshops for teachers also included developing a deep understanding of young adolescents and the kinds of learning environment and experiences that they thrive on and relish.

The Workshop Model: Tweaking Its Routines

For me, writing workshop provides the effective framework for meeting the recommendations from important research, including that of Graham and Perin in *Writing Next* (2007a), NCTE's "Writing Now" (2008), and Moffett and Wagner's curriculum in *Student-Centered Language Arts and Reading, K–13: A Handbook for Teachers* (1983). In a workshop:

- Teaching includes explicit modeling of writing strategies;
- Learning is collaborative and social, tapping into the talents of adolescents;
- Scheduling writing blocks allows students to write, observe strategy lessons, and confer with teachers and peers;

- Collaborating and interacting include learning from the teacher and peer experts;
- Assessing students' writing focuses on the entire process and can lead to independence;
- Studying models or mentor texts teaches students myriad ways professional writers apply craft and technique; and
- Improving writing can happen by learning with peer experts and other adults (Vygotsky 1978). Unfortunately, the workshop approach of Calkins (1994) and Graves (2003) never caught on in middle school the way it has been embraced by teachers in the primary and elementary grades. I believe that middle school teachers thought they did not have enough time to carry it off. Calkins and Graves recommended that teachers schedule writing workshop at least four times a week. Most middle school teachers have about forty-five minutes to teach reading, writing, spelling, vocabulary, and writing conventions; they saw the workshop approach as daunting and impossible. However, the scheduling suggestions on page 108 do make the workshop approach accessible to middle school teachers.

Middle school teachers who resisted the approach also believed that it meant allowing students to choose what they wanted to do all the time. Writing workshop was misperceived as loosey-goosey, focusing mostly on fiction and personal narratives, and lacking structure. (How myths such as this get entrenched in schools and undermine brilliant innovations in education like the writing workshop approach is beyond the scope of this book, but it's something worth examining with colleagues.)

For the rest of this chapter and the next, I share the routines and lessons that define my forty-five-minute workshop—a framework that includes explicit teacher modeling and develops students' self-regulatory abilities through self-evaluation, collaboration, conferences, and time to write at school (Coker and Lewis 2008; Graham and Perin 2007a; Troia et al. 2009; NCTE 2008; Robb 2004). Both implicitly and explicitly, you'll see lessons and student writing in this book that *span* writing genres. Nonetheless, I want to underscore my belief that writing will matter most to students when we have them mess around in an array of genres, including arguments, persuasive essays, fiction, literary analysis, poetry, and so on. I bristle a bit when writing workshop gets knocked as being fiction-focused, and something that only the writerly kids can thrive in.

> "I learned how to write in fifth grade 'cause we had a writing workshop and wrote most every day."
> *Stephanie, seventh grader*

Routines that Help You Manage Writing Time

When you create a framework for your writing class, you offer students freedom and choice within a structure. You might have to tweak and adjust the routines that I find

Sample Writing Workshop Daily Schedule to Review with Students
- Demonstration: sensory images (5 minutes)
- Writer's Notebook: "Secrets" by Naomi Shihab Nye (10 minutes)
- Writing Time: students choose group work on multi-media poetry presentations or individual pieces (25–28 minutes)
- Wrap-up (2 minutes)

useful; that's fine, as long as you reserve a large chunk of time for students to write in a two-week, reading-writing cycle. It's okay to try some or all of these routines. I do them all when teaching. However, teaching is an evolutionary process that asks us to continually learn from research, conversations with colleagues, and our teaching experiences. Here's how I structure my writing classes.

Post and Review Your Workshop Schedule

During my early years of teaching, I'd keep the day's learning events to myself; the learning experiences were clear to me and a mystery to my students. As soon as I began posting and reading the daily workshop schedule, students made comments such as, "It's nice knowing at the beginning of class that I'm conferring with you today," or "I'm looking forward to having time to collaborate on writing a Readers Theater script." They experienced comfort in knowing the day's workshop map, and they were able to look forward to specific events.

Present Explicit Teacher Demonstrations

Until I read *Writing: Teachers and Children at Work* by Donald Graves (1983, 2003), my writing lessons were not explicit. Most of my direct teaching occurred in conferences, which I based on the ones my own high school creative writing teacher, Mr. Mandell, conducted. However, demonstrations and Think Alouds make your process visible to students and can enlarge their mental model of a writing strategy.

Teacher demonstrations are focused, five- to ten-minute lessons that you present on genre structure, writing plans, asking questions, revision, and editing; craft lessons such as strong verbs and specific nouns; and technique lessons such as using foreshadowing, flashback, or sidebars. You'll think aloud, share and discuss mentor texts, and model how to revise content or edit for writing conventions.

You might start with a whole-class demonstration. If students don't "get it," ask them what's confusing them, then adjust the lesson. For example, as I presented a lesson on sensory imagery to fifth graders, a large group looked confused. "Is there something you don't understand? I asked.

Figure 4.3 Studying writing criteria with a friend is great fun.

"Yeah," they chorused.

"What do you mean by *senses?*" one student asked. Not knowing the five senses certainly prevented this group from absorbing a lesson on sensory images. The next day, the group met with me, and I gave them two short lessons about the five senses to build their background knowledge (Graham and Perin 2007b).

You'll also adjust original demonstration lessons for small groups, pairs, or individuals who need reteaching or who learn best when sitting close to the teacher. Anxiety can prevent students from hearing and absorbing information during a whole-class lesson. When you adjust the model as needed, it sends the message that you care, want to help, and are willing to reframe lessons so that they "get it."

Reserve a Chunk of Time for Students to Write

Extended writing time develops writing stamina, the ability to concentrate and block out everything but the writing. Set aside at least thirty minutes of class time for students to write. This "writing" may occur in a variety of ways: gathering ideas in writer's notebooks; engaging in paired discussions about possible topics and brainstorming; drafting; conferring with a peer, small group, or the teacher; collaborating to revise, edit, or self-evaluate; reading a piece out loud to pinpoint errors; conducting research; and surfing the Internet for information and ideas.

Students who need greater quiet while thinking and writing should be able to work undisturbed. Designate a space in your classroom as a silent work area. You might also want to create a conference corner with a table or small desk and chairs for you and students to use during prearranged conferences and collaborative work. Often, as you circulate around the room and spot a need, you'll also hold an on-the-spot conference, in which you pull up a chair or bend down next to a student to provide feedback, model a strategy, or discuss a student's question.

Use Writer's Notebooks

Writer's notebooks were never part of my experiences as a student. However, at home I kept notebooks that were rich in writing possibilities. In my notebook, I'd copy favorite poems, passages from a novel that I wanted to repeatedly reread, lists of words I adored and despised, favorite songs, movies, names, pages that simply logged what I did in a day. I had dozens and reread them in high school, always feeling surprised at what I deemed worthy of noting in past years. I still jot down thoughts, ideas, and phrases that speak to me from books, poems, and the newspaper. In my classes, students complete notebooks at school. A home notebook is optional; some students are not that committed to writing. Not all of my friends kept notebooks.

Notebooks are places for students to collect ideas for their writing. If you only teach writing, you'll need a separate notebook. I prefer the composition books that don't have spiral bindings for notebooks. That way, students are less likely to tear out pages, which can end up on the floor, in a trash can, or crumpled in a locker.

Consider setting aside five to seven minutes at the start of students' writing time so they can gather ideas in their notebooks. I find that exploring ideas three times a week is sufficient, especially if you have one period to teach both reading and writing. As you read on, you'll study a few techniques that can help students discover writing ideas. You might also want to dip into the books listed in the box on page 119, which include dozens of ideas for writer's notebooks.

It often works well to collect ideas in notebooks after students read and discuss independent reading texts and mentor texts. For example, in one sixth-grade classroom I worked with, partners discussed this short poem by Emily Dickinson to deepen their knowledge of metaphor:

> His bill an auger is,
> His head, a cap and frill.
> He laboreth at every tree,—
> A worm his utmost goal.

Then each student returned to the poem to find ideas to record in notebooks. Their familiarity with the poem was an asset as they jotted down the ideas, words, and phrases that the poem called to mind. Danny wrote about his goal to play forward on a travel soccer team; Liz explained that she loves to plant herbs and her auger is a trowel; James described laboring over math homework. Students brought parts of themselves to their responses, and these differed because the poem kindled unique reactions in each one.

Besides having students use poems to discover writing ideas, offer them myths, legends, newspaper headlines, photographs, illustrations, paintings, posters, and snippets of articles. I invite students to bring in texts they would like to share. This saves me time and gives them the responsibility they seek. You can also ask students to write lists of things they love or hate, as well as to jot their questions and wonderings about life, friendship, pets, secret and imaginary places, and people.

Journals and/or notebooks remain on students' desks throughout class, even after they've completed a notebook exercise. During writing time, some students jot down ideas that have popped into their minds and note words and phrases from a mentor text or a book they're reading. Others copy poems or short paragraphs from texts. This is not plagiarism, because students internalize phrases and lines, then transform and place them in different genres and topics. As eighth grader Danny explained the process:

Figure 4.4 Peer Conferences: The Road to Independence

Some Short Texts that Stir Writing Ideas

My students rate the following short texts, artwork, and websites as top notch because of the connections they can make that in turn stimulate writing ideas. You know your students' backgrounds, humor, interests, and idiosyncrasies, but I'm including my students' favorites in the hope that you'll find some new ideas to use with your classes.

Short Texts

- "Porsche," "Instant Care," "Dead on the Road," "The Monkeys Not Seen," and "Scary Movies." From *Mama Makes Up Her Mind*, a collection of short memoirs by Bailey White. New York, Vintage Books, 1993.
- "Alien Candy," "Nightmare Inn," "I'm Not Martin," and The Black Mask." From *Nightmare Hour* by R. L. Stine. New York, HarperCollins, 1999.
- "I started early, took my dog," "I'll tell you how the sun rose," "A narrow fellow in the grass," and "I never saw the moor." From *Poetry for Young People: Emily Dickinson.* New York, Scholastic, 2000.
- "The Negro Speaks of Rivers," "Mother to Son," "Dream Variations," "The Dream Keeper," "Merry-Go-Round," and "I Dream a World." From *Poetry for Young People: Langston Hughes*, edited by D. Roessle and A. Rampersad. New York, Scholastic, 2006.
- "Apollo," "Pandora," "King Midas," "Sisyphus," and "Orpheus." From *D'Aulaires' Book of Greek Myths*. Dell, New York, 1962.

Artwork: I collect images from calendars for students to use to generate discussions and jot ideas for writing in their notebooks. Museum websites are major resources for finding paintings and photographs for notebooks writing.

Websites for Works of Art and Photographs. You can project the paintings, slides, and photographs on these websites from your computer onto a SMART Board. Google the museum's name to access their website.

- Art and Photography from the Smithsonian in Washington, DC
- Images from the Art Institute in Chicago: www.artic.edu/aic/collections/
- Images from The Metropolitan Museum of Art in New York City
- Explore and Learn Images at the Metropolitan Museum of Art: www.metmuseum.org/explore/index.asp
- Images frm MoMA (Museum of Modern Art) in New York City

Books About Writer's Notebooks

A Writer's Notebook: Unlocking the Writer Within You by Ralph Fletcher. New York: Harper Collins, 1996.

100 Quickwrites by Linda Rief. New York: Scholastic, 2003.

Notebook Know-How: Strategies for the Writer's Notebook by Aimee Buckner. York, ME: Stenhouse, 2005.

> I'm writing and remembering poems and parts of books I love. The writing stamps some words, phrases, and metaphors into my memory. But my memory is a trickster, changing authors' words into my words It's like the author sets my brain on a journey and when I arrive, the words and ideas are mine.

What Teachers Do While Students Write

One of the first tasks while students are working during class is to make the rounds to see where they are with their writing. Use the remaining time to confer with the students whose names you've written on the chalkboard. On days that you haven't planned conferences, continue to circulate, observe students, and hold deskside conferences. A simple question such as "How's it going today?" can let you know whether students need support (Anderson 2009).

Middle school students need a writer's notebook, a literature response journal for writing about their reading, and a writing folder where they can store their writing.

Routines that Help You Keep Track of Process

 To keep track of where students are in the writing process, I use a grid for each class that lists the students' names and the deadline date for each stage of the process (see the Status of the Class form on the DVD). I circulate around the room with the grid two to three times a week and note where students are in the process. It only takes about five minutes to discover which students are in danger of missing their deadlines and then give them support and/or deadline adjustments.

> During workshop time, I encourage you to meet with students. Avoid sitting at your desk and grading papers, although this is tempting when time is tight.

I do not write while students are writing. During those thirty minutes, which evaporate quickly, I believe my responsibility is to support them. I circulate and visit each student and/or I hold preplanned conferences. Moreover, not all teachers want to write or feel comfortable writing for themselves or in front of students. That's the purpose and point of teaching writing with mentor texts so students learn to read with a writer's eye.

What Teachers Can Negotiate with Students

Middle school writers appreciate negotiation. Whenever possible, include them in decisions, such as creating criteria, establishing reasonable deadline dates, and developing behavior guidelines for writing class. Negotiation develops students' responsibility for meeting deadlines and for the choices you offer, such as topic, audience, genre, and collaborations to revise and edit.

For example, when I worked with the fifth graders in Cheri Kesler's class, the students explored ideas for writing about a topic related to "obstacles" (see pages 81–83). After allowing time over two consecutive days for partners to discuss ideas, I negotiated one deadline date with students for choosing a topic to explore, and another deadline date for brainstorming a list of ideas. Take your cues from your students and the complexity of the project. I usually allow the class to negotiate as we establish deadline dates for completing a writing plan, a first draft, revisions, and so on. I recognize that some students will beat the deadline, while others might need additional time.

Once students begin searching for topics, brainstorming, planning, and so on, they quickly reach different points from one another in the writing process. Throughout the process I negotiate deadline dates with students, who have the option to extend a due date by explaining their reasons to me. Negotiating means that the class or individual students and I spend about five minutes discussing how much time they feel they'll need to complete a brainstorm or a writing plan, and so on. Since the level of writing expertise varies with each class, negotiating dates allows teachers to tap into the time frames different groups require.

Frequently, you'll negotiate the same deadline for all students in a class; at other times, deadlines will differ, depending on the scope of the writing and each student's needs. Younger students and students who struggle might require more time to work and more time conferring with you. I find it's essential to remind students of the negotiated deadline dates, which I post on the chalkboard. These reminders can support the decisions students make about using workshop time productively. Table 4.1 shows the

Table 4.1 Process Stages

Process Stage	Average Time Needed
Finding and Focusing Topics	two to four classes
Brainstorming	two to three classes
Writing Plan (includes deciding on genre and audience)	three to five classes
First Draft	two to five classes
Revising	one to three classes
Editing	one to three classes
Second Draft	two to three classes
Publishable Draft	completed at home in two to four days when you only have forty-five minutes for writing

process stages that I negotiate with students and an average of the time we agree upon; students might work on a stage for fifteen minutes or the entire thirty minutes of extended writing time. The amount of workshop time that students use depends on their writing proficiency and other projects they're completing. Every piece of writing doesn't move through the entire process.

When a student doesn't meet a deadline, check that knee-jerk reaction we all have to give a low grade. One or more low grades can create anger and frustration and can build a foundation of negative feelings toward writing. As long as you continually circulate and keep abreast of where each student is with his or her writing, you'll understand the need for extensions of time, be able to provide the support that enables students to meet negotiated deadlines, and note, from your observations and conversations, the lessons on genre, craft, and technique that individuals, small groups, or the entire class needs. To ensure that reading-writing connections are in the forefront of my mind, I plan my reading and writing units together. This imprints in my mind the reading-writing connections I want to present, and it prepares me for sharing these with students.

Learning from Professional Writers

Professional writers plan! To help you build a culture of planning writing among your students, Katherine Paterson has graciously provided me with her writing plans for *Bridge to Terabithia*, and Jean Van Leeuwen has shared her plans for *The Cabin on Trouble*

Name_____   Date_____

Planning Your Writing

Directions:

Answer each question below. Give examples when you can.

- Do you plan your writing?

- If you do plan, explain what you do.

- Would you plan your writing if this stage was not required? Why or why not?

- Why do you think professional writers plan their stories and books?

- Do you believe that planning can improve your writing? Explain your position.

Creek (see Appendices A and B). Here are some questions I encourage you to use as you explore these novelists' plans with colleagues:

> This is an ideal time to survey students on their attitudes toward planning their writing. Results can provide you with discussion ideas and ways to move students who resist planning to experiencing its benefits. Use the Planning Your Writing reproducible on page 122 to get a read on where your students are with this writing stage.

- Explain how these authors' plans are alike. How are they different?
- Why do you think having a plan helped these authors write their books?
- Did each writer stick to the original plan?
- Why bother to plan if you're going to take writing detours?
- How might you use these authors' plans to help students understand the benefits of taking the time to plan?
- How do you think planning affects the writing process?

Discuss Students' Writing

Professional Study Invitation

At the next professional study meeting, give each colleague a copy of Paterson's and Van Leeuwen's writing plans (see Appendices A and B). Use the discussion questions to jump-start the conversation. Share the survey with teachers and encourage them to ask their students to complete it. When students resist planning, and believe me, they do, I invite them to pilot this writing stage. Once they've tried writing from a plan, invite students to debrief by sharing benefits and drawbacks. Then discuss the contents of each list.

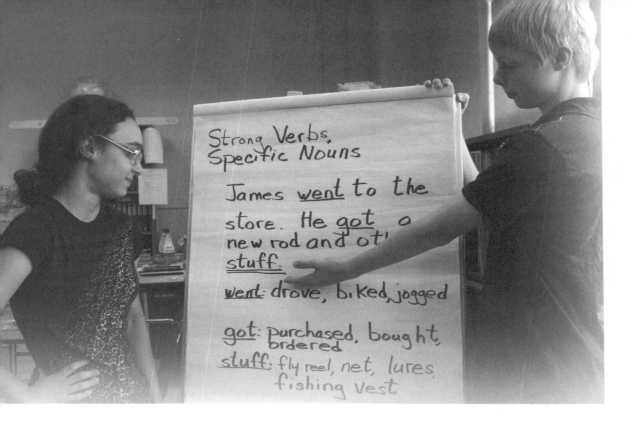

CHAPTER 5

Making Powerful Writing Happen Day to Day

Lessons that Work

In mid-November one year, a principal at a middle school in Virginia invited me to spend several weeks coaching language arts teachers. The two of us toured all the language arts classes to give me the lay of the land, and then the principal asked me to spend time in two seventh-grade English classes. Her purpose was to show me the dramatic differences in instructional approaches between teachers, and the challenges I'd face providing professional study.

The twenty-seven students who filed into the first class sat in rows; the teacher spoke from a lectern in front. Class started with a spelling test based on a unit from a grade-level basal. As I walked up and down rows, I noticed that several students did not even attempt to write some of the words. Students in each row passed their completed tests to the first person; the teacher picked up each stack and placed them in a folder. Next, three student monitors passed out a set of worksheets to classmates. "When you finish these," the teacher announced, "You can work on your piece about your favorite season. No talking." Then the teacher sat at her desk and graded the spelling papers.

I asked the teacher if I could look at the worksheets. There were five different ones. Students had to underline complete subjects and complete predicates; place quotations marks around dialogue; and complete exercises on capitalization, subject and verb agreement, and forming possessives. When I placed the set on the teacher's desk, she looked up and said, "We'll practice all year for the state writing test. They need to review this grammar—their writing has so many mistakes." When I asked a student if she had a writing folder I could look at, she whispered, "We don't have one."

The second classroom I visited was in the midst of writing workshop. I noticed that the teacher had listed the learning events for that day on the chalkboard. The seventh graders sat at tables in teams of five; twenty-five students in all. Using "Bam, Bam, Bam" by Eve Merriam and "Juba Dance," a Creole folk song as mentor texts, the teacher had just completed a minilesson on strong verbs and had asked students to find four verbs in their latest draft that could be strengthened. Group members helped one another pinpoint dull verbs and suggested alternates. The quiet hum of students' voices was like music compared to the utter silence of students in the first classroom.

The teacher circulated, pausing to help some writers and commenting enthusiastically on the more distinctive verbs.

Juba Dance

Juba jump and Juba sing,
Juba cut dat pigeon's wing!
Juba kick off Juba's shoe,
Juba dance dat Juba do!
Juba whirl dat foot about,
Jubal blow dat candle out!
Juba circle, raise de latch,
Juba do dat Long Dog Scratch!
—Creole Folk Song

Figure 5.1 This eighth grader is in the midst of revision.

During the remaining twenty-five minutes, students revised the lackluster verbs, then worked on their pieces. At a separate table, the teacher conferred with three students whose names were on the chalkboard. When he finished conferring, he asked, "Does anyone need to meet with me today?" Two hands shot up, and the teacher conducted a deskside conference with each student. Later, when we debriefed, the teacher told me, "I use mentor texts because they actively involve students in studying craft and technique. Students always choose their topic, and they do well on state tests."

What Do I Believe? The Need to Name Our Underlying Philosophy

Visiting those two classrooms back to back was an eye opener. As I drove home that day, I thought about how both teachers were succeeding in what they set out to do with their students—even though their goals for their students were very different. Earlier in my career, I would have said that key factors of effective teaching are organization, preparation, and a clear class structure. These two teachers reminded me that planning and purposefulness do not necessarily signal good teaching. What counts is the quality of the educational philosophies and the soundness of the research upon which the instruction is based.

At that point in time anyway, the teacher in the first classroom defined teaching writing largely as a matter of test preparation. She had her students complete worksheets that would improve the grammar and usage in their pieces, but there was no evidence that she helped her students develop the content of writing or reasons for writing. Her comment that students' "writing is filled with mistakes" and the dozens of worksheets they completed each week did not lead her to conclude that the isolated drills weren't working and that she should try something else (Calkins 1994; Graves 2003; Newkirk 2009). The philosophy behind her teaching seemed to be that students needed to master expected skills of writing. This is not to say her students were doomed as writers or that they were destined to learn nothing from her that year. It's more to say that they could have had a more joyful experience as writers—and grown more as writers and thinkers—had she approached writing differently.

I can't say whether this teacher always taught this way or whether she moved in that direction under the pressure of having her students perform well on state tests. I do know that an overemphasis on accountability and scoring high on state writing tests can prompt teachers to shelve the craft and technique lessons they are doing, in favor of playing it safe. It's disheartening to see backward slides like this in schools where writing process approaches had taken hold—and had helped student writers move forward.

How would you describe the educational philosophy of the second teacher? He modeled craft with real literature; students applied the demonstration lessons to their own writing; he valued collaboration, and having a block of time to write. To me, he seems to espouse a more student-centered approach to teaching writing than the first teacher. His circulating, his small-group and one-on-one conferring with students, speak volumes about his beliefs about his role as a teacher and his respect for students. He's a writing coach, an authority—but not authoritarian.

Research supports the writing instruction of the second teacher because his workshop includes lessons and conferences, student collaborations, choice, the study of mentor texts, and time to write at school (Coker and Lewis 2008; Graham and Perin 2007a; NCTE 2008). In this chapter I share writing lessons that sit well within the routines I described in the previous chapter. They aren't writing lessons I particularly knew how to "do" a decade or two ago. That is, they are actually reading and writing lessons, because more and more I've come to see the power of mentor texts as cantilevers that open up the possibilities to students of their own voice and springs of content.

Reading Lessons Inform Writing Lessons

In an interview in 2003, young adult author Walter Dean Myers said, "If you're serious about writing, you should be equally serious about reading. Read junk if you will, but also tackle the best books. After a while you will set internal standards for yourself" (Robb 2004, 39). In middle school, reading can inform writing style, content, organization, craft, and technique each time you model and students practice reading-writing connections. At school, the point of thinking aloud and discussing reading-writing connections is to develop and strengthen students' ability to understand what writers do, so they can approach their reading from a writer's perspective.

Myers challenges student writers to move beyond depending on teachers and collaborative groups to learn about writing from their reading. Students can meet Myers' challenge when teachers provide deliberate and explicit instruction in reading-writing connections. Then, as with professional writers, middle school students internalize the process, learning more and more about writing craft and technique from their reading. Sometimes the process is subconscious, with readers verifying and validating what they know. Other times the process is deliberate, and students and adults consciously consider how a professional writer handles flashbacks, foreshadowing, or uses dialogue to advance the plot of a narrative.

The ideal instructional setup is for reading and writing to be taught by the same teacher, so he or she can model powerful reading-writing connections. If reading and writing are divided between two teachers, both should plan together to mine the reading-writing connections that can help middle school writers improve. For me, reading informs writing and we write for specific audiences to read our work; the bond is as close as mother and child. Knowing, in advance, the connections I hope to make, allows my Think Alouds to be clear and thoughtful and builds a mental model for students of the process I want them to understand, and use.

In the following section, you will find parts of my plans for a reading unit that informs the teaching of writing. Knowing my mentor text(s) allows me to identify, in advance, the reading-writing connections I want students to explore and discuss. In the plan below, I've included callouts that let you step into my thinking process. Making notes before, during, and after a unit helps me recall, later on, students' and my reactions.

> "Read, read, read. Read everything—trash, classics, good and bad and see how they do it. Just like a carpenter who works as an apprentice and studies the master. Read. You'll absorb it. Then write." *William Faulkner*

Planning a Reading and Writing Unit: Eighth Grade

Genre: Memoir Through Poetry and Short Narratives

Estimated Time: Five to six weeks

Read Alouds and Mentor Texts:

- *Connecting the Dots* by David Harrison
- *Mama Makes Up Her Mind* by Bailey White

Students' Materials: Students will read two different texts

Choice of poetry, memoir, autobiography

> Note how the texts selected for Read Alouds function as teaching texts too.
>
> Students choose books at their instructional reading levels from my classroom and the school library.

Reading-Writing Connections for *Connecting the Dots*

- Topics of the poems
- Techniques: dialogue, inner thoughts, figurative language
- Introduction to each poem
- Focus is one event
- Length and shapes
- Titles of poems

> What I will help students understand with the mentor text: After I model, pairs will discuss a poem using the Reading-Writing Connections bulleted list to find examples.

Note how reading-writing connections deepen students' knowledge of craft and technique, giving them choices of what to include in their writing.

Reading-Writing Connections for *Mama Makes Up Her Mind*

- Topics of memoirs
- Length of memoirs
- The focus—number of events
- How White creates images
- How White builds characters' personalities
- Use and choices of memories
- Titles of vignettes
- Handling of time
- Show, don't tell
- Punctuation of dialogue

Writing Requirements

Because the school requires that students write an autobiographical poem, they will collaborate to plan and draft one autobiographical poem. Students will write a minimum of two autobiographical poems, more if they have the time. Or they can write one poem and one memoir.

Even with requirements, you can find ways to offer students choice.

Writing Choices

Students can pursue autobiographical poetry or write a narrative memoir. For narrative memoir they can use selections from Bailey White's *Mama Makes up Her Mind* as a mentor text.

Compelling Questions

Students will generate these after hearing several poems by David Harrison and short narrative memoirs by Bailey White.

Craft and Technique Lessons

The 300 students who answered the "Ten Questions About Writing" questionnaire raised my concerns about how much middle school students know about the craft of writing. Answers to this question "What would you like to know about how to improve your writing?" explained my concerns. The largest group, 240 students, noted that they needed help with spelling and learning grammar rules; dozens wrote, "I don't know," or "I don't want to know how to improve it," or "I want to improve my sloppy writing." Twenty-five did not answer the question.

The remaining group of 60 students asked for better ways to improve brainstorming, help find ideas, help add details, learn how to not write about everything in their heads, make stories more interesting, learn ways besides webbing to plan a story, and how to revise writing. Students' responses from both groups point out the importance of giving them a set of practical tools that can, as one eighth grader noted, make them more dependent on themselves and less dependent on their teachers. When you give students a toolbox of strategies that their favorite authors, like Walter Dean Myers, use, you offer them tools for getting started, for refining their drafts, and for gaining control over their writing.

The Prewriting Stage: Topic Selection, Brainstorming, Planning

I have watched students start to write with boundless enthusiasm, then, in less than five minutes, crumple up their paper and toss it in the trash. Others refuse to brainstorm ideas because they tell me, "It's in my head." Sometimes it really *is* all in a student's head, ready to pour out onto paper, but based on my teaching experience, this group is small. Other times, students have no ideas. They use this statement to keep the teacher at a distance and to avoid jotting ideas onto paper. To help you make students feel comfortable with exploring ideas before writing, I've included strategies writers and students use to discover writing topics, brainstorm, and plan so you can practice these with students and dismantle the avoidance patterns many have.

Graham and Harris' research in *Writing Better* (2005) expresses the need for learning disabled and struggling writers to have explicit writing instruction that offers clear steps for all stages of the writing process, especially in the prewriting stage. This includes teaching them how to find topics, brainstorm, and plan. The strategies in this section support those who struggle by providing students with mental models of each process stage.

> "Engage adolescents in activities that help them gather and organize ideas for their composition before they write a first draft. This includes activities such as gathering possible information for a paper through reading or developing a visual representation of their ideas before writing."
>
> Dolores Perin, "Best Practices in Teaching Writing to Adolescents"

Finding Topics

Whenever I watch an author or illustrator speak to elementary or middle school students, I notice that students always ask this question: "Where do you get your ideas?" Some authors tell students that a character visits them and returns again and again, compelling the writer to investigate the reasons for these appearances. Others browse in libraries and bookstores, searching for ideas from book titles, photographs, and illustrations. Nonfiction writers have a passion for and curiosity about specific topics, so they conduct research and write about them (Robb 2004).

While we can learn from professional authors, it's important to recognize that we can also learn from the writers in our midst: our students. When I asked some middle school students, in emails and interviews, where they get their ideas, their answers wowed me. I hope that their suggestions will also resonate with your students.

> I use song titles and song lyrics to find ideas for writing poems. (ASHLEIGH, GRADE 8)
>
> Sports events on television inspire me to write about soccer, football, and baseball. (RYAN, GRADE 7)
>
> Books I read, like *ttyl* by Lauren Myracle, give me ideas. (STEPHANIE, GRADE 8)
>
> Playing in a band, rehearsing, learning music, and meeting people give me ideas. (NICK, GRADE 9)
>
> I mull over things that happened to me and how I felt about them. (DILLON, GRADE 8)
>
> I write about subjects and topics I learn from movies. (THOMAS, GRADE 5)
>
> I write about my hobbies and recent events in my life. (MATT, GRADE 6)
>
> I use my dreams. (LIZ, GRADE 8)

Brainstorming

Brainstorming, which may be one of the most challenging and creative writing techniques, is a free fall of thoughts, words, and phrases. A large number of the middle school students I teach either resist brainstorming or generate a limited list of two to four ideas. However, writers know that it's better to collect more ideas than you need before writing, providing you with choices of what to include. The same rings true for middle school writers. That's why I've included three strategies that work and enable students to develop rich, brainstormed lists to return to as they design a plan and draft.

1. **Allow students to engage in conversations.** Encourage students to find topics they are passionate about—topics they find irresistible. Passion leads to writing with voice: writing that sizzles with energy and grabs the reader's interest immediately. Listen to the first stanza of Christa's poem, "Computer."

> *My computer jeers at me*
> *From the dark corner where it lurks,*
> *Daring me to come closer*
> *And outsmart it.*

Notice the verbs that personify the computer and how quickly this eighth grader creates an adversarial relationship. Christa found something that mattered to her: a love-hate relationship with her computer. That's why the four lines have energy, voice, and verbs like *jeers* and *lurks* that add stealth and attribute intent to a machine.

Once students have selected a topic they love and care about, invite partners or groups of four to chat about their ideas for five to ten minutes. If conversations are lively and productive, then let them continue. Talk has an uncanny way of reclaiming events and ideas from the deepest recesses of our minds. When students are finished talking, immediately invite them to brainstorm in their notebooks; encourage them to let ideas free-fall in any order. Organizing ideas can come later.

2. Have partners pose questions. Give students a three-inch-by-three-inch sticky note and organize them into pairs. Have partners exchange and read one another's brainstormed lists. Then ask them to write on the sticky note the questions the ideas raised. Encourage students to use their partners' questions to add more details and ideas to their brainstorming.

When Cheri Kesler used this strategy with her fifth graders, Mattea explained, "It was easy to ask questions for someone else's list." Other students needed Cheri to suggest some questions, which frequently occurs. By circulating and making herself available, Cheri modeled the questioning process for those who needed it. At first, Morgan only had one to two jots for each diary entry. Once Cheri helped her generate questions like *Why were you scared? Can you tell more about how you felt when nothing had happened?* and *Why didn't you mind staying in the house alone?*, ideas poured onto her paper (see Figure 5.2)

3. Pose questions yourself. In every grade, a few students will feel reluctant to note questions about a partner's brainstormed lists. Keep a watchful eye and jump in to support them immediately. For example, in one of my classes, Ian did not want to work with a partner, even though he was stuck. When I offered to meet with him, he explained that he wanted to write about friendship. He had listed the names of four best friends, but admitted that he did not know what else to write. We chatted for a few minutes, and Ian told me that his friends were funny and he "loved doing stuff with them." On a sticky note, I jotted several questions:

- What do you do together?
- How often do you see each other?
- Do you get into trouble? Give examples.
- What do you have in common?
- How are you different?

WRITING PLAN FOR DIARY ENTRIES

NAME_____DATE_____

THREE TO FOUR ENTRIES

my mom left meseges then I call her or P.ck up the phone int the massig bord (if home)

FIRST ENTRY
• my first time in the house aloun
• I was scared
• what is some one got hurt
• what if some one tryed to brake in
• what if I could not get my mom on the phone
• what if murray did something realy bad

SECOND ENTRY
• Nothing bad haffend my first time
• I was happy I knew I could call my mom
• I was happy I knew I could go to my naibors (if home)
• I was sill worried though

THIRD ENTRY over coming my fear
• I dident mind stying in the house
• my mom called every 10 min or so
• my nabors were normily home
• no one had go hurt a nothing bad haffend

FOURTH ENTRY
• When I stay in the house alone murray normily does something anowing like once I said pick up the phone. I thought it was going to be my mom. I thought it was not. The person asked to talk so murray did as I told h.m.

Figure 5.2 Questions help Morgan gather rich details.

Then I invited Ian to use the questions to generate ideas for writing (see Figure 5.3). When I returned to see how Ian was doing, he said, "[The questions] made such a difference. I got lots of ideas."

Always follow your teaching instincts to support students who ask for or show they need help. They won't depend on you forever because of their strong desire for independence. As soon as students have a solid mental model of the writing craft or technique, and realize that they can succeed, gradually release responsibility to them. There is no timetable; some will take longer than others. Give your students the gift of time.

Planning

As I made the rounds in Cheri Kesler's fifth-grade classroom, I watched students dip into their brainstormed lists to create plans. I find that students usually suggest genres for writing that they know and understand—genres that will work with their topics. Here, some planned for diary entries, others for a news article, and a few for a short narrative. Next, I created planning forms for each genre and told students that they could write, draw, or draw and write.

> "[Writing is] like making a movie: All sorts of accidental things will happen after you've set up the cameras."
> *Kurt Vonnegut*

Discuss Plans by Katherine Paterson and Jean Van Leeuwen

Before setting fifth graders to work on their writing plans, I showed them plans from former students and from two authors whose books they love: Katherine Paterson and Jean Van Leeuwen (see Appendices A and B for these plans). Because many student writers resist planning, it's helpful to show them what professional writers do.

I explain to students that planning writing is like using a road map for a vacation. You might stick to the map until you come upon a sign that advertises a museum or an amusement park. Then you'll take that detour, eventually finding your way back to the plan so you can reach your destination. When you are writing, you'll also take detours as you change, refine, and move ideas, but it's a comfort and a support to have the writing plan, which provides an idea of where you're going and confirms that you have a conflict for a story or enough details for diary entries and news articles.

Ideas

1 School
2 Sports
3 Friends
4 how i learned

Ideas

<u>Freinds</u>   <del>Sports</del>

Value of Friendship   Basketball
Ben — white-chocolate
Michael —   being in a game
Eric —
Brett —

Ben — we play school basketball and rec
basketball with him. We mess around
with each other and call him my
white — chocolate. we get in trouble
together. we both love football
and basketball. Go to the movies
and mall together. Have fun. He likes the Steelers
Michael — we play basketball together
at school and we get in trouble together

Figure 5.3 Now Ian has lots of ideas to develop.

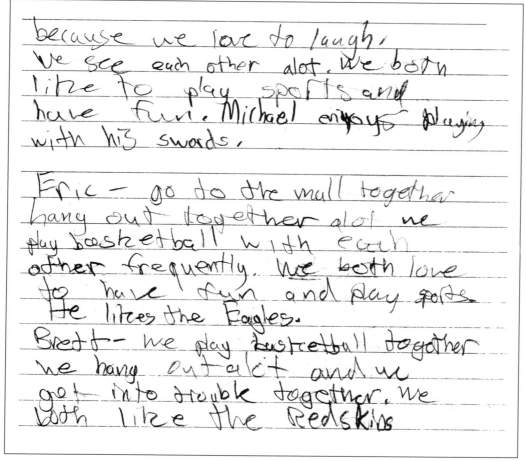

because we love to laugh.
We see each other alot. We both
like to play sports and
have fun. Michael enjoys playing
with his swords.

Eric — go to the mall together
hang out together alot we
play basketball with each
other frequently. We both love
to have fun and play sports.
He likes the Eagles.

Brett — we play basketball together
we hang out alot and we
got into trouble together. We
both like the Redskins

Figure 5.3 *Continued*

Skyler decided to write a short narrative. When he and I conferred about his plan,
I asked him what the problem would be. "There is none," he answered. I reframed my
question: "Can you tell me about the conflict?" That didn't work either. So I asked,
"What will get in the way of this character? Is there an obstacle he'll have to overcome?"

"I have special powers in the story. That's all. I don't want a problem," he said. Skyler
continued to resist adding a problem, although he agreed that in his independent reading book, the main character encountered lots of problems. He seemed to need time to
think about this, so I moved on to another student.

Two days later, at our next conference, I discovered that Skyler had thought of a conflict. Giving him time to think was the right decision. Skyler's problem is a descending funnel cloud; he solves the problem by jumping into a ditch (Figure 5.4).

Skyler was ready to draft. By supporting him at the planning stage, I enabled him to revise his plan before drafting and encountering major difficulties at that time. I was able to praise him for thinking of a problem and to reinforce the fact that one of the reasons stories engage us is that the main character has one or more problems to solve. The guidelines that follow can help students revise and develop detailed, useful plans.

Planning Guidelines

- Set aside a day or two for students to think about points previously discussed in a conference with you.
- Explain the plan's strong points, and point out one or two areas to rethink and/or revise.
- Ask, "How do you think you can improve this?"
- Listen carefully to the student's response. If you observe an unwillingness to consider changes and/or additions, let it go. Try again the next day.
- Find examples from your Read Aloud text or from the student's instructional or independent reading book. Present and discuss these. Ask, "How did this element [problem, conflict, details, differences in characters' personalities, etc.] make the reading enjoyable? Engaging?" Then move to the student's plan and ask one or two questions and/or suggest one or two ideas to stimulate the student's thinking.
- Drop the discussion if resistance hasn't diminished. Hopefully, the issue will resolve itself while the student drafts. You can discuss the issue during a revision conference, referring to the negotiated criteria for the piece (see pages 159–65).

Do All Middle School Students Use Written Plans?

No. But all middle school writers plan in some way—even if it's mostly in their heads. A few talented seventh and eighth graders plan in their heads or use a combination of notes and in-the-head plans. From my teaching experiences and perspective, I think it's important for students to experience the benefits of written planning, especially for those who are writing long stories and informational pieces. I view learning to plan in the same way that young artists must learn about perspective and painting people, or that student writers must learn about composing complete sentences before they consciously move to using fragments. Being grounded in the technique adds intentionality to breaking the rules, which surpasses breaking the rules because you don't know or understand them.

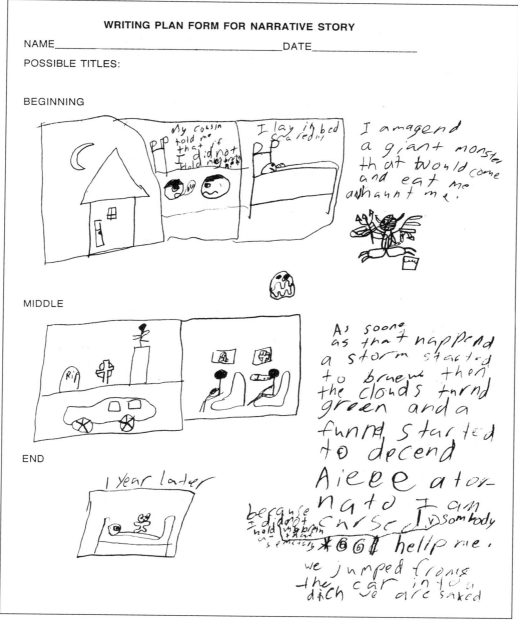

WRITING PLAN FORM FOR NARRATIVE STORY

NAME_____DATE_____

POSSIBLE TITLES:

BEGINNING

MIDDLE

END

Figure 5.4 Drawing and writing help Skyler plan.

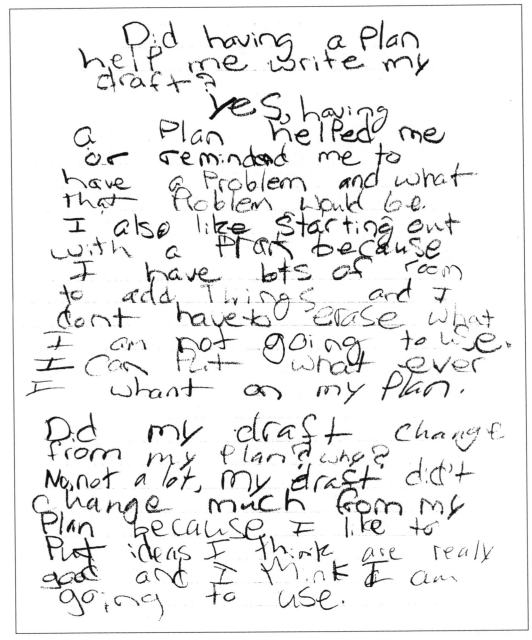

Did having a plan help me write my draft?

Yes, having a plan helped me or reminded me to have a problem and what that problem would be. I also like starting out with a plan because I have lots of room to add things and I dont have to erase what I am not going to use. I can put what ever I whant on my plan.

Did my draft change from my plan? why? No, not a lot, my draft did't change much from my plan because I like to put ideas I think are realy good and I think I am going to use.

Figure 5.5 Morgan's experience shows plans help!

Figure 5.6 This seventh grader plans her memoir.

I recommend that you require fifth and sixth graders to create written plans several times before you grant permission for them to plan in their heads. The true test of in-the-head planning is the quality of the draft.

Here are two ways that Addison and Haley, both talented eighth-grade writers, plan their stories. Addison explains it this way:

> The idea comes first. Like when we were thinking about questions for studying pressure. I knew immediately that I was going to write about the media pressuring young girls to be skinny and have the perfect figure. Once I have an idea, I must have a title or I can't go on. Then, the main character appears. I feel her presence. In the shower and at night before I fall asleep, I narrate the story again and again. When I hear the voices of the characters, I know it's time to draft. Sometimes I struggle with endings. A conference with the teacher can help because I can talk about all my ideas. The talking helps me get there.

Haley's internal planning process differs from Addison's:

> I pick the genre first. Then, I imagine the settings. Next I work on the characters. I splatter personality traits from friends, classmates, and adults I know into my characters. I need to show differences in characters, so I take these from people I know. Then, I stare off into space and think until I find the story. I listen to music and replay the story in my mind like a movie. I see it. I make changes now and as I draft. Titles are hard. I do those last.

Both girls have the hearts and souls of fiction writers. Both plan in great detail. Both understand that planning supports gathering and organizing ideas, developing characters, collecting details, and developing plots.

Four Key Writing Lessons

In addition to lessons on collecting ideas and planning, young writers need lessons on the craft and technique that professional writers use to make their writing compelling. I've chosen four lessons that I believe every middle school writer needs:

1. Show, don't tell;
2. Paint images with strong verbs and specific nouns;
3. Craft leads that grab the reader's attention; and
4. Create satisfying endings.

These are basic lessons that I want every student writer to know, understand, and be able to apply to their writing. I suggest you revisit these lessons several times during the year with the entire class and/or with small groups. Students need repeated lessons and practice in order to transfer the lessons to their own writing.

Each lesson takes ten to fifteen minutes. I prefer spreading the lessons over two or three days so students have time to absorb, figure out confusing parts, and raise questions. In my classes, the study of craft starts with learning from mentor texts (see pages 68–73).

1. Writing Craft Lesson: Show, Don't Tell

Professional writers agree that this is one of the most important lessons we can offer students. It merits repeating several times throughout the year. Studying mentor texts is crucial to understanding the concept of "show, don't tell," because writers don't show everything. Students who read widely and can make reading-writing connections eventually develop the sensitivity and expertise to know when to show and when to tell.

The Teaching Structure for the Lesson on Show, Don't Tell

Study mentor texts with the class and discuss the showing parts and the telling parts. Ask students to try to figure out why writers chose to use one or the other. I offer students this first stanza from an Emily Dickinson poem:

> *The morns are meeker than they were,*
> *The nuts are getting brown;*
> *The berry's cheek is plumper,*
> *The rose is out of town.*

After we discuss the showing, I ask them, "What is being shown here? If you were to recast this as a statement that tells, what would you say? (It's autumn.)"

Next, we look at sentences that tell rather than show in "The Negro Speaks of Rivers" by Langston Hughes:

> *I've known rivers ancient as the world and older than*
> *the flow of human blood in human veins.*
> *My soul has grown deep like rivers.*

Then I invite students to explain why Hughes' narrator directly tells rather than shows. In one of my classes, Sam, a seventh grader said, "Hughes wants us to know that his soul is as deep as the ancient rivers. His soul has been shaped by the past. Telling makes me zoom in on the comparison of soul to river." Develop students' ability to show by:

- Modeling how you transform a telling sentence into a showing sentence.
- Inviting partners to change a telling sentence into a showing one by mirroring your process.
- Having students rewrite telling sentences in their writing.

I use Hughes' poem and other examples to make students aware that telling isn't always a bad choice for a writer, especially if it's enlivened by similes and such (". . . grown deep like rivers.")

Teacher Demonstration

Next, help students recognize that a downside of telling is that if it's too direct readers can't form pictures in their minds—pictures that are similar to what the writer envisions.

Ten Telling Sentences to Rewrite

- The dog is vicious.
- The house is spooky.
- The pumpkin is rotten.
- The tree is pretty.
- The man is handicapped.
- The ocean is calm.
- The pool is cold.
- The wind is fierce.
- Mom is tired.
- My brother is energetic.

For example, I write on the chalkboard: *The tree is pretty.* Then I ask students, "What do you see?" Answers vary widely: oak, maple in autumn, pink blooms on a dogwood, cedar, birch in the winter, and so on. I explain that telling sentences are inexact and conjure diverse images. The writer's job is to use words to show readers what the writer envisions.

To continue the demonstration, I write the telling sentence on the chalkboard. "The tree is pretty." Then I tell the class that I want to transform the telling sentence into one or two showing sentences. I complete a mini-brainstorm to collect ideas before writing, adding the following words to the chalkboard: *maple, backyard, autumn, gold, crimson, orange.* Then I select words to craft one or two sentences that show. I write: "Standing tall in my backyard, limbs lifted skyward, the old maple wears leaves of gold, crimson, and orange."

Pair Practice

Pairs practice on another day. I write ten telling sentences on index cards, then ask pairs to choose one to rewrite (see the sidebar above). I write the following directions on the chalkboard for pairs to review before they collaborate.

- Complete a mini-brainstorm.
- Change the telling to showing in one to two sentences.
- Share with classmates.

We repeat this lesson during the year until students demonstrate that they understand.

Individuals Change Telling to Showing in Their Writing

As soon as you can, move students out of the practice mode to their own writing. Here are three ways to pinpoint sentences that need rewriting:

- The teacher chooses sentences students need to rewrite.
- Students select sentences to rewrite.
- Peer partners help one another identify one or two telling sentences, then revise them. By studying mentor texts, middle school writers will find that strong verbs and specific nouns can help them show instead of tell because these words paint pictures and appeal to the senses.

2. Writing Lesson: Paint Pictures with Strong Verbs and Specific Nouns

Student writers and professional writers, in an effort to pour out their thoughts onto paper, compose first drafts that often contain weak verbs and general nouns: *went* instead of *jogged; things* instead of *magnifying glass; flower* instead of *tulip; tree* instead of *birch;* or *car* instead of *convertible.* To raise students' awareness of the image-making power that resides in verbs and nouns, you can have them create word lists. I encourage you to snip five minutes off your period for two to three weeks to build lists with the class. Then hang the word lists in the classroom as writing references for students (Noden 1999). In the sidebars on this page, I've included samples of miniature word walls that feature a weak verb (*go*) with alternatives and a general noun (*things*) with specifics.

> **Replace *Go* with Strong Verbs**
>
> Sentence: I *go* to my friend's house.
>
> trudge
>
> strut
>
> amble
>
> jog
>
> run

Here are suggestions for training students' ears and eyes to the music and images strong verbs and specific nouns create:

- Pause as you read aloud to point out a strong verb and/or a specific noun and quickly share the image you see;
- Have students mine poems for strong verbs and specific nouns, since poets have to choose words wisely and carefully; and
- Ask students to dip into their independent reading to find and share a sentence or short paragraph that is brimming with strong verbs and specific nouns.

When students revise a piece, ask them to circle three to five weak verbs. Have them brainstorm alternates in the margin. A peer partner or the teacher can help them list several verbs to choose from, making sure that the verb enhances and connects to the context of the piece. For example, having a bell *toll* or *peal* creates opposite images and feelings: *sadness* and *joy.*

Follow the same revision procedure with general nouns. Avoid having students work on verbs and nouns at the same time. You'll avoid confusing them, and students will bring more thought and energy to the tasks when they are separated.

> **Replace *Things* with Strong Specific Nouns**
>
> Sentence: Look at the *things* on my wall.
>
> posters
>
> mirror
>
> photographs from camp
>
> bulletin board with messages
>
> two paintings
>
> bookshelves

Develop Best Verbs and Nouns Lists

Invite students to collect powerful verbs and nouns from their reading and jot these in their notebooks. Have students share this exemplary language. It's helpful if you find examples to periodically bring to students' attention, by noting these on a chart. Here are some of my favorites that I offer students.

Strong Verbs

"I <u>ambled</u> over, took a little run, and <u>cleared</u> it [high jump bar] with inches to spare." From *Jim Thorpe: Original All-American* by Joseph Bruchac. New York: Dial, 2006, page 33.

"I <u>balled</u> up those stockings, <u>stuffed</u> them in my pocket, and <u>waltzed </u>outdoors with my heart pounding." From *Becoming Billie Holiday* by Carole Boston Weatheford. Honesdale, PA, Word-song, 2008, page 29.

"My eyes <u>touch</u>, my fingers<u> trace</u>, The griot <u>chants</u>, <u>clicks</u> songs of the Ancestors." From "History of My People" by Walter Dean Myers, in *Soul Looks Back in Wonder*, collected and illustrated by Tom Feeling. New York, Dial, 1993, unpaged.

Specific Nouns

"The singsong <u>chants</u> of schoolchildren rang out from their sidewalk <u>classrooms</u>, and <u>carts</u> full of <u>brick</u> and <u>marble</u> rumbled through the <u>streets</u>." From *Galen: My: Life in Imperial Rome* (2002) by Marissa Moss. New York: Harcourt, unpaged.

"On the <u>lid</u> of the <u>well</u>, three black <u>stones</u> gleamed in the <u>gray-ness</u> of the <u>dawn</u>." From *Georgia Rises: A Day in the Life of Georgia O'Keeffe* by Kathryn Lasky. New York: Farrar, Strauss & Giroux, 2009, unpaged.

"I take a long <u>shower</u> and wash my pushy <u>stepmother</u> and my confused <u>father</u> and the <u>smell</u> of <u>cheese</u>, <u>sausage</u>, and <u>motel</u> out of my <u>hair</u>." From *Wintergirls* by Laurie Halse Anderson. New York: Viking, 2009, page 126.

3. Writing Lesson: Study the Essence of Leads

Middle school students who study leads in mentor texts and with their teacher's assistance learn several ways to open a story or an informational text; they never start this way: "I'm going to tell you about snakes," or "This is about the time I got lost." With a menu of leads to choose from, student writers have choices. In their first drafts, they often run with a lead to get started with the writing. It might be the perfect lead for that piece. More likely, it will need tinkering or a fresh try. Patricia McKissack's advice rings true for professional and student writers. Share it with your students: "When the shoe fits, you know it. That's the way your lead is. Play with it and play with it and don't be afraid of tearing it apart and starting over" (Robb 2004, 111).

Student writers need to practice the eight types of leads to deepen their understanding of how each works. The practice they need differs for each grade and depends on the writing skills students have. Once students can play with and revise their leads, then the need for practice diminishes. Though you'll be tempted to introduce all eight quickly, resist the temptation. Present the leads that will support the kind of writing your students do. For example, in seventh and eighth grade, when students are learning the art of writing a persuasive essay, they can practice leading with a quote from an authority or using a convincing statistic. In fifth grade, leading with a fascinating fact will benefit students who are writing articles about the rain forest. I always introduce leads by inviting students to study how professional writers grab readers' attention.

> "Once I have a draft, I go back and work on those first sentences. They have to be great or no one will read on."
> *Lucy, eighth grader*

Start with Professional Writers

Have students read and study the leads in picture and chapter books. One lesson might be enough for students who have studied leads before; repeat the lesson two to three times, using different texts, if students have little knowledge of leads and their significance.

Cheri Kesler's fifth graders were writing leads that opened with: "I'm going to tell you about . . ." We wanted to move them away from this rudimentary, boring approach, so we planned the first lesson by organizing students into pairs and giving each pair a picture book. These books included a mixture of fiction, biography, and informational texts. Pairs read the lead, discussed what they noticed, and shared their findings with classmates. Rachel and Cameron pointed out that their lead made them wonder what would happen next. Heads nodded. All agreed that their lead made them wonder or ask a question. Rachel explained, "That makes you want to turn the page."

Next, I asked pairs to try to identify the kind of lead the author used because, as partners read theirs aloud, I noticed so many differed. Here's what fifth-grade partners figured out:

- Ours had an amazing fact that made us want to know more.
- This one starts with dialogue.
- Ours build suspense.
- This one made us feel sad.

All agreed that the best leads, the ones that hooked them, had a dash of the unexpected and raised a question. Cheri and I repeated the lesson, inviting students to study the leads of their independent reading books. Repeating the lesson throughout the year is worthwhile because it raises students' awareness of what leads do—what makes a lead effective.

Next, I asked partners to develop questions they could use to study authors' leads and their own leads. Here are some of the fifth graders' suggestions, which they used to analyze and evaluate leads in their own pieces:

- How did the author grab your attention?
- What questions came into your mind?
- What details does the lead include?
- How do the details let you know what to expect as you continue to read?
- How could the writer make the lead better?

I always invite students to create their own list of questions because it shows me how much they have absorbed and understood. Moreover, when students test their lead with queries they have developed, they invest in the process and are willing to write alternates. Post the queries on chart paper or give each student a copy to paste into their writing folder.

The Basic Structure of Lessons on Writing Leads

To assist your planning lessons on leads, consider the basic structure I use. Know that the structure is flexible, allowing me to adapt it to what students show me they need. Sometimes I might do more collaborative writing with the class or a small group; other times I'll emphasize developing questions so students can evaluate their leads.

Here's the structure of lessons on leads that shows you the kinds of practice I offer. Students:

- Study and evaluate mentor texts;
- Create a list of possible writing topics;

- Collaborate to write a lead for one or more topics from the list;
- Evaluate the collaborative leads;
- Evaluate the lead in a piece of their writing; and
- Rewrite and improve leads in their writing.

As soon as possible, move students from collaborative practice to their own writing. Then, invite students to evaluate their lead and decide whether opening with a different type of lead would add zest, and hook the reader.

Eight Leads that Entice Readers

For each type of lead, I've included an example from professional writers that I consider a grabber lead. Share these examples and others that you and students find so you can observe how the lead sets the tone of a piece.

1. **Lead with a question.** Many authors open by hooking the reader with a question they know will spike the reader's curiosity.

   Example: "'Which one of Johnny Burwell's eyebrows do you think is cuter?' Sarah asked. Her light brown bangs fell into her eyes as she tilted her head meaningfully at a boy sitting two tables away in the school cafeteria, 'Don't look!'" From *The Juliet Club* by Suzanne Harper. New York: Greenwillow, 2008.

2. **Lead with a dialogue.** A brief exchange between two people or the utterance of one character can hook readers and set up a narrative that contains lots of dialogue.

   Example: "I am running. That's the first thing I remember. Running. I carry something, my arm curled around it, hugging it to my chest. Bread, of course. Someone is chasing me. 'Stop! Thief!' I run. People. Shoulders. Shoes. 'Stop! Thief!'" From *Milkweed* by Jerry Spinelli. New York: Random House, 2003.

3. **Lead with a brief story or an anecdote.** We're all tuned into stories; that's why opening with a short one can capture the reader's imagination.

   Example: "There is a saying that eyes tell everything about a person. At a store, my father saw a young jewish boy who didn't have enough money to buy what he wanted. So my father gave the boy some of his. That boy looked into my father's eyes and, to thank him, invited my father to his home." From *Passage to Freedom: The Sugihara Story* by Ken Mochizuki, illustrated by Dom Lee. New York: Lee & Low, 1997.

4. Lead with an interesting fact. Catch readers' interest with the unexpected: tell them something they didn't know; something that arouses curiosity.

Example: "As you know, in a few days I'm going to be twelve. That means two things:

1. In six weeks, you'll be nine.
2. In nine more years, I'll be twenty-one and then I'll be old enough to take care of you myself." From *Peace, Locomotion* by Jacqueline Woodson. New York: Putnam, 2009.

5. Lead with a thought-provoking quote or fact. A powerful quote or insight from an authority on a topic can make the reader sit up, read on, and take a position for or against the fact or the quote.

Example: "Experience: that most brutal of teachers.
But you learn, my God do you learn.'" C. S. Lewis. From "A Long Walk Home" by Jason Bocarro. In *Chicken Soup for the Teenage Soul*, edited by Jack Canfield, Mark Victor Hansen, and Kimberly Kirberger. Scholastic, 2007.

6. Lead with an action. There's nothing like action-packed excitement to draw readers into your piece.

Example: "The year I turned ten
I missed school to march with other children

For a seat at whites-only lunch counters.
Like a junior choir, we chanted, 'We Shall Overcome.'
Then, police loosed snarling dogs and fire hoses on us.
And buses carted us, nine hundred strong, to jail." From *Birmingham, 1963* by Carole Boston Weatherford, Honesdale, PA: Wordsong, 2007.

7. Lead with first person. This puts you into the story and immediately bonds you with the narrator.

Example: "They never call me over the intercom at school. But I can tell by the way the secretary is saying my name over that thing—I'm in trouble." From *Begging for Change* by Sharon G. Flake. New York: Hyperion, 2004.

8. Lead by setting a tone or mood. Words can create suspense, danger, mystery, or anger; tone stirs our imaginations and attention.
Example: "The house looked strange. It was completely empty now, and the door flung wide open, like something wild had just escaped from it. Like it was the empty, two-story tomb of some runaway zombie." From *Tangerine* by Edward Bloor. New York: Harcourt, 1997.

Students Find Other Ways to Lead

If you think about it, the kinds of leads writers can create are limitless. Encourage students to develop variations on the eight and to invent novel ways of opening a piece. Here are four my students have composed:

Lead with sentence fragments. Though not a favorite of English teachers, fragments can vary sentence length, startle, and grab the reader's attention.

> Student Example: "Okay, Stevie. She won't call. Won't. I know it for a fact. Snicker."

Lead with parts of song lyrics. The title or a line from a familiar song can draw the reader into your piece.

> Student example: "I will survive."

Lead by setting up a flashback. Starting at the end can raise enough questions in readers' minds to stay with the writer as he flashes back to the beginning.

> Student example: "Granddad and I sat by the fire warming our wet, chilled bodies. Why? I wondered. Why did our boat capsize at night?"

Lead with sensory images. Smells, sounds, and other sensations can reclaim the reader's memories and forge a connection for continuing to read.

> Student example: "Rotten eggs, I thought. My nose twitched, and I knew that my brother was at it again."

4. Writing Lesson: Crafting Satisfying Endings

Have you noticed how writers in primary and middle grades write "THE END" in oversized, capital letters to mark the closing of a piece? Sometimes it's their way of saying, "Look, I don't know how to create a satisfying ending, so these two words will do it." Other times, I feel that "THE END" is there to inform teachers that *I'm done and don't ask me to do any more thinking and writing.* In this section, we'll look at strategies that enable you to push students in grades 5 and up to take endings seriously and work hard to make them as effective as their leads.

> "The ending sums up the emotional journey, leading the reader to an awareness and understanding of how the person grew from experiences and how the reader grew by following it."
> *Hudson Talbot*

My students frequently struggle with ending pieces (see Addison's challenge with this issue on pages 93–95 and Laura's on pages 184-86). It's almost as if they have worked so hard on leads, on the plot, and on developing character that they rush through their endings to gain that sense of completion. Hudson Talbot's comment in the sidebar sheds some insight into this rush to finish: perhaps it's because the emotional journey for middle school writers is often exhausting and heartwrenching. They've spent their writing energy and jot the first ending that comes to mind.

Reading and discussing the endings composed by professional writers can reveal models that students can adapt to their own writing. Instead of presenting formal minilessons on crafting endings, I prefer working with the entire class and small groups; we take turns sharing a specific ending, then think aloud to explain why it's effective or ineffective. All through the year, students and I study leads and endings using these informal lessons. To help us analyze, we create questions, which I write on chart paper so we can add to the list each time we study endings.

Inquiry and Collaboration Support Analyzing Endings

I encourage you to analyze the endings from the fiction and nonfiction picture books with your students using the following questions to guide Think Alouds. Feel free to invite students to add to this list of queries as they gain experience with studying endings.

Satisfying Endings

Invite students to use some of the techniques that made their leads effective: an anecdote; a brief, memorable scene; a question or quote; closing dialogue and/or inner thoughts; the creation of a mood.

- What technique did the writer use: Anecdote? Dialogue? Memorable scene? Summary? Mood? Ironic twist?
- Can you describe the lingering thoughts and/or feelings the ending stirred? How did the writer accomplish this? How did the words make you feel?
- Did the ending surprise you? Can you explain why?
- Did the ending grow out of the story? Can you show how?
- Why was the ending satisfying? Unsatisfying?
- How did word choice affect the ending?
- How does the ending help you rethink a main concept or idea that's threaded through the book?
- Why does the ending paint vivid visual images in your mind?
- How does the ending enable you to connect to the character or person?

I prefer using picture books when I work with the entire class. That way, I can read the entire text, which allows students to experience how the ending emerged from the lead and plot. If a small group has read the same novel or informational text, I use that, too. In my Think Alouds, I include points I want to share with students. As soon as possible, however, turn the analysis and thinking aloud over to students so they gain practice using their writer's eye.

> When writers end with an ironic twist, they lead the reader to expect one type of ending, but surprise readers with a different ending.

You can also analyze the endings of students' writing. Please make sure you have a student's permission to do this if the student is in your class. If you use work from students who are no longer at your school, remove their names to maintain the student's anonymity. Here are two examples of strong endings that I use from professional writers, along with the type of Think Aloud I might do.

From *Wilma Unlimited: How Wilma Rudolph Became the World's Fastest Woman* by Kathleen Krull: "Wilma Rudolph, once known as the sickliest child in Clarksville, had become the fastest woman in the world."

Robb's Think Aloud: Krull's ending takes the reader back through her entire story of Wilma Rudolph; all the events replay in my mind. She juxtaposes Rudolph's early life with the challenges of winning three Olympic medals. I find this ending simple, yet satisfying because it helps me redefine the concept of challenge and how, through determination and endless work, it's possible to meet those that seem insurmountable.

From *Landed* by Milly Lee: "Sun could hardly wait for the launch to dock. With just a few steps up a ladder, then ten paces on the pier, Sun was reunited with his family. He had landed."

Robb's Think Aloud: The last three words, "He had landed," immediately remind me to the title, which is the focus of this story. These final sentences are short and loaded with action, a contrast to all the studying and interrogations Sun went through. By focusing on actions that show Sun has reached the goal he's worked for throughout the story, the ending is satisfying because it takes readers back to events that show the courage of a young Chinese immigrant and the importance of family.

Learning from Students' Writing

In this chapter, I've introduced the lessons and practices you need to run a writing classroom and the tools professional writers use to create texts that make readers plead, "Can't we have more time to read?" In your last professional study invitation, we discussed how having a plan enables writers to concentrate on writing well because the ideas and details have been reclaimed and organized. During this professional study session, we'll look at students' self-evaluation of their plans and drafts, and discuss students who can plan in their heads.

Once fifth graders in Cheri Kesler's class had completed a plan and first draft of their piece related to obstacles, I asked them to evaluate whether planning helped them draft:

> **Did having a writing plan help you with drafting? Explain.**
>
> **Did you depart from you plan as you drafted your piece? Why?**

Morgan plunged into her self-evaluation and wrote furiously for ten minutes. She told me that "I put down lots of good ideas and could choose from these."

Daniel explained that having a plan helped him organize his ideas (see Figure 5.7). He did add more details when drafting. Fifth and sixth graders, and middle school writers who struggle with writing, benefit from planning on paper.

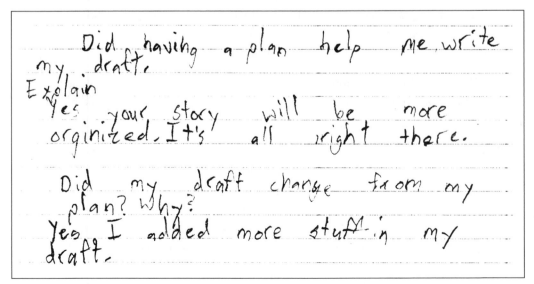

Figure 5.7 Adding to and changing plans is what happens.

The Night

Ned Selzer
*The hours pass
And the sun retreats
The forest's heart
Begins to beat
Slowly awakening
From the luminary sleep
With dreams of countless
useless sheep*

*The leaves on the ground
Start to swirl
Taking the form
of a dancing girl
Like a ballerina
The cold earth's the stage
Like a story book
Just turn the page*

*And inside you'll read
Of towering trees
Gently swaying
In the cool night breeze
And of lively creatures
Playful and fun
But each important
Every single one*

*The owl hoots
a soft lullaby
Bidding farewell
To the darkened sky
The night again
Fades away
Diminishing into
Another day.*

Figure 5.8 Ned composes poems in his head.

Some gifted writers, like eighth grader Ned, who is a poet, plan in their heads. When eighth graders discussed their ideas for writing about pressure, Ned sat in a quiet corner and spent two days finding a topic and another two days writing the poem. In an interview Ned explained his planning process: "Once I have the idea I play with writing the poem in my head. When I'm ready to write, it pours out. I can hold the plan in my head. It works for me." Ned's words, "It works for me," show us how to respond to students who refuse to plan on paper. If the writing is as Ned's (Figure 5.8 on page 155), then don't fret that the planning is internal. If it's more like Hank's (see page 97), then a written plan can help because it gives us a place to start figuring out how to support students.

Discuss Students' Writing

Professional Study Invitation

While students are writing, set aside time to ask student writers who don't complete written plans to explain how they plan inside their heads. Doing this enables you to see the relationship between in-the-head writing plans and drafts. I'm an on-the-paper planner, continually taking and adding notes, words, phrases, and new ideas. Some writers, especially those who write poems and short stories, are in-the-head planners; others are a mixture of both styles.

Invite one or two colleagues to bring plans and drafts of fledgling and strong writers as well as those writers' self-evaluations. Study and discuss these. Provide feedback that offers teachers suggestions for improving students' plans and letting go of this part of the process for students who plan in their heads.

C H A P T E R   6

Setting Criteria, Revising, and Editing

It was mid-October. I was observing a seventh-grade English class. In a daily forty-two-minute period, the teacher, in her second year, was responsible for the reading and writing curriculum. Students completed a journal entry while the teacher returned graded persuasive essays. I moved up and down the rows, checking out grades and comments. There were four marked, *A Terrific!*; eight marked, *B+* or *B Good*; five with *B–, Nice*; four with a *C* or *C+ Nice Try*; and three with *D* and no comment.

A few minutes before the class' end, a girl with a *C* marched up to the teacher. She asked why she had received a *C* and how she could improve. The teacher scanned the essay and then said that the paper was "C quality." The student pushed. She wanted to know what "C quality" meant. She pointed out that the only marks on her essay were for missing punctuation, adding, "And there's not that many." The bell rang. The teacher dismissed the class, reminding them to read the assigned short story.

The girl remained. "I want to get a better grade but I don't know how. I got a C or C+ the last two times." Students waiting for the next class piled up outside the closed door. Scribbling a late pass for the student, the teacher told her to come back at lunch.

Once the third-period class was over, the teacher and I conferred. She was nervous about the lunchtime meeting with the student. She told me that she had two measures for the grade: her gut reaction, and how the piece compared to the *A* papers. But she struggled to know what to suggest to the student. "Be honest," I told her. "Let the student know you want time to reflect. And explain that you will have suggestions tomorrow."

After school, the teacher and I discussed the girl's essay and created a list of what worked. We also identified a few areas that the student might want to rethink and revise. The teacher was open to my advice on negotiating criteria with students at the outset of each writing assignment.

When the teacher met with the student the next day, the girl mumbled that she should have known this criteria before she was expected to turn in the essay. And she was right! The teacher handled the situation beautifully. She didn't get defensive. Instead, she told the student that on the next assignment, there would be writing guidelines, and if the girl's writing showed progress, she would drop one of her *C* grades.

Have you ever had a student challenge a grade? How did you respond? In the rush of teaching, it's easy to overlook the signals students send us about the need for greater support. Again, in this case I was extremely impressed with the teacher's openness to work to make things right. The vignette also contains an important strategy: delay your response when you're unsure what it should be. It took me way too long in life to learn this tactic, but I encourage you to take it to heart. It buys you time to think and gather feedback from colleagues to support your students.

Our students can teach us a lot if we observe them at work, confer with them, and create an environment that permits them to question our practices—even those we hold sacred. Here's what I advise:

- Listen to students when they question teaching practices. Overcome those defensive feelings that lead to anger and frustration.
- Give yourself time to think through the issue and explore alternatives. Doing so respects both the student and yourself.
- Consider changing or adjusting a teaching practice that does not help students improve their writing.
- Explain to the student your reasoning for the decisions. Understanding is one path to acceptance.

Put simply, setting criteria for your students' writing will make your teaching easier, not harder. Criteria, or writing goals, allow you to define content, organization, style, and writing convention standards with students. This transparency of what you expect of them has all sorts of positive effects. When students establish criteria with their teacher before planning, it gives them powerful support and lessens the chances for unsatisfying false starts as they write.

> ". . . setting product goals is effective with adolescents who are weaker writers. Overall, assigning students goals for their written product had a strong impact on writing quality." *Steve Graham and Dolores Perin,* Writing Next

Having a set of criteria also gives you guidelines for responding to and grading students' work. Students can check drafts against criteria and revise and edit *before* turning in an essay, narrative, or poem. This act of self-evaluation is invaluable to middle school teachers who have 100 to 150 students and pieces to evaluate.

Writing Criteria: Why They're More Valuable Than Rubrics

At workshops or in coaching situations, teachers often ask me, "Why do you prefer writing criteria over rubrics?" My explanation opens with a discussion of purposes. Teachers can use rubrics or criteria to grade and respond to student work but often, teachers or publishers design rubrics whereas *teachers and students* design criteria.

Criteria incorporate what students are learning and what they've shown they can do in your writing class. Criteria support students' writing from planning to deadline or final drafts because they are a writing, revision, editing, and self-evaluation tool rolled into one neat package (see the box on page 160 for sample criteria). It can be easy for students to suggest criteria because these guidelines emerge from demonstration lessons, the study of mentor texts, and writing convention standards that students have understood and absorbed. Flexible, versatile, and responsive to students' needs, criteria change as the year progresses, and they grow out of what students know and can do as writers. My ultimate goal is for students to develop an understanding of content, style, organization, and writing convention criteria for fiction and nonfiction; this understanding provides them with the knowledge they will need to set criteria independently at school and on standardized tests.

Most often, teachers use premade rubrics, but these might not connect to what they have been teaching and what students already know. In contrast, criteria can and should be negotiated between students and their teacher. These negotiations also allow teachers to assess what students recall and understand from diverse writing lessons.

It usually takes about five minutes to create the criteria for a piece of writing with students. In the criteria, I include the name of mentor text or texts we've studied. Note

Sample Criteria for Autobiographical Poems

I include the mentor text or texts we've studied in the criteria. Students have copies of these in their writing folders and can refer to them as they draft, revise, and edit.

Criteria for Sixth-Grade Autobiographical Poems
Mentor Text by David Harrison: *Connecting the Dots*

Content	Content and Style: 70%

Note that all statements are positive, which encourages and motivates students.

- Preview to your poem has writer's age and explains this event.
- Include a short title that lets reader know the topic.
- Focus on one event, one moment.
- Include dialogue.

Style and Organization

- Shape your poem.
- Include stanza breaks.
- Use figurative language: simile, onomatopoeia.

The teacher can adjust the criteria for struggling writers since the criteria are not divided among a rubric point.

Writing Conventions: Mechanics and Usage	Writing Conventions: 30%

- Punctuate dialogue.
- Punctuate poem.

that all statements are positive, which encourages and motivates students. Students have copies of the criteria in their writing folders and can refer to them as they draft, revise, and edit. Also, the teacher can adjust the criteria for struggling students since the criteria are not divided up among rubric points.

The Disadvantages of Rubrics

Since a rubric moves from high to low points, many statements are negative. Students who earn a 1 or 2 often feel hopeless instead of hopeful. Moreover, the rubric locks teachers and students into specific statements; rubrics are difficult to adjust for writers who struggle.

Teachers tend to translate the rubric into grades: 4 = A; 3 = B; 2 = C; 1 = D. For me, giving students Ds and Fs in writing can discourage them to the point where they will make comments like, "Just give me the F; I won't bother to write." Students who struggle with issues such as writing dialogue correctly or shaping a poem need our help. In a few conferences, we can move them forward, and at that point, grade them on their progress, effort, and desire to improve. I'll take this one step further and encourage you to explain what you expect from students as you work with them. Let them know how meeting your expectations will affect their grade. For me, giving a child an F without stepping in to offer support sends a very strong message: "You're hopeless, so I'm not giving you extra time."

> Helping students at the brainstorming and planning stages can prevent those Fs that we all find painful.

Criteria: Naming the Attributes Common in All Genres

When you teach students about criteria, you raise their awareness of the attributes that are common to good writing in any. genre, as well as those that are genre-specific. Students need to be involved in setting writing criteria, which offers these benefits:

- Students can choose a genre and pairs or groups can set criteria based on what they have been learning.
- Students receive guidelines before planning, which helps them self-evaluate their writing to decide whether they have included each guideline.
- Students share with their teachers the responsibility for and control over an aspect of writing that supports their process.

Negotiated criteria or criteria set by the student with the teacher's approval also supports the teacher and can eliminate vague feedback such as "B– Nice," which doesn't let the student know the parts of the writing that worked and the parts that need revising. In addition, criteria give teachers the language for responding to and evaluating a piece. Teachers who use criteria experience these benefits:

- They can adjust criteria to meet the needs of a class with diverse writing abilities;
- They can grade more objectively by referring to criteria;
- They can respond to students' writing using criteria, forming responses that are specific and more objective; and
- They can reflect on whether a few students or the entire class had difficulty meeting one or more criteria, then use this data to make reteaching decisions.

> "When my teacher fixed the criteria for a memoir so I could do it, I felt good about starting to write."
> *Andy, seventh grader*

Not-to-Be-Missed Books About Writing

In addition to reading and discussing with colleagues books on writing by researchers and teachers, you can check out some of my favorites by professional writers.

- *Bird by Bird* by Anne Lamott. New York: Anchor Books, 1994.
- *Learning by Teaching* by Donald M. Murray. Portsmouth, NH: Boynton Cook, 1982.
- *Write to Learn* by Donald Murray. New York: Holt, Rinehart and Winston, 1984.
- *On Writing Well: The Classic Guide to Writing Nonfiction* by William Zinsser. New York: Quill, 2001.
- *Writing to Learn* by William Zinsser. New York: Harper & Row, 1988.
- *Writing with Power: Techniques for Mastering the Writing Process* by Peter Elbow. New York: Oxford University Press, 1981.
- *Writing About Your Life: A Journey into the Past* by William Zinsser. New York, Marlowe & Co., 1998.

Think of criteria as the beacon of composing for student writers. The criteria are rays of light that provide students with clear and exact illuminated points for improving content, style, and writing conventions. As they brainstorm, plan, draft murky sentences and paragraphs, they can turn to the criteria to know what to tinker with, revise, and edit, bringing clarity to each piece.

Some Content Criteria for a Short Narrative

- Focuses on one big problem.
- Has protagonist solve the problem.
- Handles changes in time.
- Builds the plot to a climax.
- Includes dialogue.

DVD CLASSROOM RESOURCES

Explore Fiction and Nonfiction Criteria

On the DVD, you'll find a list, Some Criteria for Editing and Evaluating Nonfiction, Fiction, and Poetry, that can apply to a wide range of fiction and nonfiction genres. The list offers you criteria that can assist you with developing genre-specific guidelines for paragraphs, essays, diary entries, short narratives, short stories, or poetry. Use this information to plan writing demonstrations and for studying mentor texts. Then negotiate and establish specific criteria with your students. I've included a brief sampling in the sidebar on the left.

Criteria for Fifth-Grade Journal Entries

Mentor Texts by Marissa Moss: *Rose's Journal: The Story of a Girl in the Great Depression* and *Galen: My Life in Imperial Rome.*

Content

- Include three journal entries.
- In each entry, discuss and elaborate on one event or incident.

Content & Style
75%

Style and Organization

- Date each entry.
- Include doodles, diagrams, and drawings with captions in margins and between entries.

Writing Conventions: Mechanics and Usage

- Mark paragraphs.
- Use complete sentences.

Writing Conventions
25%

Criteria for Eighth-Grade Memoir or Personal Essay

Mentor Text by Ralph Fletcher: Excerpts from *Marshfield Dreams*

Content

- Include a short, catchy title.
- Focus on one event and the people who were part of it.
- Create a lead that quickly draws reader into the piece.
- Make sure dialogue reveals character, advances plot.

Content & Style
65%

Style and Organization

- Use active voice.
- Show, don't tell in appropriate parts.

Writing Conventions: Mechanics and Usage

- Mark paragraphs.
- Use complete sentences; no run-ons.

Writing Conventions
35%

Criteria for Seventh-Grade Persuasive Essay
Mentor Texts by Students and by Newspaper Columnist Leonard Pitts

Content

- Use a short title that introduces the topic.
- Create a lead that grabs attention and introduces position.
- Include and develop three arguments for the position.
- Address one or opposing arguments.
- Include statistics and/or quotes from experts.

Style and Organization

- Use active voice.
- Vary the sentence openings.
- Organize ideas logically and showcase best arguments.

Writing Conventions: Mechanics and Usage

- Mark paragraphs.
- Use complete sentences.
- Use correct pronoun references.
- Use commas to separate compound sentences, and to follow introductory clauses, direct address, or adverbs at the start of the sentence.

Avoid the temptation of offering students too many criteria; this can overwhelm them and shut down their desire to write. For grades 5 and 6, I recommend that you include one to three items under each heading; for grades 7 and up include two to four. As the school year progresses, resist continually increasing the number of guidelines you include. Instead, respond to where your students are with their writing, and always modify criteria for students who struggle, helping them experience the success that pushes them to work hard. Consider the lessons you've presented, and negotiate criteria that can light the way for middle school students by providing them with a focus for revising and editing.

The boxes on these pages contains three sets of criteria you can review and discuss with a colleague. Notice the flexibility you have with grading and adjusting statements for particular students. If you've stressed content and style, those areas should receive more points than writing conventions. If you've worked diligently on writing conventions, then assign more percentage points to those.

Criteria Help You Respond and Grade Fairly

It's a comfort to you and your students to arrive at a grade based on criteria that has already been set. Stick to the criteria to be fair. For example, let's say that while I am evaluating sixth-grade stories, I notice an abundance of run-on sentences. Since run-ons were not part of the criteria, I don't take points off for those errors. Instead, I note in my plan book that I need to present demonstration lessons on spotting and repairing run-ons. After the demonstration, students can use these existing stories to repair run-ons. Depending on the progress students make, criteria for the next writing assignment might include repairing run-ons. However, they might not gain the required skills that soon. Avoid including criteria that students can't meet.

> **Finding Persuasive Texts by Leonard Pitts**
> - Leonard Pitts is a syndicated columnist; he might be in your local newspaper.
> - Pitts is a columnist for the *Miami Herald*. You can Google Leonard Pitts/Miami Herald and search for editorials that work for you students.

Our responses to students' writing should include what they did well and areas that require revision. Criteria enable me to write these responses with ease. An example of my response to a sixth grader's memoir can be seen in Figures 6.1a and b.

Notice how I couch the need for revision and/or editing in a question. Questions offer choices that I would like students to consider. Questions are kind because they don't say, "Here's what you *must* do." Students know these are questions to reflect on, discuss with me or a peer, and use to adjust their work. Writing feedback initiates students' rethinking about specific questions, but it also builds on what they did well. This honors the writer and develops the self-confidence students need in order to overcome their resistance to revising and editing. The process of giving written feedback also compels me to consider whether the student will be able to work successfully with a peer or will need my support to revise and edit or to get started with the task.

Along with detailed feedback on students' writing, I give two grades. The first is for content and style; the second is for writing conventions. This system allows me to praise students whose content has energy and engages readers, even though their mechanics and usage are weak. Both grades appear on first drafts that students will revise. This provides them with an idea of where they are, helping them decide where they want to go.

The Benefit of Students Turning in All Phases

Before I collect papers that I will grade (the deadline or final draft), I have students turn in all stages of their process. During each stage, they have conferred with peers or me to gather suggestions for improving their writing. From the bottom up they include brainstorming, plans, peer feedback and evaluations, drafts, revisions, edits, self-evaluations,

> Because you brainstormed, planned, sought peer feedback, your first draft focused one one main event in your life: your best friend jumping off the high dive when he couldn't swim. Your revisions followed the criteria, and you improved your lead; you also rewrote 2 telling sentences as showing! Can you read aloud to hear 2 run-ons and some missing words? A-/A-

Figure 6.1a Teacher's questions drive writers to revise.

and the deadline draft. My purpose is to grade students on their progress, their improvement. To accomplish this, I have to review and skim all the stages that led students to their early or publishable draft.

Let's look at a choice piece of writing completed in the spring by Amylee, an eighth grader. Amylee, who has learning disabilities, entered my eighth-grade classroom with an IEP (Individual Educational Plan) that required me to review directions with her personally after giving them to the class. The IEP report stated that Amylee, an avid reader, needed support with writing, especially brainstorming, planning, and elaborating ideas. With

Your thesis is strong
because you back it up
with the surveys you
took in 6, 7, 8. These
support your position
that personality and
values are more important
than appearance. I like
the way you used survey
data to rebut the
arguement that looks
are everything.
Can you work on
your concluseon so that
it leaves readers with
more to think about? Can
you repaer the 2 run-ons? A-/B+

Figure 6.1b *Continued*

choice writing, I allow students to set their own criteria and run it by a peer. If a student
needs my feedback, we discuss the criteria. Here's the list that Amylee set for her poem:

- Title, shape it
- Stanzas
- Figurative language and strong images
- Punctuate the poem

Figure 6.2 Self-confidence blooms when peers work together.

Breath Method
Student reads the piece out loud. Each time she pauses to take a breath is a line break.

Amylee worked on brainstorming to find a subject for her poem (Figure 6.3), but found that she still needed more ideas. She worked with Christa, a classmate, to enlarge her list, and on the sticky note, Christa jotted additional points (Figure 6.4). For her first draft, Amylee wrote a paragraph (Figure 6.5). We conferred, and I used the breath method of dividing ideas into poetic lines (Figure 6.6).

To help Amylee shape her poem, I handed her an anthology of poems and asked her to work with Christa. The pair read a few poems and discussed how the poet shaped each one. Having a model from professional writers supported Amylee as she wrote her deadline draft. In a conference, I told her, "I'm pleased you read your publishable draft out loud and completed one more edit." Next Amy and I discussed her self-evaluation (Figure 6.8).

With the support of a peer or myself, Amylee did "a lot of revising." I agreed with her grade choice because she invested time and hard work to meet her criteria and write a poem that she felt ". . . is rich and interesting." The research of Graham and Harris

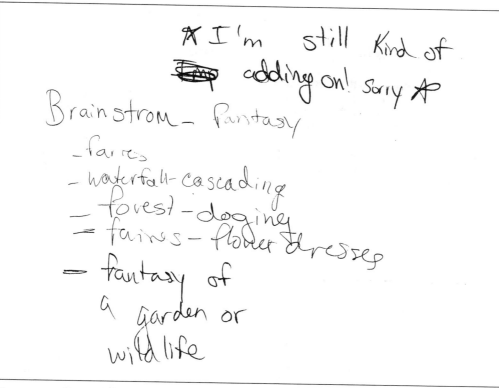

Figure 6.3 Amylee needs some help with brainstorming.

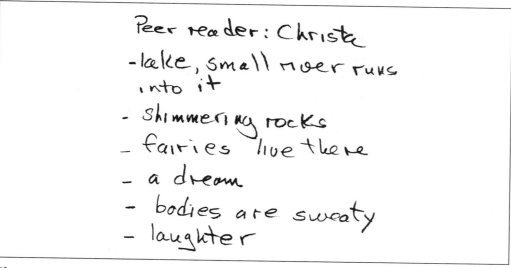

Figure 6.4 A peer reader offers support.

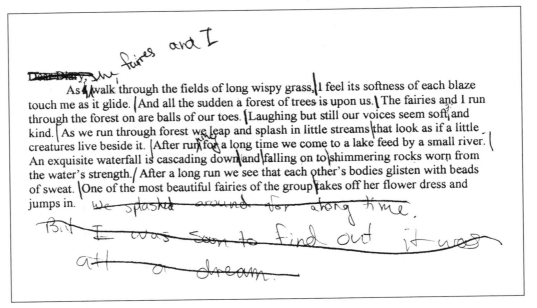

Figure 6.5 Amylee's Paragraph

(2005) and Perin (2007) all point to the success of having adolescent writers support one another, as Christa supported Amylee. In addition, these researchers urge teachers to build and/or enlarge students' mental models of a writing stage by providing support and feedback that enable them to fine-tune, rethink, and revise.

Deciding What Students Revise

Another question that rattles around teachers' minds is "Who decides what writing to revise?" Sometimes it's the teacher and other times the student. Required writing, such as a memoir, persuasive or personal essay, lyric or narrative poem is the teacher's decision when the school's curriculum states that students must bring a specific genre to a final or publishable draft. No negotiation room here. However, students can choose which one of their choice pieces of writing to revise. Choice is crucial here because revision demands that students work hard, rewrite, tinker, add, change, delete—a slow and thoughtful journey. Choice is the first step to investing in a tough but satisfying process. In my classes, students:

- Complete (including revising) one piece of required writing per trimester or semester;
- Use the remaining time to compose writing on topics and genres students choose;

Amylee

Fantasy

~~the fairies~~
~~As I~~ walk through the fields of long wispy grass,
I feel its softness of each blade touch me as it glides by. ~~my blade of grass~~

And all the sudden a forest of trees is upon us.

The fairies and I run through the forest on are balls of our toes.

We're Laughing but still our voices seem soft and kind.

As we running through forest we leap and splash in little streams

that looks as if a little creatures live beside it.

After run for a long time we come to a lake feed by a small river.

An exquisite waterfall is cascading down

and falling on to shimmering rocks worn from the water's strength.

After a long run we see that each other's bodies glisten with beads of sweat.

One of the most beautiful fairies of the group

takes off her flower-dress and jumps in.

The fairies start to blur but I try hard see clearly.

Soon they disappear all together in blackness.

I awake my bedroom ceiling staring down at me,

and wishing my fantasy would come true.

Figure 6.6 Listening to a draft read aloud supports revising and editing.

Amylee

Fantasy

As the fairies and I walk through the fields of long wispy grass,

I feel ~~its~~ softness of each blade of grass touch me as it glides by.
the

of a
And all ~~the~~ sudden a forest of trees is upon us.

the   feet
The fairies and I run through the forest on ~~are~~ balls of our ~~toes~~.

We're laughing but still our voices seem soft and kind.

As we are running through the forest, we leap and splash in little streams

That look as if little creatures live beside it.

After running for a long time, we come to a lake feed by a small river.

An exquisite waterfall is cascading down

And falling onto shimmering rocks worn from the water's strength.

After a long run, we see that each other's bodies glisten with beads of sweat.

One of the most beautiful fairies of the group

Takes off her flower dress and jumps in.

to
The fairies start to blur but I try hard see clearly.

Soon they disappear all together in blackness.

I awake to my bedroom ceiling staring down at me,

and wishing my fantasy would come true.

Figure 6.7 Corrections are natural even on the final draft.

SELF EVALUATION OF CHOICE WRITING

Name_____Date_____

Title and Genre___Fantasy_____a Poem_____

• <u>Comment on your process.</u> Include the time you gave to this piece, your brainstorming, planning, first and second drafts.

Time is 4 hour or more. I didn't brain-storm alot because this was a fantasy already in my mind. I did a lot of revising.

• <u>Comment on your idea.</u> Why did you write about this? How did you arrive at the idea? Do you feel that the content is rich and interesting to others? Why?

I thought it was a great dream that had great description. I was thinking about a book and this came up. I think it is rich and interesting.

• List all the things you like about this piece and all the elements that make it a strong piece.

I like the fantasy things that wouldn't really happen in real life.

• Discuss one to two ways you feel you can improve this piece.

I could make it more in poem form.

• Give yourself a grade and defend your grade.

and it A because I did alot of revising, it is creative.

Figure 6.8 Self-Evaluation: One Road to Better Writing

- Collect two or three drafts, then choose one in which they want to invest the time and energy it takes to revise;
- Use the criteria developed for that piece to decide on revisions;
- Meet briefly with the teacher to discuss revision possibilities if specific criteria weren't set; and
- Revise in class so they can receive feedback from peers and the teacher.

Throughout the year, demonstration lessons for the class or small groups continue on genre structure, craft, technique, revision, and editing. To provide the opportunities young writers need to make sense of a complex process, offer repeated modeling with mentor texts and Read Alouds. Also ask students to share examples from their reading.

Criteria Ease Revision and Editing

Keep in mind that revising and editing are daunting tasks for student writers—tasks that are often accompanied with anxiety, frustration, and avoidance. Student writers want to move on to another piece; they don't want to navigate the roads of revision and editing alone. Repeatedly, students describe their feelings toward revision and editing with these words and phrases: *won't do it, hate it, don't know what to do, don't know where to start.*

In some school cultures where teachers feel pressured into rewriting and editing students' papers themselves, then returning the papers for students to recopy, resentment increases in geometric proportions. The students' anger emerges from the loss of control they experience when they receive a marked-up paper; in turn, angry teachers spend hours doing the students' job. This situation creates teachers, not students, who are skilled revisers and editors. As students recopy corrected papers, they think about texting a friend, meeting at the mall, attending the after-school basketball game. They are not motivated to learn about revising and editing from what their teachers have done.

"Improving the writing abilities of adolescent students has social implications far beyond the classroom. Helping these young people to write clearly, logically, and coherently about ideas, knowledge, and views will expand their access to higher education, give them an edge for advancement in the workforce, and increase the likelihood they will actively participate as citizens of a literate society." Graham and Perin, *Writing Next*, page 28.

At a two-day workshop on writing I taught for teachers in and around Ann Arbor, Michigan, sixth-grade teacher Leslee Cassel-Bonilla, a reflective teacher, said, "When you explained why the student, not me, the teacher, should revise and edit, you gave me my life back! Now I have revision and editing lessons and they do the work. I can support them in conferences." I'd like to pause to explore why Leslee's shift from the teacher feeling she had to correct everything on students' writing to asking students to revise and edit worked for her.

> Revision and editing can become students' Mount Everest if their knowledge of writing craft and technique is limited. That knowledge, combined with your modeling and thinking aloud, can provide students with mental models of how to improve their writing.

Here are some suggestions that Leslee integrated into her writing workshop. I encourage you to try some so that you can show students the *how* of revision and editing.

- With students, establish criteria or guidelines for content, style, and writing conventions for each piece. Criteria set limits on what students will revise and edit. Partners can use criteria to make the process social, palatable, and doable.
- Model, in a minilesson, how you revise for one content or style element. These minilessons will come from the criteria you establish with students. So you might model how you revise to improve verbs, develop sensory images, or show more instead of telling. Consider repeating these lessons using passages from past students' writing and the collaborative writing you and students have competed during the year.
- Use minilessons to model how to edit for writing conventions. Show students the benefits of editing for one convention at a time: correcting the punctuation of dialogue, paragraphing, repairing run-ons and fragments, and so on. Again, I suggest that you model the conventions that were part of the criteria for that specific piece.
- Continue modeling and thinking aloud, making your process visible to students.

> "When students use criteria to revise and edit, the piece has been improved before I read it. With more than one hundred students, this strategy makes a difference!"
> *Andrew Frye, eighth-grade English teacher, Shelburne Middle School*

To be effective teachers, we all need a rich, personal life. For me, Leslee, and other teachers I work with, this school-life balance occurs when we shift the responsibility for revising and editing on to the students. Through continual modeling, we show them how the process works.

One at a Time: Separate Revising and Editing

I'm always battling the temptation to ask students to revise *and* edit, to make their writing better all at once. It doesn't work for many professionals and it is a daunting task for middle school writers. First, create criteria to show students the revision and editing guidelines they need to tackle. Revision can come from content and/or style and organization criteria. Help the students choose the two or three areas that require revision. Stick to the established guidelines. For example, you notice that several students need technique lessons for varying sentence openings, yet this is not part of the criteria you and students negotiated. Make note of this need, plan and teach lessons that model this technique for students, and include it as criteria in their next piece.

Have students revise the content, style, and organization criteria first, then work on all or part of the writing convention criteria. Some students might only be able to revise one of the criteria; that's fine. The amount of revision can differ because what's revised should respond to what each student can do well and absorb. Students use the criteria for a piece to reread, revise, and edit before you read the draft to give feedback and a grade. You can also ask partners to read one another's work and use the preset criteria to offer suggestions.

When you invite students to edit, ask them to edit for one criteria at a time. Explain that this feels like extra work, but it's an effective strategy for catching errors in mechanics and usage. Separating content, organization, and writing conventions means students will reread their work multiple times. Can you hear the groans? Feel the resistance? Best to do this in class and not as homework. This permits you and student experts to provide all the support and encouragement that's needed.

The Big Ten Revision Strategies

Grading papers for English or language arts teachers is overwhelming because in one week, they can have one or two sets of 120-plus papers to read. The Big Ten Revision Strategies give teachers a much needed break because these strategies ask students to start the revision process. You might invite students to complete a few of the Big Ten or to use all of the strategies before you read their papers. First, this places part

Advice on Publishing Student Work

If students' writing goes public, in a magazine or on a school bulletin board, then you *should* act as the editor and correct elements not in the criteria. You can explain to students that correct writing, mechanics, usage, and spelling are school requirements for writing that goes public. Professional writers also have editors correct their writing conventions before their texts are published.

of the responsibility for revision on students and shows them how they can revise on their own. Second, since students have revised and improved their writing in advance, it will take you less time to read their papers. For example, look at the revision that Christa, an eighth grader, completed on her own and with the support of a peer. First, Christa showed her peer partner a draft of her writing. Her partner pointed out that the lead could be less wordy but hold more meaning. (Both students used criteria for identifying revision needs.) Next to the lead, Christa wrote "Intro stinks" and scribbled through it (Figure 6.9). She also numbered three parts that needed rewriting. She revised on separate paper, numbering her revisions to correspond with numbers on her draft (Figure 6.10). Christa turned in the draft, which I read on top of her brainstorming, plan, first draft, and revisions. This allowed me to note the progress she made, read a revised and edited draft, and either respond and grade or call for additional revisions and edits.

Christa's Compelling Question

Why are some friendships so good, so close, that you want to remember them forever?

"Develop instructional arrangements where adolescents work together to plan, draft, revise, and edit their compositions. Such collaborative activities have a strong impact on the quality of what students write."
Dolores Perin, "Best Practices in Teaching Writing to Adolescents"

Teacher Feedback for Student Revision

Fifth and sixth graders will need more teacher feedback for revision and editing than seventh and eighth graders. At each level, you'll find students who can use the Big Ten independently to revise and edit well, and all you will need to do is comment and grade. Others will need your suggestions as they work through the Big Ten and when you read revised and edited drafts.

The Big Ten strategies on pages 179–83 show students how to rewrite and improve drafts *before* you read them. As students use the criteria to self-evaluate and improve, they move closer to independence because they develop the skills needed to fine-tune their writing. Sharing the Big Ten strategies with students is an important aspect of creating an effective writing curriculum.

First Friendships

Every person, guaranteed, had a simple friendship at one point or another throughout their childhood which they still have fond memories of. The friend from that friendship was the kind who you can do anything with and tell everything to, no matter what. Whether you're still in contact with that person or not, you will probably remember them friend long after you have moved on to a newer, more complicated lifestyle. I have three such friendly memories, from a time predating kindergarten when I lived in the kind of neighborhood that no matter where you go or what you do, you are welcome.

Intro Stinks

All of the little girls in the neighborhood had pink, fluffy, white-walled rooms. In every one there were cute stuffed animals, fancy pillows, and, of course, lots of lace and frills. The biggest, brightest, and by far the coolest bedroom in my eyes was Paige's, a girl who lived up the street and around a corner. She even had a skylight right over her bed! Paige also had a walk-in closet, with a secret passageway from her stuffed animal-filled closet to who knows where. You entered it through a little door behind a projecting piece of wall, which only a small child could fit into. Once you entered and pulled that door shut, you could go anywhere you wanted, real or made-up. We had thousands of adventures through Paige's little white door. The best by far was when we traveled by boat to Disney World and got to walk in a parade with Mickey and Minnie Mouse. Paige also had a fluffy white dog. It was the kind of dog that is always named Muffin or Marshmallow or some such thing. This particular dog was the Muffin type, and lived up to its namesake one day by eating all of the blueberry muffins which Paige's mom had just cooked for us. That was the only time anything was ever out of order in Paige's perfect house.

On the first day of summer when I was four, a girl, her brother, and her mother from down the street appeared on our doorstep with a bucketful of freshly picked blackberries and raspberries. They grew wild all over the neighborhood and behind our house, but it was such a friendly deed that we invited them over that day, sealing our families' friendship. That girl was Rebecca Bacon. From then on, we would hang out, play together, and later, unbeknownst to us until we met there, go to school together. We are still friends today.

My best best friend in the old neighborhood was Abby Rogers. She lived a few doors down from me. One day, during the summer, we sold lemonade to the small handful of people

Figure 6.9 Christa numbers places to revise.

who passed by ~~on their way to their various obligations~~. One of Abby's next door neighbors came over and chatted with her mother for a bit, then came over to us and gave us a fifty-cent piece for a cup of lemonade. When we split up the money afterwards, Abby tried to give me the fifty-cent piece. My eyes flew wide open and I told her in an astonished tone that she shouldn't give it to me because fifty cent pieces were worth more than ordinary money. I think I had learned this from my sister a few months earlier, ~~when she~~ *My sister* gave me one *a 50¢ piece* and told me that, since it was a fifty cent piece, I should pay her back fifty cents and then some to make up for it.

During spring collection right after Easter one year, I remember walking down the street with Abby, Easter baskets and candy in hand. Stopping by everyone's piles, we picked out priceless treasures and giggled at how dumb people were for throwing out the things that they did. Our parents and neighbors were throwing out chairs, baskets, mattresses, and even a basketball hoop! We picked a basket out of a pile and put all of our Whoppers Easter Eggs in it, so that we could share all of the eggs instead of one of us having more. We soon found out why the basket was in the junk pile. The bottom fell through, spilling our precious sweets all over the damp ground around us. We ate them anyway.

Memories like these are always there, whether you want them or not. Even if they're tucked away in a dusty corner of your mind, you're bound to stumble across them one day. When you're stressed out or under a lot of pressure, they help you to recall a time when you had not a care in the world, because you didn't have to. ~~If you're sad, being reminded of them will make you smile. The first buddies you remember having~~ *They* will always be the truest and closest as you remember them. No matter ~~how many times you move or make new friends, you will always remember your first and best.~~ *what they're doing now,* *I know mine are.*

Figure 6.9 *Continued*

The Big Ten Revision Strategies

1. **Let the writing rest.** Before students reread a draft to revise it, it's helpful to let a few days pass. Like professional writers, students will love their work immediately after composing. Two days later, they are more likely to see the pitfalls and the need for rewriting. Cooling off time provides the distance that can enable student writers to play and tinker until they can craft a lead or refine a conflict so that it's clear and engaging.

2. **Read the writing out loud.** This is an easy strategy for detecting missing words, incorrect words and phrases, repetitions, switches in verb tense, and misspellings.

① Did you have any really close friends when you were a child? Most people did, even if they don't remember now. I still remember mine, from my first ~~family~~ neighborhood. We all lived within a few houses of each other, and ~~pretty much~~ were allowed to roamed freely together all summer.

② Memories like these are always there, whether you want them or not. Even if they're tucked away in a dusty corner of your mind, you're bound to stumble across them one day. When you're stressed out or under a lot of pressure, they help you to recall a time when you had not a care in the world ~~because you didn't have to~~. You'll smile when you think of having had such faithful friends. They will always be the ~~truest~~ and closest as you remember them, no matter who or where they are now. I know mine are.

③ One day, during the summer, we sold lemonade to the trickle of people passing by her house.

Figure 6.10 Rewrites display the power of revision.

Older students, like eighth grader, Carter, often resist doing this. Carter rolls his eyes when I suggest reading his story out loud. Several girls hear me and chorus, "I'll look freaky!" Even after modeling, there's no way I can or should try to coerce students to adopt this revision technique. So I sit with Carter and have him read his story out loud. "If I'd done that with my really rough draft, I would have caught all of these before you read it," he says. My point is that it pays to work side by side with these students, allowing them to read their work aloud *to you*, so they still experience the benefits of a strategy they will otherwise avoid because it's not "cool." This also shows students that we'll meet resistance with support.

3. **Use questions to edit and revise.** The revision and editing questions on the DVD can help students identify revision needs and spark ideas for re-writing. Questions also enable students to spot writing conventions that need repairing. Moreover, questions are kind and consider middle school students' fragile self-images. Questions are a positive way to send students back to their writing to make it clearer for their audience.

4. **Use the numbering strategy.** Before revising, student writers tend to scratch out the weak verb or even several sentences, which makes it impossible to read the original writing. Instead, I ask students to number, on their drafts, places they intend to revise. Then they revise on separate paper, numbering rewrites to cor-respond with the numbers on the draft.

   When students revise on a computer, I require that they print each page that they change so I can reflect on and if necessary weigh in on their rewrites. It's beneficial to keep reminding students to run off changes because it provides you with parts of their process.

5. **Reread the brainstorming and plans.** Before and after drafting, I ask students to reread their list of ideas and their plans. This helps them identify information they omitted and decide whether and where they should add more details. Invite students to consider the needs of their audience when making these decisions.

6. **Use the criteria to self-evaluate an early draft.** Invite students to study their early drafts and measure these against content and style criteria. Jen, a seventh grader, discovered that she had two supporting para-graphs for her essay. The criteria called for three; Jen added a third paragraph. "The process lets me catch something I need to add before I turn in a paper the teacher will grade."

Encourage students to use the Peer Evalua-tion form from the DVD to evaluate each other's work. Peers can jot their suggestions on sticky notes or complete a revision form that lists the criteria on the left and comments and questions on the right.

7. **Rewrite parts related to the criteria.** Ask students to rewrite parts that they, you, or both of you have selected based on content and style criteria. If you

Peer Evaluation

Student's Name_____ Date_____

Peer Evaluator's Name_____

Directions:
1. Under each heading list the criteria for the piece you're evaluating.
2. List what the writer did well first.
3. Select one to two areas that would benefit from revision and note these as questions.

Content Criteria	Comments and Questions

Style Criteria	Comments and Questions

Writing Conventions Criteria	Comments and Questions

May be copied for classroom use. © 2010 by Laura Robb from *Teaching Middle School Writers* (Heinemann: Portsmouth, NH).

have a self-contained class, you can read students' revisions and then confer with them. Middle school teachers with 120-plus students can read revisions and offer feedback on sticky notes since it's impossible to confer with every student about every piece of writing. This frees you to confer with writers who struggle.

8. **Confer early in the process.** Confer early in the process. Start by organizing students who can help one another into pairs and/or small groups so you can have time to confer with the students who most need your support. Send these independent learners back to the criteria for the piece; they can also use the questions on the DVD to provide constructive feedback to one another. Listen carefully to the handful of students who need to confer with you. Ask them, "How can I help you? What parts do you feel need additional work?" When we take our cues from students, they let us know the level of support they need. For the few who can't verbalize their needs, start the conversation by returning to the criteria to compare the content, style, and writing convention guidelines with students' work.

9. **Edit for writing conventions.** Help students understand that they need to edit for one writing convention at a time. This means students might have to read

Figure 6.11 Sixth graders confer to revise content.

through their writing two to four times. Conventions come from established criteria. Next, a peer edits the piece.

10. **Have the teacher read.** Most students in time will do a beautiful job of bringing a piece to a polished point through self-evaluation and peer conferences, and I can't emphasize enough how the questions and criteria you negotiate support this independence. However, if a student wants a particular piece to receive a final grade, you'll need to confer with them, reading the piece and giving advice on sticky notes about content, style, word choice, and so on. The student then revises accordingly and hands it in to you.

> "Knowing I can revise— make my piece better—is the real part of writing. I try my best on the first draft. But I always have to rewrite and add details. "
> *Kate, eighth grader*

Asking Questions: A Revision Strategy That Works

Professional writers and editors ask questions such as: Does the ending logically emerge from the plot? Do I need this information? This character? This event? Can my reader follow my train of thought? Can I say this using fewer words? Does this word/phrase enhance or weaken the sound of the sentence? Kathryn Lasky captured the essence of

---

Scaffold by Writing and Thinking Aloud

Basically, I'm a hands-off-correcting-students'-writing teacher because the students learn from doing the work. There will be times, however, when you will have to rewrite part of a student's work, such as a lead or paragraph opening. Be sure to do this on separate paper. This makes visible what you're trying to show students with words and mentor texts. Don't hesitate; do it! Some students learn best by seeing what you want them to try. For example, Brian, an eighth-grade student, had difficulty finding verbs to strengthen. I circled three on his paper, then modeled how he could note a list of alternates in the margin. Next, I used a Think Aloud to show Brian how I chose a verb that worked best for what he was trying to communicate. I set up four consecutive conferences with Brian and two other students to review verbs, because I recognized that part of their problem was that they could not pinpoint this part of speech. When students show you they need extra teaching and modeling, find the time to help them, then gradually move them to independence.

this aspect of revision when she wrote, "In fact revision is tightening, kissing good-bye to something you think is great" (Robb 2004, 254).

Show students how questions can guide revision. Ask questions during conferences and on sticky notes when you offer feedback. Let me show you how helpful questioning was to eighth grader Laura Renzi. She wrote a short story centered around the idea of peer pressure, but her ending seemed melodratic and unreal (Figure 6.12). I be-

---

I wouldn't have come to school today either if I were you. We are all so happy. We didn't have to look at you wobbling around all day.

-Holly

I start to cry. I can't take this anymore. I run to my medicine cabinet and put a handful of Benadryl in my mouth and swallow. Before I can spit them up, I know that I shouldn't have done that. I know that overdosing isn't going to make Holly like me anymore. But it's too late now. I can't hold myself up any longer. I fall to the ground and make a loud noise. My mom runs up the stairs and sees what I've done. She pulls out her phone and all I hear is "I need an ambulance." I lay there lifeless. I don't know why I did it. It's too late to go back.

I wake up and I don't know where I am. It's a plain room with not much in it except a few machines. I look to the left and I see a heart monitor. I have a flash back the night before when I tried to end my life.

Ever since then I have been in a rehab center. When I think about it I don't feel like that was enough to make me that depressed, but sometimes you have nothing else to do. Every minute I can't believe that I judged Holly to be such a good friend and ended up completely wrong. I've gotten a few apology letters from my old friends and a visit from Holly. I know that nothing will go back to the way it used to be. It's too late for that.

Figure 6.12 First Ending—A Bit Dramatic

lieved that Laura was using this melodrama to wrap up an ending that she wasn't quite satisfied with. Like many middle school students who lack life experience and practice with writing short stories, Laura settled on an easy solution. During our conference, I asked her, "What do you think of the ending?" Silence. In my head, I counted to 150. I wanted Laura to think this through.

Then she said, "I guess it's a bit much."

I nodded and offered her questions to help her revise the ending. "What else could Dani do that would follow from her experiences? Can you step into Dani's feelings when she reads Holly's hateful note? What other way can you show that Dani is miserable, wretched, and isolated?"

"It's hard," Laura blurted.

"I know. Take as much think time as you need. You can try possibilities on one or more classmates and consider their feedback."

It took Laura three revisions of the ending until she found one that satisfied her (Figure 6.13). Laura's final revision contained a remarkable insight—Dani is in control of her life and decisions. The pressure exerted by Holly and her gang no longer irritated Dani.

"I didn't think I'd get there," Laura said, as she handed me her last rewrite. "The questions all helped me try to be and feel like Dani. But it took time."

Questions for Content and Style

Laura's words, "But it took time," remind us that good writing is hard work that takes time. Time equals revision. Revision equals posing questions. I want to reconnect students with their questioning selves and exploit their sense of wonder to benefit their writing. With this in mind, I've included ques-

tions (Content and Style Questions that Support Revising) on the DVD that you can ask students to provoke thinking about revision.

> "... there is no greater object than building effective writing programs that will equip young people to succeed in school, to contribute to a vibrant global economy, and to participate in an increasingly pluralistic civic life—all facilitated by the power of the written word."
> *David Coker and William E. Lewis, "Beyond Writing Next"*

Questions for Writing Conventions

Let's face it, proofreading our own work to identify errors is tough. As mentioned, students can read their work out loud to pinpoint errors, and they can read each other's

work to find spelling and usage errors. In addition, teach them to use the Questions that Help Students Edit for Writing Conventions (on the DVD) and present the editing demonstration lessons on pages 187–92.

I start to cry. I can't take this anymore. I run to my medicine cabinet pull out a bottle of Benadryl. I put if up to my mouth, then stop and think. What would this do for me? How far would it get me to try and kill myself? This wouldn't make people like me anymore. This wouldn't make Holly forgive me. It would just end up ruining my life. I would either end up dead or end up in a rehab center. My parents would be devastated and probably blame this all on themselves.

I feel like it's the first time in my life where I actually think about someone else. In my past I have worried too much about fitting in and what people would think of me. This time I am going to worry about how my decisions will affect other people. I'll think about my parents and my friends.

I empty the rest of the pills in the bottle and place them into my hand. My hands are almost over flowing with pills. I walk to bathroom and open the toilet. With know hard decision I throw them in the water. It takes a bit of time but I finally flush the toilet. I take the bottle and burry it in the mess under my bead. My worst nightmare is gone. There is no temptation.

As I get ready for school the next morning I think back to the decisions I made last night. I have never been so proud of the person I was. I cared about the people I loved and that was all that mattered.

Maybe being the bigger person in this fight would help me and Holly. I would hope to teach her a lesson. I hope that she will learn the same thing I learned. For now I have no friends, but I do have a few people that love me. I do have a house, two legs, two arms, and enough things that will get me through the rest of high school. Until then I will be stuck with the same reputation, but as soon as I am off to college that reputation will be gone, along with all the drama.

Figure 6.13 A satisfying ending to Laura's story.

Four Editing Lessons that Benefit Middle School Writers

I find that middle school writers have difficulty marking paragraphs in their stories and essays, finding and repairing run-on sentences and fragments, and varying sentence openings. Introduce the following lessons to the whole class, since review benefits everyone. For each lesson, ask students to use their own stories or essays. Repeat lessons for groups or individuals who show you they need reteaching. These lessons, which teachers and professional writers have used and continue to use, can help students develop their editing skills.

For each of the four editing lessons, have students use their own stories or essays.

Editing Lesson 1: Paragraphing Your Essay or Story

While drafting, most student writers focus on content and don't paragraph. This lesson helps develop students' awareness that paragraphing shapes meaning for readers.

First Day: Write Guidelines for Students

Write these paragraphing tips on large chart or construction paper. Make them available for students as they search for paragraphs.

- Use the editing symbol to mark places where new paragraphs start (¶).
- Separate the lead or introduction into its own paragraph.
- Begin a new paragraph when you:
  - Switch to another idea or topic.
  - Make a new point.
  - Change the setting.
  - Change time.
  - Switch speakers while writing dialogue.
  - Change the plot.
- Separate the ending or closing into its own paragraph.

Second Day: Provide a Demonstration Lesson

- Use an uncorrected student paper (remove name) by someone who is no longer in your class.
- Think aloud and model how you use the paragraph symbol to show when a new paragraph starts.
- Repeat the lesson for the entire class or small groups until they can help you mark the paragraphs.

Another Day: Ask Students to Edit Their Writing for Paragraphs

- Ask students to use a piece of their writing to mark paragraphs.
- Have pairs read each other's work and confirm the paragraphing and/or make suggestions for other places that require paragraphing.
- Confer with individuals who need your support to complete this editing task.

Editing Lesson 2: Repairing Two Types of Run-on Sentences

When middle school students fill their early drafts with run-on sentences, know that they are trying to use compound and complex sentences. Celebrate. Your students are ready to receive instruction. However, be mindful of expecting students to apply these lessons quickly. It won't happen. Repeat them. Middle school writers benefit from continued rewriting of their run-ons.

Present a Common Run-on and Ways to Repair It

- Write this sample run-on sentence on chart or construction paper. This type of run-on is prevalent among students in grades 5 to 8.

  Richie climbed the mountain he ate lunch sitting on the grassy peak.
- Explain that even though the ideas are related, this is a run-on because each idea has its own subject and verb.
- Write the four ways to repair this kind of run-on on chart paper so students can use it as a resource when they rewrite.

On Another Day

1. Write two complete sentences.
   Example: Richie climbed the mountain. He ate lunch sitting on the grassy peak.
2. Add a conjunction or connecting word and remove the subject in the second sentence.
   Example: Richie climbed the mountain and ate lunch on the grassy peak.
3. Add a conjunction or connecting word and a comma. Keep the subject of the second sentence.
   Example: Richie climbed the mountain, and he ate lunch on the grassy peak.
4. Use a semicolon to replace the conjunction or connecting word.
   Example: Richie climbed the mountain; he ate lunch on the grassy peak.

On Another Day: Ask Students to Repair Their Run-on Sentences

- Have students place brackets at the start and end of this type of run-on. Bracket off run-ons for students who can't locate these.
- Ask students to choose one of the four ways to rewrite each run-on sentence.
- Have students compose their rewrites on sticky notes or number the run-ons and their rewrites.

On Another Day: Present a Lesson on Runaway Run-on Sentences

- Write this runaway run-on on chart or construction paper.

  We walked into the forest at dusk and continued on the path until we came to a huge log that blocked our path and then we decided we should turn back but then it was too dark to see and then it was lucky that Jim had a flashlight and then we walked back to the camp.

- Point out that there are two ways to find this type of run-on:
  - Check to see if the sentence goes on for three-plus lines.
  - Read it aloud. Listen for and circle these words: *and, and then, and but.* These are connectors young writers use in place of punctuation.
- Circle the connector words.
- Tell students that this kind of run-on has two or more sentences written as one sentence.
- Explain that when rewriting, we have to decide if all the ideas are related. If unrelated, delete them. We also have to separate ideas for clarity.
- Make sure students understand that they will need to combine, reorder, and even add ideas to make these sentences work. Some students simply remove connector words and plunk in periods; this strategy doesn't work.
- Pair students up and have partners rewrite.
- Model and think aloud to build or enlarge students' mental model of the process.
- Invite partners to try a rewrite of the same run-on or a different one.

Here's a rewrite that I modeled and one that eighth-grade partners offered. Point out to students that there are several ways to rewrite this run-on. I like to model and then have partners show what they did. This helps students understand that there's not one correct revision.

> **Robb's Rewrite:**
>
> *At dusk, we hiked into the forest and continued until we came upon a log across the path. At this point we agreed that it was time to turn back. However, the last rays of the sun were setting, and soon it would be too dark to see. Luckily, Jim had packed a flashlight that we used to guide us back to camp.*
>
> **Eighth Grader's Rewrite:**
>
> *We hiked deep into the forest just as the sun was setting and continued to walk until we bumped into a huge log that blocked the path. Because it was getting dark, good sense helped us decide to turn back. Jim saved the day with his flashlight which helped us safely return to camp.*

Continue thinking aloud and inviting partners to rewrite sample run-on sentences until students can revise these independently.

On Another Day: Ask Students to Repair Their Runaway Run-ons

- Have students bracket off sentences that are three-plus lines and test these for run-ons.
- Ask students to rewrite these. Emphasize that they might have to rearrange the words or add or delete words.
- Confer with students who need to work with you to rewrite this type of run-on.

Editing Lesson 3: Repair Those Sentence Fragments

When writers include a fragment to create an effect, they are conscious of what they are doing. In *Hatchet*, Gary Paulsen (1987) is the master of fragments; he uses them to highlight important words and thoughts; he uses them to show the pattern of Brian's thinking. Students can use fragments, too, as long as the use is intentional.

Share the following passage with students. Then ask them to discuss why Paulsen used fragments.

> The burning eyes did not come back, but memories did, came flooding in.
>
> The words. Always the words.
>> Divorce.
>> The Secret.
>> Fights.
>> Split. (5–6)

To deepen students' experiences with literary fragments, ask them to bring in other examples from their texts and share these with classmates. Ask three or four students to share each time the class meets. By spreading these sessions out, you offer students opportunities to deepen their insight into this writing technique.

First Day: Write and Explain Three Causes of Sentence Fragments

Write these three types of sentence fragments on chart or construction paper. Post when students need to use this information to edit. Under each item, I've included an alternate way of presenting this for students who don't know these terms.

Cause #1: When a subordinate clause stands alone, it's a fragment.
<u>Alternate</u> #1: A group of words can be a fragment if they stand alone and start with *if, when, since, until, because, as soon as,* etc.

> *If our team wins this game.*

Cause #2: When a participial phrase stands alone, it's a fragment.
Alternate #2: A phrase or group of words that stands alone and is introduced by the present or past form of a verb is a fragment.

|| *Stung by an angry wasp.* ||

Cause #3: Two consecutive prepositional phrases become fragments.
Alternate #3: Two phrases in a row that start with small words such as *with, on, in, by, at, for, after, next to, into* can become fragments.

|| *On the beach by the lake.* ||

Explain that each fragment can be completed by telling what happened next. For older students who know their grammar, you can add that when a sentence opens with a subordinate clause, participial phrase, or two prepositional phrases, it's a fragment until you add an independent clause.

On Another Day: Invite Partners to Rewrite the Fragments
Ask partners to rewrite the fragments. Here are some examples written by fifth, sixth, and eighth graders.

|| If our team wins this game, we play for the district championship.
|| Stung by an angry wasp, the toddler screamed and ran to her mother.
|| On the beach by the lake, we spotted several decomposing trout.

Editing Lesson 4: Vary Those Boring Sentence Openings
Sentences that repeatedly open the same way turn readers off because they are boring. This lesson enables you to provide students with the tools that can help them vary those monotonous, repetitive sentence openings.

First Day: Give Students the Tools
Write this list of words on large chart or construction paper and post it so students can use it as a writing repair resource:

as soon as	suddenly	immediately	when	during
since	if	while	afterward	then
next	near, nearby	now	later	before
after	both	instead	unlike	yet
finally	meanwhile	as	until	around
under	below	over	tomorrow	in front of

Older students might know these as adverbs, prepositions, and subordinating conjunctions. All students should know that these words can revise a series of consecutive sentences that start with the same word.

Second Day: Present Your Demonstration Lesson

- Write an example on the chalkboard such as:

> I heard a noise in the basement. I went down the basement steps. I used my flashlight to look for the cause of the noise. I saw the cat next to a trash can that fell. I saw the cat was scared.

- Think aloud and show students that every sentence begins with *I*.
- Rewrite the example by dipping into the words on the chart.

> As soon as I heard a loud crash in the basement, I grabbed a flashlight and gingerly walked down the stairs. Finally, I spotted the cause. My cat, back arched, tail tucked under its belly, stood next to a trash can that had tumbled over. Nearby, old papers, rusty nails, and a hammer without its handle covered the floor.

- Ask students, "Why was the rewrite an improvement over the original sentences?" Here are comments seventh graders made:

> You combined ideas in short sentences into one sentence.
>
> You used the words from the chart and that helped make it interesting.
>
> You added details about the cat and what was in the trash can.

This third point is important for student revisers to understand, absorb, and practice. Rewriting includes adding specific details and stronger verbs to bring vigor to the revision.

On Another Day: Ask Students to Edit Their Writing to Vary Sentence Openings

In conferences, I use selection questions and criteria to initiate the revision or editing process. After I model, students frequently gain the confidence to revise with a peer, and they succeed at improving their piece.

- Have each student place a check next to sentences that start the same way.
- Remind students to use the words on the chart to help them revise.

Discuss Students'
Writing

Learning from Students' Writing

For professional writers, revision and editing are the best parts of writing because there's time to improve and shape a piece. We want students to feel this way as well.

Let's observe and reflect on teachers' feedback on Hattie's news story, which she based on *So Far from the Bamboo Grove* by Yoko Kawashima Watkins. Teachers reviewed Hattie's plan, first draft, and final draft (Figures 6.14 through 6.16). Hattie self-evaluated her first drat and included revisions in the final draft. At that point, Hattie's teacher had two options: send her back for additional revisions or grade and comment on her work.

Here's the writing criteria that Hattie and her teacher had agreed upon:

> <u>Content and Style:</u> effective headline; lead that grabs reader; article to answer the 5 Ws

> <u>Writing Conventions:</u> paragraphing—keep these short as in newspapers; compete sentences, vary sentence openings

Here's what teachers thought Hattie did well throughout her process:

- Includes strong headlines
- Uses notes for 5 *w*s
- Focuses on the one event
- Uses newspaper style

The group made this revision suggestion:

- Read the piece out loud. Too many sentences and paragraphs begin with "Mrs. Kawashima." Hearing the writing helps identify repetitions.

They noticed these writing convention strengths:

- Separates writing into paragraphs
- Uses complete sentences

Finally, they identified these writing convention editing needs:

- First paragraph could be separated into two paragraphs to maintain journalistic style.
- Revise to eliminate opening three consecutive paragraphs with "Mrs. Kawashima."

News Article

Head line : Grabs attention, short + to the point
        announce topic

By line · Name of Author

Opening ¶
    Boyce, VA - Begin Article
    City, country

Head line - Young Daughters left with
        Nothing

By line - Hattie R. Schiavone

Place - Seoul, Japan

Who -   Where

                    How

What -

                    Why

When -

Figure 6.14 Ease of writing is in the writing plan.

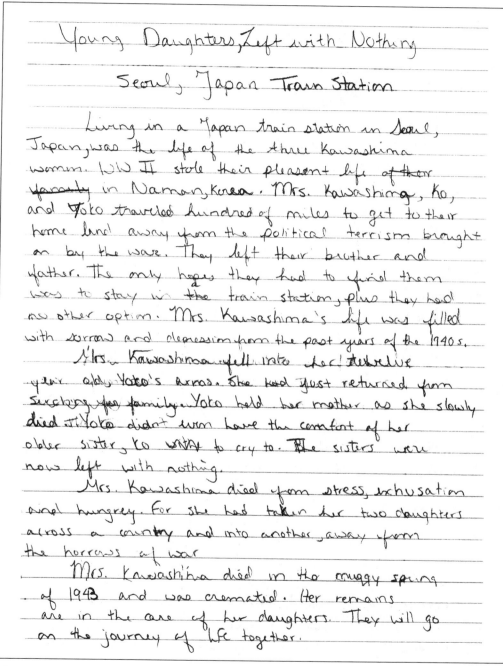

Young Daughters, Left with Nothing

Seoul, Japan Train Station

Living in a Japan train station in Seoul, Japan, was the life of the three Kawashima women. WW II stole their pleasant life of their ~~family~~ in Naman, Korea. Mrs. Kawashima, Ko, and Yoko traveled hundred of miles to get to their home land away from the political terrism brought on by the war. They left their brother and father. The only hopes they had to find them was to stay in the train station, plus they had no other option. Mrs. Kawashima's life was filled with sorrow and depression from the past years of the 1940s.

Mrs. Kawashima fell into her twelve year old Yoko's arms. She had just returned from ~~Searching for family.~~ Yoko held her mother as she slowly died. Yoko didn't even have the comfort of her older sister, Ko ~~what~~ to cry to. The sisters were now left with nothing.

Mrs. Kawashima died from stress, exhusation and hungrey. For she had taken her two daughters across a country and into another, away from the horrors of war

Mrs. Kawashima died in the muggy spring of 1943 and was cremated. Her remains are in the care of her daughters. They will go on the journey of life together.

Figure 6.15 Translating Part of a Book to a News Story

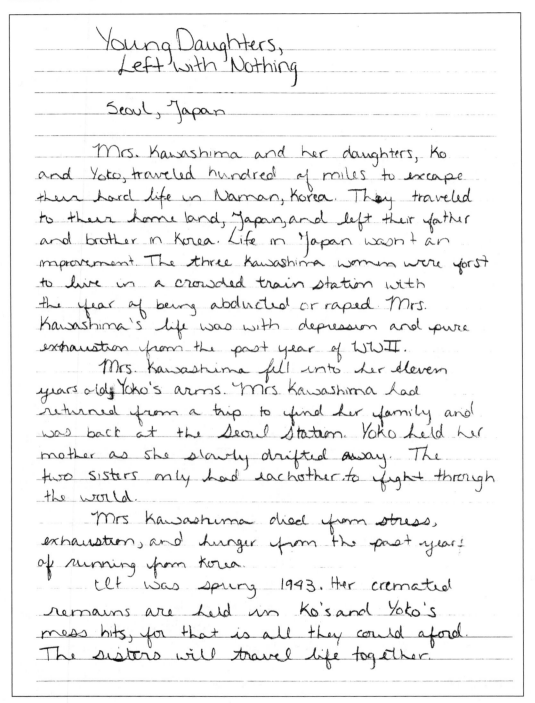

Young Daughters, Left With Nothing

Seoul, Japan

Mrs. Kawashima and her daughters, Ko and Yoko, traveled hundred of miles to excape their hard life in Naman, Korea. They traveled to their home land, Japan, and left their father and brother in Korea. Life in Japan wasn't an improvement. The three Kawashima women were forst to live in a crowded train station with the year of being abducted or raped. Mrs. Kawashima's life was with depression and pure exhaustion from the past year of WWII.

Mrs. Kawashima fell into her eleven years old Yoko's arms. Mrs Kawashima had returned from a trip to find her family and was back at the Seoul Station. Yoko held her mother as she slowly drifted away. The two sisters only had eachother to fight through the world.

Mrs Kawashima died from stress, exhaustion, and hunger from the past years of running from Korea.

It was spring 1943. Her cremated remains are held in Ko's and Yoko's mess hits, for that is all they could aford. The sisters will travel life together.

Figure 6.16 Final Draft of Hattie's News Story

Note that when pointing out needs, teachers did not waver from the criteria. If there are additional writing convention needs, Hattie's teacher could attend to them during a conference or with a group who displays the same need.

Professional Study Invitation

Ask two teachers from different grades to each bring a student's first and final drafts of a piece of writing, along with the criteria for each. Make enough copies for everyone attending. Ask teachers to read each student's work, compare it to the criteria, list what each student did well, and then create a list of revision and editing needs. The purpose here is twofold. First, for teachers to experience what they ask students to do in order to understand the class time needed to accomplish this. Second, to go through a process that you will use while reading papers that requires your feedback. Moreover, doing this will sharpen your ability to revise and edit.

- Choose the revision and editing questions from the DVD that the group believes will support each student's rewrites.
- Add these questions to the generic self- and peer revision sheet.
- Decide whether the student can revise and edit independently or if he or she requires your assistance.
- Bring the results back to your next meeting and discuss.

CHAPTER 7

Conferring

Answering Middle Schoolers'
Need to Collaborate

When I invite groups of teachers to share their experiences with conferences, silence either overtakes the room, or I hear a chorus of comments like "I can't confer in a forty-two-minute period" or "I've tried conferences, but they don't work for me." I understand their plight, so I've arranged this chapter to show you routines and resources that will make conferring manageable. Here is a highlight of what you'll find:

Types of Conferences
- Making the Rounds Conferences (pages 202–13)
- Scheduled Conferences (pages 213–16)
- Pair Conferences (pages 216–18)

Forms and Routines that Make Life Easier

See "Tips for Conferring with Writers" under Teaching Take-Aways in the DVD and watch the conferences in action.

Conference Topics I Will Model

- Planning
- Adding details
- Clarifying genre structure
- Improving use of conventions
- Deepening student's ability to evaluate their writing

The Benefits of Teacher and Student Conferring

There's a powerful reason for us to find ways to confer with students: conferring is the most efficient way to teach and support student writers (Anderson 2000; Cramer 2004; Rief 2007; Routman 1999). This one-on-one work moves a student's writing forward beautifully because it's custom tailored to who the student is as a learner and as a person. I can smooth the student's way through a writing stage that's become an obstacle; listening to the student's take on the writing enables me to know and understand the writer's needs, strengths, and interests. We can laugh together while discussing a piece and exchange stories the piece brings to mind. We develop a connection that helps me see what aspects of craft, technique, and writing conventions I need to teach the individual student and, in turn, the class.

You See Your Teaching Reflected Back

As an assessment window, a conference is unparalleled. While I assess a student, I use the exchange to hold a mirror up to the effectiveness of my teaching. If the student doesn't yet fully understand something, then this might be because I haven't yet taught it well enough. Should I nudge the writer to rethink that section? Will the student embrace this advice or find it deflating? Do I quickly model rewriting now or do a lesson tomorrow on it, so the writer has an example? This student is so good at dialogue; whom might I pair her with so she can share her expertise? As I confer with a student, questions flicker and I make dozens of decisions.

Your Students See Themselves Reflected Back

Conferences build a writing intimacy between teacher and student, a bond that can only develop through a series of nurturing conversations. Teacher conferences and peer conferences help everyone involved become responsive learners. We listen to each other's tone of voice, and we watch facial expressions and body language. Middle school students thrive on this special attention both because it's collaborative and because it helps them get closer to the answer of "Who am I?" In the moment of conferring, students know they matter to you, and they sense your respect and admiration; you are helping them define who they are in the world of school and beyond.

You Exercise Empathy

Conferring is the art of careful listening and thoughtful response. After forty-five years of teaching, it's something I'm still improving. To be good at conferring, we must be comfortable living on the edge in our moments with students, because we never know how a student will respond to what we say. We have to be comfortable in our own skin, and comfortable with the silences of the student thinking beside us. When a student says, "I don't want to confer about my writing," we need the flexibility to move on and return another day, and the empathy to relate to where that learner is at a given moment (Anderson 2000; Pink 2005).

Figure 7.1 An on-the-spot conference clarifies students' questions.

The Benefits of Adding Student-to-Student Conferring to the Mix

Now, step into my eighth-grade classroom and observe the varied kinds of conferences taking place during writing workshop. As students move through different parts of the writing process, they confer with classmates. Writing and thinking mingled with informal chats occurs daily:

> "... nothing can replace the influence of teachers as they confer with children, reflecting back to them a sense of how writing is proceeding, how to think about writing, how to improve it."
>
> *Ronald L. Cramer (401)*

- Kaleigh and Christa take their writing folders to the oversized pillow at the back of the room. With pencils poised to mark repetitions or add omitted words, they read their drafts aloud to each other.
- Liz and Amylee discuss their writing plans.
- Danny and Ben sit next to each other and trade possible endings to their stories, each hoping to find a satisfying one.
- Mike and David are on the one computer, helping each other decide on images to include in their articles.
- Mary concentrates on drafting her narrative. She stops, walks to Erin's desk, and says, "Listen to this and tell me what you think."

Throughout the room, groups of two and three are drafting. Some write silently during workshop; others chat with a peer about a verb, an image, or dialogue, or they check their writing against established criteria.

While Students Confer, You Gain More Time to Confer

While students work together, I circulate and answer questions in what I call "Making the Rounds" conferences. I also hold scheduled conferences with students. Once workshop routines have been established during the first three weeks of school, this blending of casual student chats, impromptu teacher-student discussions, and formal scheduled conferences occurs during all or part of writing class.

Logistically, teachers will find that including more peer and small-group conferring lightens the load. Whether you have a forty-two- or sixty-minute class period, you can make it work. (See pages 203–4 for a strategy that compels students to reflect on the purposes of their conferring.

Your Workshop Gains Greater Interactivity and Structure

Conferring is an ongoing process that's woven into the fabric of my workshop. It allows me to stay in touch with students and create a writing community where students value positive support. Here's how I weave a variety of conferences into the forty-five-minute period each day:

- **Conferring begins sooner than later.** In my writing workshop, once I've reviewed the day's schedule and presented a demonstration lesson, the remaining time is for students to work on writing while I confer.
- **Three or four scheduled conferences occur each day.** On the chalkboard, I list the names of students whom I will meet with that period—usually three or four in about thirty minutes of workshop time. See page 214 to explore what students who aren't conferring with the teacher can do.
- **"Making the Rounds" conferences occur twice a week** or more. I circulate around the room to note where students are with their writing and if any require my help.
- **Peer conferences occur daily.** Students who are not conferring with me often confer with a peer partner, since peer support is an integral part of my workshop.

Students Get to Collaborate

The fluidity of class experiences like these quench middle school students' thirst to literally bounce about the classroom and figuratively bounce ideas off of peers. Earlier in my career I feared noisy chaos if students moved about the room and collaborated too much. I've discovered that giving them this freedom helps them become responsible, productive writers who rarely abuse the opportunity.

Make Teacher-Student Conferences Count: Guidelines for Success

The primary purpose of conferring is to help students explore solutions to writing problems, because when the students do the thinking, they begin to develop the skills to confer with themselves, edit and revise their own work, and gain independence. Whether the conference is impromptu or has been scheduled in advance, the suggestions on pages 203–4 will ensure a nurturing, constructive exchange.

"Making the Rounds" Conferring

Purpose: quick coaching and cheerleading
Frequency: three times a week, and as time allows
What the rest of the class is doing: writing, peer conferring
Craving affirmation and validation is common to writers, musicians, athletes, dancers, painters—well, just about anyone who invests in producing something. As Laura, an

Guidelines for Teacher-Student Conferences

Keep it short. No more than five minutes, six at the most. This enables you to meet with ten to twelve students a week. The student should talk the majority of the time.

Question to pose: Is there anything else you wanted to get feedback on?

Choose a single topic. Zoom in on one element: the lead, the ending, significant details, paragraphing, voice, and so on. Students won't get overwhelmed, and they can often intuitively apply insights on one particular matter to another issue in their piece. If you or your student haven't chosen an area of focus, observe the writing and decide whether to move on or ask a question.

Question to pose: Looks like you're really into this piece. Anything you need to chat about now?

Be positive. Start by pointing out what the student did well. Use the established writing criteria to help you address specific content, style, and writing convention areas if you're conferring about a draft.

Question to pose: Can you see how strengthening the four verbs helped readers? Now, can you find a place where dialogue would be more effective than telling?

Count to 120. When you pose a question, count to 120. The tendency is for teachers to fill the silence with talk and solutions. This doesn't support students. Though your wait time might feel like an eternity, students need time to think before responding.

Question to pose: Do you need more think time?

Be a *really* good listener. Avoid interrupting a student—at all costs. Listen carefully and jot down questions you have; ask these once the student has finished talking. Throughout, use your sense of this student to make further comments and ask questions that boost confidence and entice the student to speak more fully.

Affirming comment to make: I noticed how well you explained your reasons for changing the ending.

Question to pose: Can you reread to make sure the ending grows out of the plot?

Pose questions that prompt students to recall prior lessons. Review a demonstration lesson through discussion and/or by revisiting a chart with the lesson. This can help students explore solutions to a snag in their piece or process. Moreover, when you point students to a specific lesson, you shift the focus away from their own piece, which sometimes frees them up to pluck the solution from the lesson.

Question to pose: Do you recall the excellent job you and Eddie did with changing a telling sentence to a showing one? Can you find two places in your story where you tell and it would be more effective to show? Now, rewrite those parts on separate paper and show me when you're done.

Pose questions that target the writing process. Similarly, asking questions about

any part of the writing process can lead students to discover a solution. (Use the classroom resources on the DVD) If you listen carefully as students talk about their writing, you will be able to pose questions that directly relate to their needs.

Question to pose: How did you know you were finished with your piece? or Can you try to make the lead raise some questions? or Can you reread your story and find a place where dialogue would work well? or Can you reread your arguments that support your position and reorder them more effectively?

Model by writing. Use this technique only when all of the others haven't helped the writer see a solution. On a sticky note or a separate piece of paper, show the student how you rewrite, how you circle strong verbs and find alternates, or how you read the piece and figure out where to mark paragraphs using the paragraph symbol. When students sit by your side, hear your thinking, and watch as you write, they are often able to understand the revision.

Questions and Prompts for Positive Conferring

Questions and comments are kind; they are gentle and offer choices. Use the ones I share here to generate your own versions. Keep these in a notebook and bring them to conferences in case you need to refresh your memory.

Prewriting

- I noticed that you are enthusiastic about your topic.
- I'm pleased that you used questions to add more ideas to your brainstorming.
- How does this help?
- I noticed that you have been thinking about your writing. Can you tell me about it?
- You have so many terrific ideas on this list. Do you need to talk to someone to figure out which idea you want to develop?
- It seems that there are many ideas for stories here. Do you have a favorite?
- Would you like to chat about these to find the one you want to pursue?

- Can you work with a partner and ask that person to generate questions about your brainstorming?
- Does your plan provide the map you need to draft?
- Can you tell me why you included four possible outcomes in your plan?
- Does your plan have enough details to develop the support for each paragraph?
- Can you skim the text to find specific details for your plan?

Narrative

- Can you define the setting with more details?
- Can you show how the dog/character/person felt at that moment?
- Does the ending grow out of the events in your story?
- Can you think of two or three possible endings to this story?
- How do you feel about the problem?
- How does your main character change? What causes these changes?
- Can you add dialogue? Where might dialogue be effective?
- What do you want the dialogue to do in this story?
- Can you help me understand the differences between both characters?
- Do you feel that your ending is believable?

Poetry

- Why did you choose to write a poem?
- Does your poem have shape?
- Can you tighten the lines and images by eliminating words?
- Can you read your poem out loud and listen for the sound and rhythm of your words?
- Can you find a simile that's more unique? That startles and speaks to readers?
- What mood are you trying to create?
- Are your details and images doing the job?
- Are you including too many (or too few) details to tell this story?

Essays and Articles

- Should those details go in a sidebar?
- Can you find more details to support your position?
- Do you feel that you need to elaborate and develop the details?

- What ideas do you want readers to come away with?
- Does your conclusion leave readers with more to think about?
- Do you have an anecdote that supports your point?
- Does your introduction set readers up for your essay?

Revision/Editing

- Can you circle the general nouns in this paragraph and make them specific?
- Can you circle the repeated verbs in these paragraphs and find strong ones?
- Your lead includes excellent details. Try writing an alternate that either sets a mood or uses a short anecdote.
- I noticed you bracketed two run-ons; great spotting. Would like me to help you rewrite one and you do the other?
- Reread and use the paragraph symbol to mark paragraphs.
- Can you read your piece out loud and listen for missing words? For repeated words?
- Can you circle the openings of sentences in each paragraph? How can you vary these?
- Can you check to see that the lengths of your sentences are varied?

eighth grader, explained during a conference: "You put yourself out there with your writing. It's scary. My first reaction is I don't want anyone to read my stuff. But then I wonder if anyone will like it. I'm writing for myself and for others. But getting that feedback—I always think they [classmates] will hate it." Laura's anxiety and ambivalence is characteristic of many middle school writers.

"Making the rounds"—circulating among students, responding to a raised hand—means that daily, your students receive positive strokes while writing. To continue to build middle school writers' self-confidence as you make the rounds, it's crucial to maintain a positive tone, even if it's just a gentle pat on the back or a few words of general praise: "I've noticed that you've been concentrating on your writing." When I observe students and then tell them what I've noticed, I am able to offer honest, confidence-building comments—even if it's something like "I noticed that you're trying to enlarge your list of ideas" or "I noticed how you are trying to complete your draft." This reminds students that we care about their work.

"Making the Rounds" in Fifth Grade

Cheri Kesler tells her fifth graders that she and I will be walking around the room, offering help. Right now, the fifth graders are drafting an informational paragraph with two or three nonfiction features. Morgan raises her hand and asks me to read her draft (Figure 7.2). I bend down next to Morgan and tell her how pleased I am that her draft includes two sidebars and illustrations. She smiles. Next I ask Morgan to read her paragraph out loud, listening to the beginning and the ending. Here's how the conference proceeds:

> Morgan: *I'm not so sure about the ending.*
>
> Robb: *Can you tell me why? [I count to 120.]*
>
> Morgan: *Well, if someone reads it, they're interested.*
>
> Robb: *Can you think of another way to end this?*
>
> Morgan: *Hmmm. [No response. I count to 120 again.]*
>
> Robb: *What would you like to do now that you know about these planets?*
>
> Morgan: *[Thinking] I know. [She places the number 1 in the text and on her blank paper; see Figure 7.3.]*
>
> Robb: *I'm so pleased that you remembered this revision strategy! Now, read what you wrote out loud.*
>
> Morgan: *[Reads] I hear it. "Get."*
>
> Robb: *Great, Morgan! Can you find alternate verbs? [Morgan brainstorms* ride *and* board *for the first* get *and eliminates the second* get.]
>
> Morgan: *I'll read it once more. [She reads.] That sounds better.*
>
> Robb: *Can you tell me what you mean by* things?
>
> Morgan: *[Crosses out* things *and writes* planets.] *There. That's better.*
>
> Robb: *I noticed how well you solved each writing problem as soon as you saw it.*
>
> Morgan: *Reading out loud helped me.*
>
> Robb: *You're right! Keep it up*

Robb's Comments

Reading out loud enables Morgan to pinpoint some needs and then rewrite without me jumping in to do the thinking for her. Counting to 120 helps me avoid thinking for

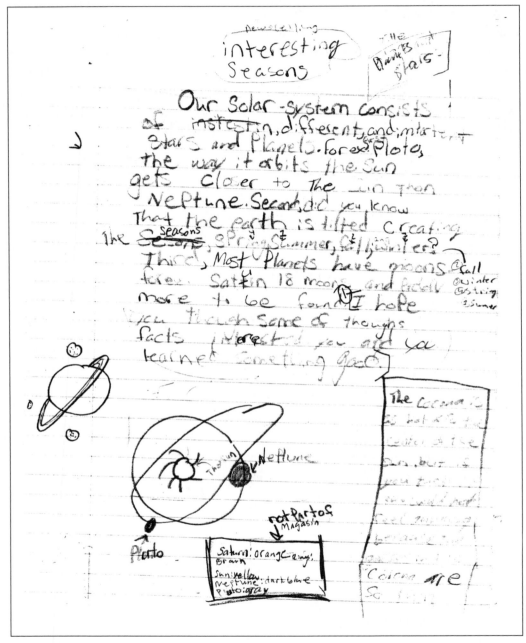

Figure 7.2 "Adding nonfiction features makes the writing more interesting," says Morgan.

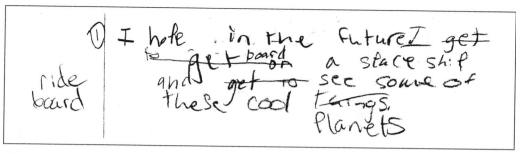

Figure 7.3 Revised ending has more pizzazz.

Morgan, which is important so she will learn to use these strategies independently. The tone is positive, and Morgan remains in charge.

"Making the Rounds" in Eighth Grade

I circulate among the eighth graders. As soon as Ben finished *Max's Logbook* by Marissa Moss, he planned his own version. Ben's cover showcases his love of fantasy and U.S. army equipment (see Figure 7.4). Today, Ben is labeling the army tank he designed as part of his logbook. I pause and ask, "How's it going?

> Ben: *I'm almost done with the labels. Next, I'm doing a page of jokes.*
>
> Robb: *I can't wait to read your entire logbook, Ben.*

Ben doesn't stop writing; he doesn't need me today. I move on to Danny, who's adding details to his plan for an analytical essay. I pull up a chair and sit next to Danny.

> Robb: *What did your peer editor suggest?*
>
> Danny: *The big thing was to add details to my list of supports. [See Figure 7.5.]*
>
> Robb: *Great idea!*
>
> Danny: *[Takes his short story book out of his desk.] I'll skim to make sure I have lots of details.*
>
> Robb: *That will help you when you draft. I like the feedback your partner gave you on your conclusion notes. You've thought about going beyond repeating the thesis, and you have strong points that will keep readers thinking. I know you'll find the details you need. When you've done that, start your draft.*

Danny nods, and I continue making the rounds.

Figure 7.4 Ben's cover shouts "This is me!"

PLANNING AN ANALYTICAL ESSAY

Name_____ Date_____

Lead Paragraph: Thesis statement. Note what ideas you will include in your transition
sentence.

Seth discovers to be cool you can still be yourself

Details to Include in the Body: *Trying to be*

Opening general statement: "being cool can get you in gigantic trouble *you did a fine job adding details*

List 3 pieces of support here: *the smoking* *bragging about making out*

Seth thought it was wrong and to be cool

Seth felt uncomfortable around Adam and lying to his parents

Adam flinging the cigarette butt on the car *cigarette landed on car and the people bent Seth up and tried to get him to lick the cigarette off*

Adam blaming Seth because Adam was chicken

Show how you will connect ideas to your thesis: *do this on draft*

Conclusion: Note ideas you will include. What did you add that will enable the reader to
think further about this issue?

- thesis statement ⟶ *don't need. repeat main point in a different way.*
- repeat general statement
- desire to be cool lead to beating ✓
- catchy last sentence — seth couldn't pick his friends, can you! ✓

Figure 7.5 Revising a plan improves the essay.

Robb's Comments

In my eighth-grade class, not only are students at different points in the writing process,
but also they work on varied projects. In this instance, all students had to complete an
analytical essay. Ben and several others completed this required task a week before the
deadline date, then turned to their independent writing projects. Notice, too, the helpful

---

The Good, The Bad, and the Beating

Seth discovers something important; he discovers to
be cool you can still be yourself. In the story, "On the Bridge",
Seth learns he should probably listen to his gut instinct.

Trying to be cool can get you into gigantic trouble.
Seth felt uncomfortable around Adam and lying to his
parents. For example, Adam smoked and always bragged
about making out with girls. Adam flinging the cigarette
butt on the car was not cool. Smoking also was pretty
uncool. Back to the cigarette flinging, Seth felt that this
act was hurtful and wrong. Instead of saying this, Seth
stayed quiet because he wanted to be cool. In result, the
people in the car drove up to them. Adam was nervous and
scared. This led to him (Adam) blaming Seth. Seth was
definitely keeping his pride, and he didn't lick the cigarette
butt off the car. Seth, definitely learning the hard way,
found that it's much cooler to be yourself than someone
else.

Seth's desire to be cool led to his downfall (beating).
Peer preasure and yearning led him to think that Adam was
his friend. At the end, he finally proved to himself he
was cool just the way he was.

Figure 7.6 Analytical thinking deepens understanding.

peer feedback that Danny received. With a thought-out and detailed plan, Danny could focus on the writing of his essay because he had support (Figure 7.6).

I always book talk and display texts such as *Max's Logbook*, hoping that a student will read it, bond to the book, and use it as a springboard for original writing. Eighth grader Laura Renzi shows me how the dialogue in her short story, "Pressure," mirrors *Speak* by Laurie Halse Anderson. "I took it right from *Speak*," Laura tells me (see Figure 7.7). "It's cool." I liked the way she [Anderson] makes the dialogue look like a drama script."

Me: Hey mom. Everything is great. I actually like it here.

Mom: Well I am glad because you went into this move with such a negative attitude.

Me: Yeah I know hah. I didn't give it much of chance at first though. But anyways I was invited to a party tonight. Do you think I could go?

Mom: Oh that's why you're being like this today haha. Well give me the details. Where is it and whose party?

Me: My friend Lilly is having a party and it's at her house. Her parents will be home.

That one little lie changed my life forever. My mom believing me changed who I would be. That single conversation would affect me for the rest of my life.

Figure 7.7 Inspired by *Speak*

Scheduled Conferences

Purpose: One-on-one scaffolding for the student at any stage of the writing process

Frequency: Three or four students a week

What the rest of the class is doing: writing, peer conferring

I treasure one-on-one time with students. But my main goal, of course, is to help students dialogue with themselves about their work. Isn't that the point? Independence. Teachers can structure conferences to place a great deal of responsibility on students, which leads to great peer coaching and independence. Of course, gaining independence is a slow process and takes time. Be patient.

> **Many Similar Errors**
> If I notice several papers that need support with leads, transitions, or repairing run-ons, I gather those students into a group for a reteaching conference.

Preparing

How I ask middle school students to prepare for a conference differs by writing skill and grade. In grades 5 and 6, and with older writers who struggle, I usually give the conference a focus based on what I observed while making the rounds or after reading a writing plan or draft. I often invite writers in grades 7 and 8 to note questions they would like to discuss and turn these in prior to the conference. To assist students with posing questions, I write these queries on chart paper:

- What do you like best about your writing?
- What's working well for you?
- Is anything giving you trouble?
- Is there any aspect of the criteria that you're having difficulty meeting?
- How can I help you?

Opening

Because I always tell students what I liked about their piece, I want them to open in the same way. It's interesting to see what they liked and compare it to what I enjoyed. More-over, this ensures that we start with a positive tone.

Note Taking

I document all scheduled conferences on the Writing Conference form.

I prefer to keep the forms in file folders stored in a cabinet: one folder for each sec-tion. I tell students that I'm jotting down things as we chat so that we can have accurate notes for reference. We sit side by side and I let students read my notes as I jot them, so they understand that my notes are in no way critical or secretive. Before each new conference, I can review the notes on previous forms. My goal is to point out progress, improvement, and the students' growing ability to resolve their writing problems.

Keeping Other Students Engaged

There are several learning experiences that students engage in while I confer with their classmates. Students need to be able to work independently, so before these writing ex-periences become work-on-your-own, I make sure we have practiced them together.

- Work independently on writing.
- Confer with a peer partner on writing.
- Collaborate in a small group on writing, such as Readers Theater.
- Review a mentor text independently or with a peer partner.
- Peer revise or edit using criteria.
- Self-evaluate progress in writing.
- Read a book or magazine.

- Read and research a project on the computer.
- Post a book review on a class wiki (for more about wikis, see the DVD).
- Respond to a question on the class blog.
- Create a text for a podcast.

Student's Name_____ Date_____

Writing Conference

Conference Focus:

Positive Comments: Student

Positive Comments: Teacher

Student's feedback and questions:

Teacher's suggestions:

Agreed upon goals:

Check one of the statements:

____Needs more support   ____Can work independently

Set times for follow-up conferences:

Quick Consults

All students must work quietly so as not to disturb others. Students who discover that they require my assistance can place their names on the chalkboard under the title "Needs Help." After each conference, I check to see if there are any names listed. If so, I help those students before going on to the next conference. I may help the student myself or find a peer to give support. If the writer will need my help for more than a few minutes, I ask the student to work on something else until I am available later that period or the next day. My students know that if they are stuck on one project, they can always work on something else or read until I can address their issues.

Scheduled and impromptu conferences can cover any aspect of the writing process. My guiding rule is that whatever a student needs help with is worthy of a conference and my support, especially when the student requests help. Figure 7.8 shows a completed conference form for sixth grader Annie. The conference reviewed the brainstorming and planning she did for a short narrative about an eleven-year-old girl who has to live with an annoying younger brother.

My purpose was to show Annie her progress with gathering details and creating a plan. I assumed that Annie needed little support for drafting her piece. However, she had another agenda: Annie wanted help on where to start her narrative. I quickly switched gears and asked questions that would help her find a great way to open her story. Always listen to the students and take your cues from them, adjusting your plans to meet students' needs and concerns.

Pair Conferences

Purpose: to use criteria to help each other gather ideas, revise, edit

Frequency: every day

What the rest of the class is engaged in: independent reading and writing, conferring with the teacher

Partner conferences build on adolescents' desire for and need to socialize and focus their talk on improving writing. The research points to the benefits of student-to-student conferences. Dolores Perin (2009) states that peers can improve each other's quality of writing as long as we offer clear guidelines. In addition, Graham and Perin, in *Writing Next* (2007a), call for collaboration where students support one another through each stage of the writing process. Daniel Pink (2005) points out that collaboration can lead to creativity and unique solutions to problems—in this case, writing problems.

Some students ask to partner throughout the year. If the partnership benefits both writers, then let them. Remember, it's okay to separate such partners for a project, but make sure you explain why you've made this decision. The point with partners is to

Student's Name_____**Date**_____

Writing Conference

Conference Focus: Discuss progress with listing specific details for her story and creating a plan of the beginning, middle, end.

Positive Comments: Student

-Talking to Sarah and Cate helped. They asked questions. Then I wrote more. You helped with questions.

Positive Comments: Teacher

- Praise for seeking peer help.
- Praise for recognizing that questions can help a writer find more ideas.

Student's feedback and questions:

Annie felt she had lots of ideas for a story about an annoying younger brother. "I'm stuck on how to begin."

Teacher's suggestions Do you want to show in the lead that you're annoyed? Do you want to lead with dialogue, an anecdote, warning? (I got these ideas on a sticky note + give it to

Agreed upon goals: Annie.)

Annie says, "I'll get back on this tomorrow."

<u>Check one of the statements:</u>

__Needs more support   ✓Can work independently

<u>Set times for follow-up conferences:</u>

- Work with a peer partner to see response to her leads. Meet with Annie tomorrow.

Figure 7.8 Build self-confidence with a conference.

Figure 7.9 In a positive writing environment, students learn the art of giving constructive feedback.

ensure that they can support each other. There are times when I choose partners, especially in grades 5 and 6 and with groups who've not conferred with classmates. As you facilitate informal and formal conferences, and as students gain extensive experience with both, they will develop the independence and expertise to choose a partner and chat about their writing because they understand the benefits of gathering feedback.

In your classroom, post the suggestions that follow for your students, and review these periodically so student-to-student conferences are positive and productive.

Pair Conference Guidelines
- Ask partner to read piece out loud. Be a good listener.
- Say positive things—use the criteria to do this.
- Ask questions to help your partner think.
- Jot down suggestions on a sticky note for your partner to mull over.
- Let your partner do the revising.

Learning from Students' Writing

Invite teachers on your team or in your department to bring a piece of students' writing, such as a plan and first draft, a final draft, a draft with a peer and/or self-conference. Pair up and take turns being the student and the teacher in a conference. While role-playing the student, use the piece of writing from your class. With your partner, decide on a focus for the conference and experience the process.

Next, as a group, discuss what worked and what needs refining and practice. Identify any insights, such as "be a better listener" or "ask the student how he would revise, before jumping in to fill the blanks." As conference leaders, we need to devise ways to motivate students to do the thinking and talking.

Professional Study Invitation

For your next team or department meeting, gather in a classroom that has a computer and SMART Board. Then, one-by-one, play, analyze, and discuss the student-teacher writing conferences on the DVD. Here are some general questions to use that can jump-start meaningful conversations:

- Why was the conference productive or unproductive?
- Why would you schedule a follow-up conference?
- How do students react to conferences? Show a range by citing specific ones.
- Why was the student at ease during the conference?
- What are some things about writing you felt the student understood better?

CHAPTER 8

Writing Conferences in Action

Conferring is an art—the art of careful listening and thoughtful speaking. By observing and listening we can make decisions as we confer—decisions about how much nudging we should do, whether we should reschedule, or whether we should model rewriting so the student has an example to refer to and study.

In this chapter, let's look at some student work and the conferring that occurs. Think about how these kinds of conferences might play out with your students.

Confer to Help Students Add Details: Ian and Michael

On two consecutive days, I notice that eighth grader Ian sits and stares into space. Twice I ask Ian, "Can I help?" Each time he shakes his head and explains that he's thinking. I decide not to push but to see if he can gather more details on his own.

On the day the first drafts are due, students self- and peer edit for content. I circulate. I read Ian's draft about his friend Ben (see Figure 8.1) and decide to schedule a conference with Ian to help him add details. Here's part of our exchange:

Robb: You made me laugh when you wrote about the names and betting, but not paying up. I can sense how much you and Ben love basketball.

Ian: Yeah. I like being funny.

Robb: You have three short pieces. Can you choose two and add details to those?

Ian: I guess. I'll work on Ben and Michael.

Robb: Let me ask questions and see if you can take some notes.

Ian: Can you write? I'll talk. [I nod. The questions I pose come from the draft (see sidebar below). Ian's ideas flow freely, and I write them down for him.]

Robb: You have so many details to add, Ian. It's helpful to find sentences that are general, that don't tell the whole story, then ask questions to get more details.

Ian: [Nods]

Robb: I'd like you to ask questions based on your draft about Michael, then take notes. [I point out how many details Ian has dictated about Ben.] You've shown me you can do this.

Here's an example where the teacher takes over the writing and shows the student his rich ideas as well as the power of posing questions to gather these. Ian's rewrite of Ben and Michael reflects his ability to find the details he needs to help us see the friendship bonds (Figure 8.2). When I read Ian's final draft, I note that our next conference will address paragraphing.

> **Questions I Posed to Ian About Ben**
> - Where do you play basketball?
> - How did you both get on the same team?
> - What's your team's name?
> - How skilled a player are you? Ben?
> - How did you come up with the name White Chocolate?

Confer to Listen and Follow Students' Leads

Michael has volunteered to read his poem, which does not have a title. Just before sharing his poem, Michael finds the title and tags it onto his final draft: "Distant Snow Dropping." He prints it, then reads (Figure 8.3). Sitting in front of the class, wearing a bright red fleece, baggy khaki shorts, sneakers without socks, and a pink boa wrapped around

> BEN- Ben and I play basketball together both and school and in the Frederick county rec league. During basketball practice Ben shouts in a playful manner "Hey Ian I bet you a dollar I can make this shot" I accept his offer and even if he does make it I always fail to give him the money. One day Ben decided to call me his brown bear and I decided to call him my white-chocolate and the names just stuck. Ben and I both enjoy draining three pointers and crossing people up on the basketball floor and we love the feeling when you throw a perfect pass or catch a touchdown playing football just laughing and smiling all the way.
>
> MICHAEL- Michael and I also play on the same basketball team at school. Michael enjoys slaughtering invisible monsters with his Spartan sword and his bow while he runs around his backyard which happens to be a country club golf course. A few months ago Michael and some friends and I ventured to McDonalds and we all decided to eat five cheeseburgers each. When we placed our order the man at the counter said "are you serious? You guys are going to eat all of those cheeseburgers?" We all nearly died of laughter and our stomachs were sore as we

Figure 8.1 Ian's First Draft

his neck, Michael revels in defying convention. No one comments on his attire. That's Michael; he's wearing the outfit of the day. Tomorrow, it might be a collared polo shirt and long pants.

Michael began working on this poem in January, when the class and I started a writing workshop unit on coping with pressure. For a week, Michael thought about the subject, jotted down notes, and abandoned several attempts at writing. As I made the

Ben- I have known Ben since kindergarten and in our younger years we always fought and I would always tease him because he did gymnastics but we were still friends. Now that we are older Ben and I play on the school basketball team and we also play together in a Frederick county rec basketball league. Our rec league team has breezed by in our games using our team speed and flying around the court weaving in and out of defenders looking for the open man to hit the shot. The Powhatan school team has struggled, throwing poor passes and not playing together as a team and not looking to put pressure on the opposing team. Whenever Ben and I are standing around in layup-lines waiting to receive the ball so we can shoot. We always shout "I bet I can make this shot" or "I bet you a dollar you will miss" with laughter in our voices. One day Ben and I were standing around with some of our other friends and all of the sudden Ben told me that he was to call me his "Brown Bear" and that I could think of a nickname for him when a good one came to mind. I decided on the name "White Chocolate" for him because he frequently states that he is black from the waist down and I just thought the name would be fitting. Recently Ben and I were at a friend's house and we saw a commercial where one of the characters name was "Brown bear" and the other characters name was "White Dove". After seeing that commercial we were laughing so intensely that tears started streaming down our faces and I

Figure 8.2 Wow! Revision makes a difference.

rounds, he asked me to read the poem, which at that point did not have a title. I praised his strong images, such as "magical cradle" and "screeching of daily outbreak." Michael told me that there was a golf course behind his house, where he went to find peace, to relax.

Distant Snow Dropping

The falling of the vapors,

Forecloses the restless, screeching of daily outbreak.

The golf course makes an excellent repellant for clamorous noise

The soft ground,

Gives me a cold, but magical cradle,

As i slowly fall.

I lay down, letting the cool, icy touch, brush my face.

I am motionless.

The only movement, my heartbeat.

There is nothing more serene.

As i lay there, I find the harmony I was searching for.

Waiting for a sign, to regain my mobility,

I find the will

And strength,

To once again rise and face the world.

Figure 8.3 Word choice paints images.

"What an important detail," I said. "Can you weave that into the poem? It will give readers a visual sense of the place." Michael nodded, but he turned to revise another poem first.

Eventually, he had two conferences on "Distant Snow Dropping" with his regular classroom teacher. After those, Michael added: "The golf course makes an excellent repellant for clamorous noise" and "Gives me a cold, but magical cradle." The last line to find its way into the poem was "The only movement, my heartbeat."

Michael's process teaches us to be patient and resist the temptation to take over a student's piece. Like professional writers, students benefit from time to think, mull over ideas, and make decisions. Michael also told me, "When I read it to some friends, they wanted know where the heck I was. That did it for me." So often, revision results from a combination of suggestions from the teacher and peers.

Not all middle school writers want to wrestle with details, then revise. That's okay. If we rewrite or insist on a specific revision, that student will struggle to reach independence. In fact, we will encourage dependence on us. Consider the three suggestions that work best for me—suggestions that showcase the diversity of the writing process and lead students to rethink and revise.

- Have students confer with peers about different stages of their writing.
- Design bulletin boards that feature stages of writing so everyone can tap into one another's process. Here are titles I use: *See Our Brainstorming and Writing Plans; Here's Our First Drafts; Revisions Make a Difference.*
- Invite students to read their deadline drafts to classmates.

Confer to Revise Genre Structure: Jessica

When middle school writers wrestle with finding an ending or defining a specific genre, they handle their writing problem in one of two ways:

- They decide to toss their work and start over.
- They require time to muster the desire and energy to revise.

Before I dismissed class, eighth grader Jessica tucks her writing into my book bag. "Can you read it tonight?' she asks. "I need feedback."

Before I can say, "What kind of feedback?" Jessica dashes out the door. That night I read "Everything Happens for a Reason." I love the story, but I am unsure whether the text is all journal entries, or if Jessica is mixing journal writing with straight narrative. My confusion arises from sections in the text that are rich in dialogue.

The next day, Jessica and I confer. To begin, I celebrate that she took the perspective of Jake, a high school senior. "I love that you chose to write from a guy's perspective. You really stepped deep inside Jake. When he vents his thoughts and reactions to his friend, Chad, who dumps problems on Jake, and to his breakup with Heather, Jake's former girlfriend, you hold the reader with problems that teens face. Finding Nicole was perfect; it was realistic the way you had Nicole cheat on Jake with Chad. You used flashback effectively several times, which gave me the background I needed to better understand the conflict between Jake and Chad, Jake and Heather." Then I begin asking questions.

> *Robb: Can you help me understand the genre? [I purposely do not offer my hunches about genre to Jessica; I want this to be her reply.]*
>
> *Jessica: It's Jake's journal.*
>
> *Robb: Is that the purpose of the illustration of the guy kicking a soccer ball? I notice that visual separated parts frequently.*
>
> *Jessica: Uh huh.*
>
> *Robb: The visuals don't tell me the day each entry was written. Why might that be important?*
>
> *Jessica: [Long pause. I count to 200, because it's obvious Jessica is thinking about my question.] I think I get it. Having dates would show if entries were written the same day, or one day after another, or if there was a space.*
>
> *Robb: You got it. What else can the dates show?*
>
> *Jessica: Well, if they're written the same day, Jake might really be upset or excited. If there's a space of a few days, it could show things are going well.*
>
> *Robb: Now, use this terrific insight to return to your piece and carefully consider dating entries.*

Jessica does this, making it clear that the genre is a journal, and the dates help readers tune into Jake's emotional state. There is a break in entries from January 5 to January 12, which opens with "Big news, big news! I haven't written in a while, but things have been going pretty well." In addition, Jessica adds a subtitle: "Jake's Journal," which helps readers prepare for the genre before reading.

Confer to Improve Writing Conventions: Haley and Carter

Haley gives me her story to read at the start of workshop. "I'll read it tonight," I tell her. She nods in agreement, boots up her laptop, and works on a new piece.

My response to Haley's story appears in Figure 8.4. Note that the revisions I want Haley to focus on are written as questions. This is a gentle way to foster thinking and choices. Moreover, such a strategy increases the time you have to support students who require more scaffolding, and frees students like Haley to confer with peers.

The next day, Haley and I have a brief chat about creating a title and starting a new paragraph each time the speaker changes. Since Haley has excellent revision skills, the conference is short: She has my praise and questions on the note I write that's attached to her draft (see Figure 8.4).

Dear Haley,

This is truly an original and unique story! You've captured teen relationships & romance in fantasy. Your use of dialogue to drive plot reminds me of the Fletcher mentor text the class studied. I like the tension in the plot and the way it builds to the ending! Your ending — so tender and sensitive.

You also write well from the young man's perspective.

Here are questions to consider:

1. Can you think of a title?
2. Can you adjust the dialogue & indent when the speaker changes?
3. Can you read it aloud to add some commas?

Figure 8.4 Questions nudge Haley to revise.

Haley: Oh, yeah. I didn't indent. I'll fix that. Easy. [Haley uses arrows to remind herself when to indent as she revises.]

Robb: Have you thought of a title?

Haley: I hate titles. I always have trouble with them. [Her classmate, Addison, who sits near us and overhears my query, suggests, "Stupid Elf."] That'll work. I say that phrase in the story lots. Thanks, Addison.

For some students, finding missing writing conventions such as commas, end-of-line punctuation, and quotations marks feels like an insurmountable task. Using writing convention criteria, I urge you to ask the student to edit for only one convention at a time. If the student requires additional support, then, in the margin, note the missing punctuation. Editing symbols, placed on the line that needs punctuation, narrows the search and helps students correct their work.

You'll find that there will be a wide range of the level of support students require. Some, like Carter, can place the punctuation correctly using editing symbols as a beacon (Figure 8.5). Others will benefit if you sit beside them and think aloud, first modeling how you pinpoint missing commas, then releasing the editing responsibility to the student. Your students will show you the kind of support you should offer.

You may feel frustrated at times because some students will need so much support from you. Keep in mind that repeated practice can gradually move these young writers from frustration to independence (Vygotsky 1978). Knowing, in advance, that the timetable for gaining independence varies can help you avoid correcting students' work and instead continue modeling and gradually turning the process over to them.

Confer to Discuss Self-Evaluation and Grading of Choice Writing

Since choice writing has a prominent place in my writing curriculum, and since it's tough for me to read and respond to all of the students' writing, I've developed a project that students complete at the end of the year. This time is ideal because students now have a deeper understanding of their writing process and a greater knowledge of craft and technique. Here are the guidelines I provide in a handout for each student.

- Look through your writing folder and choose a piece of writing you'd like to bring to a deadline draft.
- Start a new choice project if you don't find one you want to revise and set criteria for it.

The Bullseye Operation

"Excuse me Mrs. Robb" I pause briefly to get her attention "Can I go to the bathroom?"

"Make it quick Joey, were about to learn about the physics of spheres."

I walk to the bathroom trying to remember what homework I didn't do last night so I have time to do it during study hall. I push the door open and go to the stall, and I lock the door. I hear the door open and hear two voices talking.

"Oh my God Rodger is going to kill us!!"

Whenever I hear the name Rodger, I shiver. One time he beat me up when I walked too close to his locker.

"What are we going to do? He said he'll beat us up once a week 'till we get him a new upod!"

"How about we ask our parents for some money?"

"No my mom is already furious from last time I asked her for money, I needed new books for school and I bought videogames."

I quickly realize it's Chris and Scott, they do everything together. I'm about to open the stall door when I hear something.

"We steal one."

I step back from the door intrigued by the idea.

"I know Bullseye has terrible security on upods."

I don't know why I'm still standing here.

Figure 8.5 Editing symbols point the way for Carter.

- Keep all parts of your process: brainstorming, revisions, deadline draft.
- Complete the self-evaluation form. Do this thoughtfully and honestly. Use the back of the form or a piece of notebook paper if you need more writing space.
- Give yourself a grade and defend your grade.
- Turn in your choice writing with the self-evaluation form at the top, and all parts of your process under it.
- Set up a conference time for us to discuss your self-evaluation and grade.

Jeannette, a talented eighth grader, chooses to write a poem. She brainstorms for two poems, but decides to pursue "Summer Night" (Figure 8.6). After conversations with two peers, Jeannette revises parts of her poem (Figure 8.7). She writes "READ ALOUD" in caps, so she can use her ear as part of the revision process. "Both peer partners reminded me do this," Jeannette tells me. "That's why I write it in caps—don't want to forget."

Jeannette's deadline draft and detailed self-evaluation form show me that she is in tune with her process and thinks deeply about it (Figures 8.8 and 8.9). Our conference goes like this:

> Robb: You are totally in tune with your process. I notice that you explained why you chose to focus on cicadas and "other summer ideas." You're right about being able to visualize! I appreciate your honesty about cicadas not coming out at night. It's helpful to check these points out when you brainstorm and draft.
>
> Jeannette: I want to make sure you know why I didn't include punctuation. I wanted the ideas to flow and not be stopped or cut off.
>
> Robb: I agree with your grade, Jeannette. What impresses me is the specific details on your self-evaluation. These tell me what you've learned and absorbed about writing.

Note how short this conference is; it's possible to complete four or five each class. That's because I quickly review the writing stages, then focus on the self-evaluation and grade. Students are honest. Grades they gave themselves ranged from C+, where the student explained that the writing was completed at the last minute and suffered from rushing, to top-notch grades like Jeannette's.

Self-evaluation and grading of choice writing is an indicator of the level of independence a student has reached. It's the kind of writing that the students' next teacher should see because of the process story each piece tells. By eighth grade, I'm hoping most students have developed independence, for they will need to use their understanding of the writing process in high school.

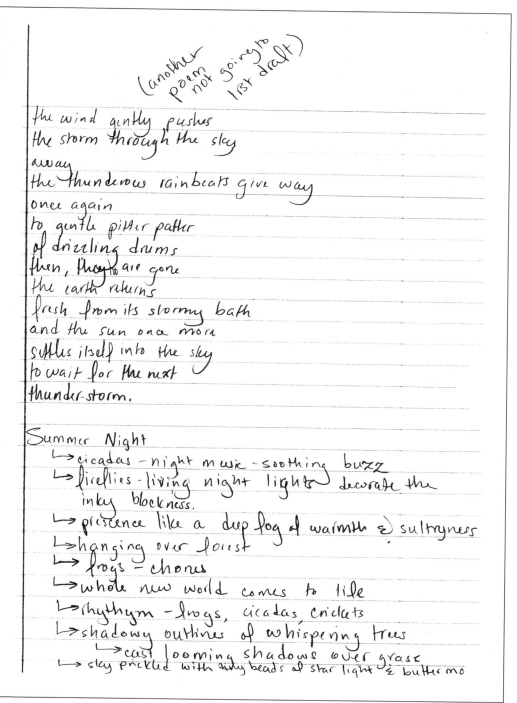

(another poem not going to 1st draft)

the wind gently pushes
the storm through the sky
away
the thunderous rainbeats give way
once again
to gentle pitter patter
of drizzling drums
then, they are gone
the earth returns
fresh from its stormy bath
and the sun once more
settles itself into the sky
to wait for the next
thunder-storm.

Summer Night
→ cicadas – night music – soothing buzz
→ fireflies – living night lights decorate the
   inky blackness.
→ presence like a deep fog of warmth & sultryness
→ hanging over forest
→ frogs – chorus
→ whole new world comes to life
→ rhythym – frogs, cicadas, crickets
→ shadowy outlines of whispering trees
     → cast looming shadows over grass
→ sky prickled with tiny beads of star light & butter mo

Figure 8.6 "Which poem should I pursue?"

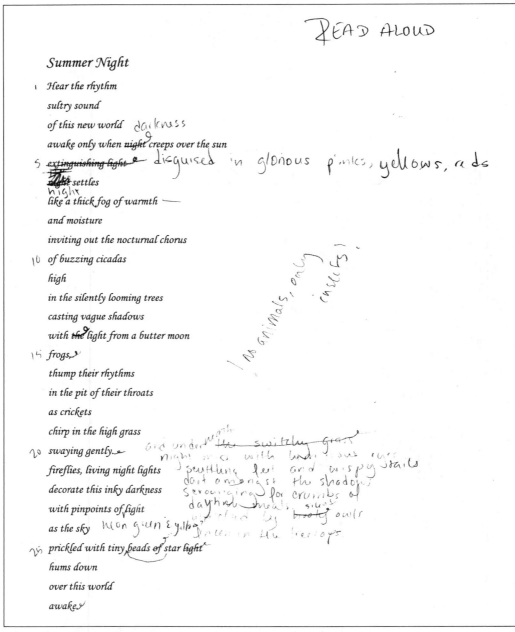

Summer Night

1 *Hear the rhythm*

  sultry sound

  of this new world ~~darkness~~

  awake only when ~~night~~ *creeps over the sun*

5 ~~extinguishing light~~ *disguised in glorious pinks, yellows, reds*

  ~~night~~ *settles*

  night

  like a thick fog of warmth —

  and moisture

  inviting out the nocturnal chorus

10 *of buzzing cicadas*

  high

  in the silently looming trees

  casting vague shadows

  with ~~the~~ *light from a butter moon*

15 *frogs,*

  thump their rhythms

  in the pit of their throats

  as crickets

  chirp in the high grass

20 *swaying gently.*

  fireflies, living night lights

  decorate this inky darkness

  with pinpoints of light

  as the sky

25 *prickled with tiny beads of star light*

  hums down

  over this world

  awake.

(no animals, only insects)

and underneath the ~~switchy~~ *grass*
night is a with ... our eyes
scuttling feet and wispy tails
dart amongst the shadows
scrounging for crumbs of
daytime meals silent
... owls
... in the treetops.

neon green & yellow

Figure 8.7 "READ ALOUD" means listen to revise.

Summer Night

hear the rhythm

sultry sound

of this new world

awake only when darkness creeps over the sun

disguised in glorious pinks, yellows, reds

night settles

like a thick fog of warmth

and moisture

inviting out the nocturnal chorus

of buzzing cicadas

high

in the silently looming trees

casting vague shadows

with light from a butter moon

frogs

thump their rhythms

in the pit of their throats

as crickets

chirp in the high grass

swaying gently

in the underbrush

night mice with luminous eyes

scuttling feet and wispy tails

dart amongst the shadows

scrounging for crumbs of daytime meals

watched by silent owls

frozen in the treetops

fireflies, living night lights

decorate this inky darkness

with pinpoints of neon green and yellow

as the sky

prickled with tiny star beads

hums down

over this world

awake

Figure 8.8 The final draft sings summer night songs.

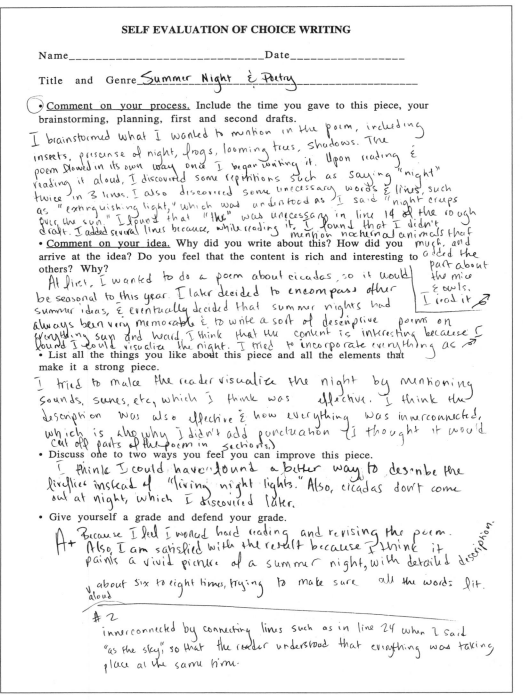

SELF EVALUATION OF CHOICE WRITING

Name_____Date_____

Title and Genre Summer Night & Poetry _____

• Comment on your process. Include the time you gave to this piece, your brainstorming, planning, first and second drafts.

I brainstormed what I wanted to mention in the poem, including insects, presence of night, frogs, looming trees, shadows. The poem slowed in its own way once I began writing it. Upon reading & reading it aloud, I discovered some repetitions such as saying "night" twice in 3 lines. I also discovered some unnecessary words & lines, such as "extinguishing light," which was understood as I said "night creeps over the sun." I found that "the" was unnecessary in line 14 of the rough draft. I added several lines because, while reading it, I found that I didn't mention nocturnal animals that

• Comment on your idea. Why did you write about this? How did you much, and arrive at the idea? Do you feel that the content is rich and interesting to added the others? Why?

At first, I wanted to do a poem about cicadas, so it would be seasonal to this year. I later decided to encompass other summer ideas, & eventually decided that summer nights had always been very memorable & to write a sort of descriptive poems on everything sun and heard I think that the content is interesting because I found I could visualize the night. I tried to incorporate everything as

part about the mice & owls. I rated it

• List all the things you like about this piece and all the elements that make it a strong piece.

I tried to make the reader visualize the night by mentioning sounds, scenes, etc, which I think was effective. I think the description was also effective & how everything was interconnected, which is also why I didn't add punctuation (I thought it would cut off parts of the poem in sections.)

• Discuss one to two ways you feel you can improve this piece.

I think I could have found a better way to describe the fireflies instead of "living night lights." Also, cicadas don't come out at night, which I discovered later.

• Give yourself a grade and defend your grade.

A+ Because I feel I worked hard reading and revising the poem. Also, I am satisfied with the result because I think it paints a vivid picture of a summer night, with detailed description

√ about six to eight times, trying to make sure all the words fit.
aloud

#2
interconnected by connecting lines such as in line 24 when I said "as the sky," so that the reader understood that everything was taking place at the same time.

Figure 8.9 Grading yourself brings a lot of reflection.

Confer to Check Notes for an Analytical/Personal Essay

A group of eighth-grade students are reading *California Blue* by David Klass. They discuss what memories they believe would linger in the minds of John, the protagonist; his mom; Miss Merrill; and Dr. Eggleson. Why were some memories alike for these characters and others different?

The students and I develop content guidelines for an analytical essay that will discuss and compare memories students feel the protagonist of a book might recall to a personal memory the student chooses. Comparisons can show likenesses and differences. Before students begin drafting their essays, I ask them to complete detailed notes on:

- Three things the students think the protagonist would remember;
- A memory from their life and how it is alike or different from the protagonist; and
- Ideas to include in an introduction to the essay.

The more detailed the notes, the more connections students make prior to writing. Detailed notes provide students with ideas for composing a clear and well-organized essay filled with specific examples and analytical thinking expectations.

Danny chooses *Bad Boy* by Walter Dean Myers for his essay. I read his notes before our conference so I can praise what worked and focus the conference on one or two needs. Danny's notes are detailed (Figure 8.10). Our conference focuses on adding ideas to his introduction notes and explaining the similarity or difference between his memory and those of Walter Dean Myers.

First, I praise Danny for the way he offers specific details under each example from *Bad Boy* and his personal memory. Here's part of our exchange:

> *Robb: You end your intro notes with, "I do not try to think about the past."*
> *Can you explain why?*

> *Danny: [Danny thinks and I count to 120, giving him time to mull.] Can I*
> *write it?*

> *Robb: Of course. [Danny adds the paragraph about the past, labeling the section "intro"—see Figure 8.10.] One more item. Can you show how you will connect memories from Myers to yours?*

> *Danny: Well . . . I think we had bad attitudes, but then we grow out of them.*
> *Now we're happy.*

> *Robb: You have the connection. Jot it down when you return to your seat.*

Bad Boy

Danny

• I would remember:
   — his english gift; because he was so gifted with anything to do with english and he loved it to; he still does, obviously, because he's an author
   — school vs. life; because he dropped out of high school his jr. and sr. year because he was so stressed and confused
   ⭐ — attitude; because of his hot temper and attitude, he got in many fights and couldn't focus on his education; he got through because he was gifted with brains
   — special school; he was so smart he got into a special class for smart kids; but attitude kicked in and they were the naughtiest and most terrible special class in the history of that school

• memory;
   When I was in 2nd and 3rd grade, I was considered the "bad boy" of my class. I went to Red Bud Run, a public school that was down the street from my house. I was unhappy, and took my unhappiness out on others. That's why my parents sent me to Powhatan, my unhappiness.

• Intro: When ever I'm not doing something, I usually go outside and swing a golf club. I think about what's going on today and what I will do when I'm older. I try not to think about the past. The past isn't coming back, and neither are the bad memories. But when I do end up thinking about the past, I think of wonderful moments. The day I won a golf tournament, the day I hit a single, double, and a triple more my baseball team. And I think of my friends and family, then I go in.

   3rd paragraph notes— attitude similarity; we both grew out and are happy now

Figure 8.10 A Treasure of Memories and Notes

Writing this essay transforms students' views of writing fiction and biography. During a debriefing, Liz explains, "Knowing the memories of your protagonist was key [to connecting to yours] because these came from events and interactions with others. Plotting your own narrative from memories and knowing the histories of characters [or people] is the stuff that makes memories."

Ben begrudgingly adds, "It's a lot of work that I don't always want to do. But I see why we should do it."

Moments like this surprise me. The students' revelations teach me that analytical writing, born of reading, can deepen students' understanding of character development and its relationship to plot.

Confer to Discuss Students' Self-Evaluations

Researchers agree that when teachers help students develop their ability to self-regulate various stages of the writing process, young writers can better recall the process, deepen their understanding of why the process supports them, and develop independence (Coker and Lewis 2008; Graham and Harris 2005; Troia et al. 2009). You can invite students to self-evaluate and set goals for any stage of the writing process: finding topics, brainstorming, focusing, knowing your audience, drafting, revising, and editing.

Self-evaluation and goal setting can lead to self-regulation as long as what students write reveals an understanding of a specific writing stage. Sometimes self-evaluation asks students to look over two or three brainstormed lists, writing plans, drafts, and so on, then write about their progress, improvement, and new understandings. Along with her classmates, Jaime, a fifth grader who lives in Winchester, Virginia, worked with me for several weeks on writing. Her self-evaluation (Figure 8.11) of her first story and revised draft reveals a deep understanding of the need for details in her lead and the body of the text. She sets a goal to gather more details before writing, which reflects lessons on planning and thinking that she observed. Once Jaime applied these lessons to her own writing, she experienced the benefits. Now, there's a better chance she will continue to use details in her writing.

I purposely taped my conference notes to the bottom of her self-evaluation so she could read these before embarking on a new piece of writing. The notes indicate that Jaime sees the need for details. But she also includes a technique—flashback—we've been studying as another possible goal to use in her next piece.

In her self-evaluation, Jaime also set a goal to gather more details before writing, which reflects lessons on planning and thinking that she observed. Once Jaime applied these lessons to her own writing, she experienced the benefits. Now, there's a better chance she will continue to use details in her writing.

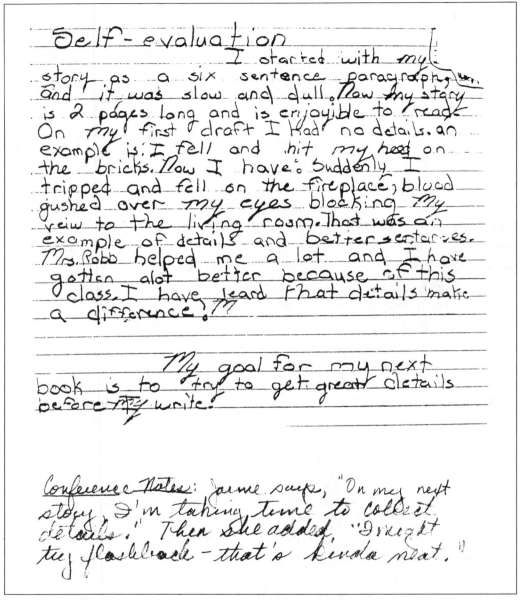

Self-evaluation
     I started with my story as a six sentence paragraph. And it was slow and dull. Now my story is 2 pages long and is enjoyible to read. On my first draft I had no details. an example is: I fell and hit my head on the bricks. Now I have: Suddenly I tripped and fell on the fireplace, blood gushed over my eyes blocking my veiw to the living room. That was an example of details and better sentences. Mrs. Robb helped me a lot and I have gotten alot better because of this class. I have leard that details make a difference.

     My goal for my next book is to try to get great details before my write.

Conference Notes: Jamie says, "On my next story I'm taking time to collect details." Then she added, "I might try flashback - that's kinda neat."

Figure 8.11 Jamie looks at drafts and recognizes the power of revision.

Figure 8.12 Rewriting this lesson gears this sixth grader up for revising his piece.

Conferring with your students is the ideal opportunity to scaffold, revisit a lesson, and reteach to unconfuse students about sensory imagery or using flashback. For me, those five minutes of one-on-one time can move a student forward because I can listen to their tone of voice, the content of their responses, observe their body language, and respond to individual needs. Conferring affords me multiple opportunities to reteach and model. It's the closeness, the sitting side by side that enables me to establish trust and send the message that "I care and want to help," and ultimately, reach each student. Classroom teachers like me, Nancie Atwell, Carl Anderson, Linda Rief, and Regie Routman know, from personal experiences, that conferring works.

Confer and Guide the Writing Process Through Email: Kate's Story

I taught writing and reading to Kate and her eighth-grade classmates at Suffern Middle School during my consulting visits. My email exchanges with Kate taught me the power of using this tool to meet the writing needs of middle school students who, because they write well, often end up working independently while the teacher meets with less able students.

From:
Subject: **Re: Writing**
Date:
To:

On   wrote:

Christie Anne and Julia have been best friends forever. Julia was always the outgoing one throwing parties.Christie never missed one of Julia's parties. Julia was beautiful, she had full red curls, freckles and green eyes. Christie was always well, plain. When Christie Anne and Julia enter high school, Julia automatically becomes popular with the guys.Julia automatically ends up with a steady boyfriend Will. Julia begins spending less and less time with Christie Anne. Christie Anne begins to feel lost, rejected, and friendless. Christie Anne had befriended Will. Will texted Christie Anne and asked what time she was going to Julia's party. Julia hadn't invited Christie Anne. Christie Anne's heart dropped. She thought she was going to throw up. Was her friendship with Julia really over?

okay this is fun!

Figure 8.13 Plot and Characters: The Soul of a Story.

A talented and enthusiastic writer, Kate agreed to plan and write a short story through a series of emails to me. She first created a compelling question that she wanted to investigate through her narrative: "What causes great friends to break up?" She decided that her story would be about how a misunderstanding almost ended a friendship. In an email, I asked Kate to think of a problem, a conflict with no more than two main characters. Figure 8.13 shows Kate's email reply.

Here's what I emailed back to Kate:

This is the beginning of a great plot, and you've woven in texting. Here are a few more questions to think about.
- What kind of a party is this?
- Can you think of reasons why Julia hasn't invited Christie Anne— it's important to think of a few reasons.
- What kind of a relationship does Will have with Christie Anne? Friends? Helps with homework?

What I'd love you to do this week is create profiles for each girl addressing these issues and any others you think of:
- Clothes
- Family members
- Subjects each likes, dislikes
- Kind of house each girl lives in
- Favorite foods, bands, singers, sports, etc.
- Keeps a diary?
- Hopes and dreams

From:
Subject: **Re: Writing**
Date:
    To:

It's Julia's annual end of the year swim party. Julia didn't invite Christie Anne because she is embarrassed by Christies social status. Julia also believes Christie Anne has a thing for Will. Christie Anne and will talk on the phone , and text constantly, even during class. Christie has no feelings for Will but Will is beginning to like Christie Anne more than Julia.

Julia

Clothes- Designer fashionable, big jewelry
Family members- adapted. Lives with adaptive mom, dad and sister.
Subjects each likes, dislikes - hates school doesn't do well, failing math.
Kind of house each lives in- A large mansion, in the wealthiest neighborhood of the town.
Favorite foods, movies, bands, singers, etc.- Always on a diet. Loves the band Linkin Park
Keep a diary? Yes, she writes down everything, who she likes, enemies, it would be a disaster if it got out ecspecially with all the things about Christie Anne in there, and how annoying she gets.
Sports they do and like- Very athletic she plays softball and volleyball
Hopes and dreams - Wants to be a mother, adapt.

Christie Anne

Clothes Very modest always in a T- shirt and jeans
Family members- Mom, da d, older brother
Subjects each likes, dislikes- A+ student, hates math, loves English
Kind of house each lives in- A high ranch across from their high school
Favorite foods, movies, bands, singers, etc.- Loves Italian food, especially Chicken Parm.
Keep a diary? Yes, writes down everything, Julia and Christie Anne has matching Diaries, Christie Anne writes down all her confused feelings about Julia, gosh forbid they got switched.
Sports they do and like Plays volleyball with Julia
Hopes and dreams- Wants to be an author, has a passion for writing.

Figure 8.14 Kate casts her characters.

Kate's reply (Figure 8.14) reveals the details and thought I'd hoped for. She starts her email by presenting the central conflict of her story. She shows me clear differences between the girls—differences that will help Kate explain how and why the conflict developed and escalated.

Next, I asked Kate to think of two, even three, possible endings. I told her that she might not use any of these—that her story might point her to a different ending. But thinking through possible endings lets Kate know that she could resolve the conflict. Three days later, Kate sent me two possible endings (Figure 8.15). In each one, notice how Kate drew from experiences in her life and the lives of friends. She was ready to write, and I emailed Kate that message.

A week later, Kate emailed me a draft. I wrote back, celebrating the plot and her use of figurative language, inner thoughts, and dialogue. She said that the "writing was a cinch" because of all the thinking she had done. "I actually had a great time," she explained. "I got into the characters—could see them and feel like them. Maybe it's because I spent time creating them."

Gently, I invited Kate to return to her first draft and paragraph the text, which arrived as one long paragraph. Figure 8.16, on pages 244–45, shows Kate's edited version of her story, "The Heartbreak Phonecall."

From:
Subject: **Re: Writing**
Date:
To:

ENDING 1:
Julia and Will break up because Will was so flirty with Christie Anne. Julia was really mad at Christie Anne and shunned her more. But one day at volleyball practice Julia and Christie Anne accidentally spilled the contents of their backpacks. When cleaning up they accidentally switched their matching diaries. Julia couldn't take the temptation and tore the diary open with anticipation. Almost every entry was about how Christie Anne missed Julia and felt awful and responsible for the situation with Will. Julia prepared warm sugar cookies and hot chocolate then asked Christie Anne to come over. Christie Anne cautiously walked into Julia's house. The familiar smell of lavender bringing back memories of her childhood. Julia sat with Christie Anne on the couch and explained how she fell into the whirlpool of teen pressure. "But you left me, a real friend is always there" murmured Christie Anne. Tears welled up in Julia's eyes, she wanted the comfort of Christie Anne after her break up with Will more than ever. "Christie you will always be my friend, I made a terrible mistake, all you were doing was texting Will, I was too dramatic." Anger rose in Christie Anne's voice, " Do you want to see the text messages?, because all they say is what a wonderful person you are!" Julia knew if she lost Christie Anne it would be the biggest mistake in her life. "I know you wouldn't, you're "Take that cheater!" Christie Anne ran to the bathroom tears poring down felt them hot behind her eyes, like when you get a cut and use disinfectant. "I'll forgive you, but I don't know if I can trust you again" Christie stated doubtfully. "I'll take it!" Julia smiled giving into the burning tears. "Come on I made you cookies." Julia laughed as the reminisced about times they went to the zoo, and their summer job at the local day camp.

ENDING 2:
Volleyball practice was excruciatingly difficult. The coach was yelling as they ran sprints. "Julia, Christie Anne partner up!" screeched Coach McCormick. Julia slammed the volleyball down angrily as she strolled toward Christie Anne showing off her skills. Christie served up the volleyball, as the 1 on 1 game began; it was the perfect time to vent her anger on Julia. They had a good volley going, when the ball came to Julia she smacked it hard and yelled "Take that cheater!" Christie Anne ran to the bathroom tears poring down her blushed face. Julia felt her stomach twist as a surge of guilt overcame her. What was she thinking? Christie Anne had been her best friend. Julia ran to the bathroom, now crying herself apologizing for all her actions. Christie Anne braced herself as she flipped open her rhinestone and showed Julia all her innocent texts to will. They had a long hug, and jogged back to volleyball practice smiling all the way.

Figure 8.15 Kate knows how her story can go.

Kate's last comment, "Maybe it's because I spent time creating them," shows me that deep planning and thinking, whether on paper or in the author's mind, supports the writer and the writing and assists the creative beacon that lies within.

Assessments of Writing Stages and Students' Behaviors Support Interventions

If you're interested in evidence-based practices read: *Instruction and Assessment for Struggling Writers* edited by Gary A. Troia. New York: Guilford, 2009.

In the chart that follows you can explore suggestions for helping all of your students, because there will be times when even students who write well will need your support. Through conferences with students and conversations about students' writing with colleagues, you will be able to add to this list. The more suggestions for supporting students, the better you and I can help them become the writers, thinkers, and problem solvers of the twenty-first century and beyond.

What We Take Away from Kate's Story

Kate taught me that email is the ideal tool for conferring with outstanding writers who frequently don't receive enough guidance and feedback from us because of the demands of a large class with several writers who require one-on-one conferences to improve. Receiving emails with suggestions, feedback, and praise builds students' writing power and self-confidence. As well, the process of sending those emails showed me how to break down assignments.

Always remember that teaching through email demands clarity. We need to write the email feedback clearly so that students can understand our suggestions without confusion. This process helps us build our own communication skills.

You can find time to email students during planning periods or one or two evenings a week. The big payoff is that by conducting email conferences and lessons with our proficient writers, we offer them the time they need and deserve—time that improves their craft and technique, time that enlarges their self-confidence, and time that inspires them to write beyond curricular requirements.

SCAFFOLD AND INTERVENTION CHART FOR PROCESS WRITING STAGES

Writing Stage	Student Behaviors	Interventions/Scaffolds
Finding Topics	• Says "There's nothing to write about." • Responds negatively to teacher's suggestions • Says "I'll take an F."	• Encourage student to draw cartoons to find topics. • Do an oral or written interest survey with student. • Send to library to find magazines of interest and browse them to find topics. • Suggest surfing sites on Internet like manga. • Invite student to use video games as inspiration to find ideas. • Have student talk to peers to find out what they're writing about. • Have peers discuss video games, comics, and movies to find topics.

The Heartbreak Phonecall by Kate Rella

I stood alone in the hallway soaking in the pain. I have no best friend. The powder blue walls around me seemed to blur, as they faded into memories of looking at clouds with Julia. Everything seemed to remind me of Julia. I looked down at the tiled floor fingering our best friends bracelets. I was the only one wearing it. She had thrown hers out right in front of me on Tuesday. She ripped it off held it over the garbage can and said in a strong voice "Don't you ever speak to me again!" I faked a headache to go to the nurse and think it over. Julia. She was stuck in my head. The girl who I ran to whenever I had a problem, like when my parents got divorced. Then came Will her first boyfriend.

We entered high school with an inseparable bond like crazy glue. Julia was instantly popular with all the guys. She was the definition of beautiful. She glowed. She had locks of curly red hair, piercing green eyes, and a dash of freckles across her face, with natural blush. She was the outgoing athlete. Julia loved being the center of attention. Then there's me Christie Anne, the idiot who called Will. Since when is it okay to text, but not call? I mean he just wanted to know what to get Julia for Valentines Day. I am plain, I have pin straight brown hair with hazel eyes, I am as pale as a marshmallow. I thought I would be forever known as the girl who sat near Julia. But I was okay with that.

Now Julia is gone. It feels worse than when I broke my arm in 3rd grade when I jumped off the swings. I felt a paper football smack my arm, I instantly grabbed for it, Will was standing right above me. "Chris, you never answer my texts any more, I mean I know Julia and I broke up because of our conversations, but you and I know they were only about Valentines."

I felt like my throat was going to close, "Yeah, but you didn't lose your best

Figure 8.16 Final draft: "What a great feeling!" says Kate.

friend over a bunch of texts and a phone call Will." I grabbed my books, and fumbled to find my pass, as I tried to contain my anger. I thought about Tuesday nonstop during math. I would never steal my best friend's boyfriend. Why would Julia think I was capable of that? She was so okay with us texting. Why did I call him? All I wanted to suggest were pink roses and a surprise visit to her bedroom window at night. I guess I could have texted the message. I have no idea why I called. I didn't think about it. WIll and I were just friends, and we both knew that. I guess I thought Julia trusted me more.

Tuesday night, I got a text from Julia. All it said was "you are a horrible friend, I broke up with Will, take him, you obviously want him." I was mortified. My jaw dropped. My chest felt like I hurled a hundred pound weight on it. I love Julie, I don't want her boyfriend. Will was just a good friend.

The I got the text from Will, "Julia went through my phone and saw my texts and phone record."

I answered faster then ever, " Did she read them"

I got an answer before I even had time to process the situation. "No, otherwise she wouldn't of cared." Of course! I reasoned and rationalized if she read them there wouldn't be an issue. They were all about Valentines Day.

Volleyball practice I forgot. I ran to the locker room, and changed. I took a deep breath and tried to prepare myself for seeing Julie. Volleyball practice was excruciatingly difficult. The coach was yelling as they ran sprints.

"Julia, Christie Anne, partner up!" screeched Coach McCormick. Julia slammed the volleyball down angrily as she strolled toward Christie Anne showing off her skills. Christie served up the volleyball, as the 1 on 1 game began; it was the perfect time to vent her anger on Julia. They had a good volley going, when the ball came to Julia she smacked it hard and yelled "Take that, cheater!" Christie Anne ran to the bathroom tears poring down her blushed face.

Julia felt her stomach twist as a surge of gulit overcame her. What was she thinking? Christie Anne had been her best friend. Julia ran to the bathroom, now crying herself and apologizing for all her actions. Christie Anne braced herself as she flipped open her rhinestone cell and showed Julia all her innocent texts to Will. They had a long hug, and jogged back to volleyball practice smiling all the way.

Figure 8.16 *Continued*

SCAFFOLD AND INTERVENTION CHART FOR PROCESS WRITING STAGES (CONTINUED)

Writing Stage	Student Behaviors	Interventions/Scaffolds
Brainstorming	• Writes little. • Unsure of what to write. • Turns in blank paper. • List doesn't match topic.	• Think aloud and model how you brainstorm. Record on a chart. • Share brainstormed lists from past students. Remove names. • Pair students. Have peer write questions about topic and any ideas on the list. Student adds to brainstorming by answering questions. • Ask student to discuss topic with peer, then add ideas to the list. • Ask "How do ideas connect to topic?" Student might make connections you don't see. • Have student talk through the brainstorming as you write what student adds. Then, discuss the rich ideas. • Help student understand that brainstorming can make the writing easier.
Focusing Ideas	• Wants to use all ideas. • Unsure of audience. • Unsure which ideas to include and which to leave out. • Inexperienced with focusing and selecting.	• Model focusing your list of ideas. • Ask "What are you trying to say? What details help you say this?" Write while the student talks, then discuss the positive points. Support student and slowly release responsibility over to writer. Be prepared to continue support until student is on solid ground with this stage. • Have student work with a peer who has expertise to help. • Keep supporting writers who need to build their experience with figuring out what they want to say, then selecting details that help them say it. • Discuss audience. Who does student want to read this? • Discuss how audience can decide the details writer selects. • Provide positive feedback about progress.

SCAFFOLD AND INTERVENTION CHART FOR PROCESS WRITING STAGES (*CONTINUED*)

Writing Stage	Student Behaviors	Interventions/Scaffolds
Planning	• Says plan is in head. • Doesn't know what plan looks like. • Doesn't see how planning supports the writing.	• Show brainstorming and a variety of plans from past students. Discuss. • Share the plans of Katherine Paterson and Jean Van Leeuwen (see Appendices A and B) and discuss why writers do this. • Model planning using your focused brainstorm list. • Plan with the student to give the writer support. • Have student complete plans with a peer expert. • Collaborate with the whole class or a small group to show how plans emerge from selected brainstormed ideas.
Drafting	• Unsure where to start. • Has several false starts. • Writes very little. • Unsure what a draft looks like. • Overly concerned with correct spelling and usage.	• Complete a shared or collaborative writing with the class and have students help you write a draft based on your brainstorming and plan. Have students discuss the process. • Show students drafts of past students. Discuss misspellings, crossed out words and phrases, etc. Explain that spelling, etc. can be corrected during the editing stage. • Have a student talk through a draft. Write as the student talks to show the close relationships between talking and drafting. • Encourage students to reread notes and plan after a few false starts to bring ideas back. • Let students who struggle with the physical act of writing use a computer to draft. Make sure all draft changes are saved. • Have student start after the opening and write that later. • Let student talk through the draft with a peer, prior to writing. • Provide positive feedback and let the student know what's working.

Scaffold and Intervention Chart for Process Writing Stages (*Continued*)

Writing Stage	Student Behaviors	Interventions/Scaffolds
Revising	• Feels unable to revise. • Doesn't know what to revise. • Wants to rewrite the entire piece.	• Model how the content and style criteria for the shared writing piece let you know what to revise. • Provide students with a revision strategy such as numbering. • Sit beside the student, think aloud, and model how you use criteria to know what to revise. • Show student how you revise. • Ask or help the student to find another criteria to revise and support the process. Continue helping with revisions and gradually release responsibility to the student. • Have the student revise with a peer expert. • Adjust the amount of revision for writers who struggle. Help them succeed with one or two revisions before asking them to do more. • Review revision lessons that you've taught and are on chart paper. Ask students to tell you what they do and do not understand.
Editing	• Feels unable to edit for writing conventions. • Unaware of the number of spelling and usage errors.	• Explain that the criteria show students which writing conventions to edit. • Work on one convention at a time. • Have student read the piece out loud to edit. • Sit side by side and show student how you edit and that the process takes time. • Give students editing symbols for paragraphing. • Have student edit with a peer expert. • Use students' errors to plan group lessons and practice sessions. • Provide positive feedback for successful editing.

SCAFFOLD AND INTERVENTION CHART FOR PROCESS WRITING STAGES (*CONTINUED*)

Writing Stage	Student Behaviors	Interventions/Scaffolds
Self-Evaluating, Self-Regulating, Setting Goals	• Unable to explain a writing process stage. • Doesn't recognize progress, improvement. • Doesn't know how to set goals.	• Show how you explain a writing process stage and why this helps with the writing. Then, on chart paper, write your thoughts. • Have partners discuss a stage of the writing process that they're learning and practicing. Then ask students to write, read one another's work, and offer feedback. Feedback should include why it's helpful to remember the process. Then students add ideas to their self-evaluations. • Have students look through their writer's notebooks, discuss the value of notebooks with a partner, then write. • Ask students to look at the work in their writing folder over several weeks and the criteria for each piece. Then, have them make a list of their strengths as writers and areas they've shown improvement in, and set one goal for their next piece. Review these and meet with students who need your support.

Discuss Students' Writing

Learning from Students' Writing

Conferring is a teaching art form that includes focusing a conference, being a great listener, and helping students solve writing problems by posing questions that stir their thinking and discussion. I've included an early and deadline draft of an autobiographical poem by Jen, an eighth grader (see Figures 8.17 and 8.18). With a colleague, department members, or your grade-level team, mull over the early draft, compare it to the deadline draft, and determine the focus of the conference between Jen and me. Would you have decided on a different focus? What would it be? Why?

What I'm emphasizing here is that the focus of a conference emerges from your teaching demonstrations and the criteria you and students negotiate. So my focus, punctuating a poem, might differ from yours. That's the way it should be because the conference topics emerge from your lessons, students' needs, and district requirements.

Miss Smith   english

The first time trying to go on
a water slide, I was afraid to go,
but with encouragement ⬤ I
finally went down now I love
water slides.

   I am 12 I am afraid to go
down the water slide at great
wolf lodge & my cousins and brother
help me go down.

      They got me to the top
      ~~~~what more do they want?
   "Come on jen you can do it"
   my cousin said
   "Theres nothing to be afraid of"
   says you.

      I look down
      Take a big gulp
      "no I can't!"

   "Yes you can, come with me"
   my older cousin annemarie said
   "Oh" I said wimpishly.

      I sit in the ~~~~tube
      more nervous then ever
      "Ready?" annemarie said
      "yeah" scared and soft I spoke.

   woosh!/off I fly down
   like a kid on red bull.
   water flying all over

      An abrupt stop
      It's done.
      "was that fun?"
      "Ya!"/I said with extreme ~~~~ excitement
      "lets go again!"

Figure 8.17 Can you see David Harrison's influence?

<u>Waterslide.</u>
I am afraid to go down the
water slide at great wolf lodge
and my brother and cousins
help me go down.

They got me to the top
What more do they want?
"Come on Jen you can do it!"
My cousin said.
"There is nothing to be afraid of."
"Huh, says you!"

I look down
Take a big gulp,
"No I can't!"

"Yes, you can; come with me."
My older cousin Annemarie said
"O.K." I said wimpishly.

I sit in the tube
more nervous than ever.
"Ready?" Annemarie said.
"Uh, yeah," scared and soft I spoke.

Woosh!
Off I fly down
like a kid on red bull.
Water flying all over.

An abrupt stop.
It's done.
"Was that fun?"
"Ya!"
I said with extreme exitment.
"Let's go again."

Figure 8.18 Ready for the bulletin board!

Figure 8.19 Kathie Schain confers with her sixth graders on the art of paragraphing.

Discuss Students' Writing

Professional Study Invitation

Invite teachers to bring a sample of a writing plan, a first draft, and a revised first draft to a meeting. Make copies of each or make overhead transparencies of each piece. Here are some questions that can stir conversations among the group:

- What are the criteria for this piece?
- What do you feel is the most important need based on the criteria?
- What will the focus of your conference be?
- What positives can you pinpoint to share with the student?
- What questions can you pose to help the student explore solutions to the problem?
- Do you need to schedule follow-up conferences with you or a peer partner?

CHAPTER 9

Analytical Exchanges Online

Blogs and Beyond

Jared, an eighth grader in Suffern, New York, wrote me a letter in response to questions I posed to him about writing outside of school, and texting in particular. I share it here because it possesses some pretty terrific confirmations about what we need to do to reach middle school writers.

> Dear Mrs. Robb,
>
> I do like to instant message, write to my friends on Facebook, and text message. Besides that I don't do much writing in my free time, not that I really have any. When I was younger my parents made me write, and I did not enjoy it at all; it was torture for me. Whenever I went on a vacation, my parents made me write about how it was, what it was like,

what I thought was exciting, what the boring parts of my trip were, and anything else I did on my vacation. It all used to be the same thing. I titled it, "My Vacation" or something similar to that and everything, to me, was very repetitive and not at all amusing. I wrote because I had to, and that was the only reason.

It was after my father Ting Chin, who I saw on the weekends, moved that I sought out a reason to write, and it wasn't because I had to. Even though he was moving closer to where I lived, I was devastated from the move to a new house and I didn't know what to do. I was angry and miserable so I wrote in a journal. I wrote of all my feelings and thoughts that saddened me. It was a new way to express myself, to make me feel better. I felt much better after expressing my feeling on paper and now enjoyed writing.

Soon enough I stopped writing in my journal. I was feeling better and didn't have the urge to write anymore. That experience of writing changed my whole view on what writing was. I became much more motivated to become a better writer in school. In 6th grade I loved making crazy stories with my friend Kevin McNally about weird animals. We had such a good time writing them. Mrs. Medina was probably the best teacher I have ever had and she pushed me to become better at not just writing, but also reading.

I would definitely like to start writing again if time allows it. All that I need is a motive to get me going.

Regards,

Jared

Throughout this book, I've mused about the gulf that exists between middle school students' writing lives in and outside of school. Much of this gulf arises from the disconnection between the goals of school writing and middle school students' own reasons for writing. Whether they are writing in journals to express emotions or penning silly stories with a friend, all of the writing that middle school students do outside of school has a real use: the writing helps these students connect to something that matters a great deal to them.

How might you be a teacher who motivates a student like Jared? I suspect you already are that teacher. You see that once students are motivated to write, the skills, craft, and conventions that bring clarity and voice to their writing develops naturally and with your support.

Using Jared's letter, let's consider writing at school from an adolescent student's perspective. I've added key words from the *Writing Next* report (see pages 41–43 in Chapter 2) and the Six Fundamental Needs of Middle School Writers (see pages 104–6 in Chapter 4) to underscore the matchup between these recommendations and what Jared yearns for in writing instruction. In the first paragraph of his letter, Jared makes the point that assigned writing topics—"I had to" writing—whether at school or home, do not motivate him.

In an interview, I asked Jared, "What do you think teachers need to do to motivate their students to want to and love to write?" Immediately, Jared said, "As a student, I believe that teachers have to first give us a reason to write, other than test prompts. Then they can see how well we are able to write." Like professional writers, students want real-world reasons to write. Jared wrote in his journal, for example, because venting feelings made him "feel better." But once the need to confront and sort through his feelings left, so did this type of journal writing.

Choice

What we can learn here is that writing is an amazing, versatile tool that enables adolescents to share meaning and emotions with themselves and often with an audience, and that they intuitively know the genre that will work best in that moment or juncture in their lives. One student writes a letter to her mom filled with anger and accusations because her parents have split up. Another writes in her journal, "I feel overwhelming waves of loneliness wash over me. There are days I'm alone and days I have too many friends." One student put her journal on my desk with a sticky note marking a page. I opened the journal and read a poem called "Wishing for Death." She wanted me to read this and help, which I did. I find that writing helps troubled adolescents survive doubts, loneliness, fears, and peer issues. Writing can help them through crises because writing is self-reflection, supporting the discovery of what they know and understand.

Relevance

In his letter, Jared praises his seventh-grade teacher, Mrs. Medina, for engaging him with writing, but also for pushing Jared to write well. Jared shows us here that middle school writers thrive on encouragement, but they also crave challenge and want to improve their craft. Most important, Jared shows us that pushing students to improve their writing is a form of motivation that springs from the teacher. The message the teacher sends to the student is "Yes, with work and guidance you can turn a good piece into a terrific piece." Such messages motivate students to work hard, build their self-confidence, and increase their self-efficacy.

Writing Strategies

Like other young teens, Jared also likes to text and IM (Instant Message). For adolescents, their friends are the center of their world. Maintaining contact with friends, arranging meeting times, and passing on gossip drives adolescents to continually text and IM. "Staying connected is what it's about," Kate explained. Middle school writers also use

Collaborative

Jared Explains How Mrs. Medina Motivated Him to Write About Reading

I emailed Jared and asked him to explain why he felt Mrs. Medina motivated him to write and pushed him to revise and edit. Here is his response:

Mrs. Medina was not an ordinary teacher. She was not one of those text book teachers, though one doesn't have many of those in English, but more in social studies. Still, Mrs. Medina did different tasks in order to motivate us and want to do work.

From my past experiences, after reading a novel in English class, the teacher would normally make the class write an essay. Mrs. Medina came up with many other ideas rather than writing an essay. One memory of her class was writing skits and video scripts. She was very open to suggestions about what we did after reading a book. She understood how writing an essay wasn't the only way to show how one understands a book.

She made groups and each were assigned to do a project about their novel. One time I remember my group wrote and performed a musical. We all dressed in costumes of the characters and instead of only acting out a shortened version of the novel, we sang it. It was the most enjoyable project I have ever done. I doubt there will be one to come that is more enjoyable.

Other things we did in her class instead of essays were writing scripts for movies. This was very much like the skits but instead of a live performance, we put the movie up on the screen and showed it to the class. Another idea that one group had was writing a puppet show. None of our scripts had to be final copies. We had a rough draft and a bunch of notes. Our performance along with what our performance was about was what she had graded.

These were only a few of the many things we could have done to show our understanding of the text. These were all great! Mrs. Medina also added in some essays to have a balance in the class; but no one could complain because we got to do all of these other fun things as well. She allowed us to express how we felt about the novel and our understanding of it, but not always on paper.

texting to let family members know that they'll be late or have gone to the library or a friend's house.

Middle School Writers Weigh In on Texting

Jared's letter, which opened this chapter, raised my curiosity about texting, so I decided to interview several students. I asked, "Why do you enjoy texting? Who do you text? Why do you consider texting a form of writing?" In an email, Kate, an eighth grader, wrote:

> Hi!
>
> 1. I enjoy staying in touch with my friends because I love them and want to be with them every second. If I didn't have my friends around, I would be a wreck.
>
> 2. My parents actually learned to text. So if I have a change of plans, or need a ride home, I can text them.

Then, because Kate knows that I don't text, she created an example of what a text looks like:

Me: hey wats up?

Person: nm u??

Me: nuttin boredd =(

Person: how was skool?

Me: it was okay. i got an a on my math test

Person: nicee

Me: hahaha yea hbu

Person: ok. i got a prob

Me: wat

Person: i like this guya nd idk how to askk him out

Me: become friendz 1st

Person: okkk i gtg ttyl

Me: kkkk bibi <3

Kate and the other students I interviewed all said that texting is a legitimate form of writing. Amanda, a seventh grader at Suffern Middle School in New York, explained, "I do consider texting a type of writing. Writing requires creativity, and you have to be creative while texting. I text just about everyone I know. I never call people anymore. I just text."

Similarly, Jared wrote, "I just got back from Australia so I wanted to tell [my friends] all the amazing things I got to do and how I was doing. I could have done the same thing in the form of an essay, a school form for writing. But I used texting. In this case, texting is like a lot of parts to an essay broken up into smaller parts and sent through my phone. Both of these forms of writing have the same purpose, one is just a broken up form of the other one."

Kate, Stephanie, Brian, and Jared, all eighth graders at Suffern, all made the same point: "Texting could be a genre because you speak in a completely different language!" Kate emailed me these examples to support her position:

lol = laugh out loud;

brb = be right back; and

idts = I don't think so.

Figure 9.1 Revision is fun with peer support.

Researchers are studying texting; their findings dispel adults' concerns that texting creates poor spellers and diminishes students' writing abilities. Two recent studies reported that texting improves writing and students' phonological awareness.

Researchers at the University of Toronto in Canada found that teenagers demonstrate a strong command of grammar when text messaging. Professor Sali Tagliamonte, a linguistics professor at the University of Toronto, explained at a meeting in August, 2002, of the Linguistics Association of Canada and the United States (Alphonso 2006) that kids who text show they have a solid command of the English language.

The BBC News Channel reported on March 18, 2009 that a study on the merits of texting had been completed at Coventry University in Coventry, England. Researchers from the university studied eighty-eight children between the ages of ten and twelve. To gain insights into the impact of texting on language skill, they gave the students ten different scenarios and asked them to write about each using text messages. Dr. Beverly Plester (2006) and her colleagues at Coventry University said that the research data showed that textisms, such

> I know that there are also studies that show texting erodes students' ability to spell and write correct English. I invite you to decide whether you will integrate this new literacy into your curriculum. You might want to investigate the study on writing that Andrea Lunsford did at Stanford University (see box on page 270). Lunsford studied the writing of first-year Stanford students; she did not find one example of abbreviated texting language in an academic paper. However, remember that for students and teachers, it's all about choice.

as shortenings, contractions, acronyms, and symbols, improved literacy. Plester inferred that teens who text developed phonological awareness by using textisms. (See http://www.coventry.ac.uk/latenewsadndevents/a/2341.)

Now that we know so many middle school writers in grades 6 through 8 continually text friends and family, and studies have been done that indicate texting does not erode students' writing skills, the question to answer is "How can we teachers integrate texting into a school literacy curriculum?"

Bring Texting to Your Writing Curriculum

Don't get me wrong: I'm not advocating moving from writing in favor of texting. I am, however, inviting you to consider integrating texting into your reading-writing units when it makes sense. Doing this shows you respect and honor what students love and do well. At the same time, you can increase their enthusiasm for writing. In addition, students will be writing about their independent reading and mentor texts to synthesize, infer, and make connections (Shanahan 2009).

When I emailed Kate and asked her to create a series of text messages between two characters in a book she enjoyed, Kate immediately wrote back: "Sure! This sounds like fun!" The first time you extend this invitation in the classroom, many students will be nonplussed—unable to respond for a few moments. Once chatting starts, however, the silence will transform into rich conversations about characters, conflicts, problems, and key events. And why not? You're asking students to reflect on two characters, understand their personalities as well as the book's plot and conflicts, and then design a series of text messages the two characters might have. This is high-level thinking, using the technology middle school writers adore.

Prior to inviting students to try a text style of writing in class, review the guidelines that follow. Next, share them with students so they can create a written plan that you can approve before they start composing their text messages:

- Choose a completed independent or instructional reading book.
- Select two characters from your book who will text one another. Write the name of each character. Then, under each name, jot down some notes that show two or three personality traits.
- Create a series of text messages that stay true to the characters and the events in the book.
- Transcribe and translate the text messages, then hand them in to your teacher.

In Figure 9.2 Kate creates the text messages that Bella and Edward, the main characters from Stephenie Meyer's *Twilight*, might send one another after Edward saves Bella from being run over by a van in the school's parking lot. Notice how Kate weaves in specific details related to Bella's wonderings about Edward's strength and captures Bella's inner resolve to not let the details of this incident go.

I always invite students to translate text messages that they complete for school. The translation is for me, but also for students. While translating, students can think about the meaning in their text-speak and revise parts so that the text reflects their intention.

This exercise, texting between characters, is similar to an exercise that asks students to plan and compose a series of letters two characters might write to each other via email correspondence or on stationery. Texting will most likely result in more enthusiasm for the project. However, you might consider including both in your plans or give students choices in writing about their reading: texting, emailing, or traditional letter writing.

Like Kate, Amanda is a zealous texter, so creating these conversations using text language is easy. Figure 9.3 shows Amanda's text between characters from *Marked* by P. C. and

From:
Subject: **Re: Can you do this?**
Date:
To:

1. Twilight by Stephanie Meyer
2. Bella: insecure, quiet Edward: Intimidating, secretive
3. When Edward holds back the car so Bella would not be runover

B- i kno u held bak the car
E- Bella i was rite nxt 2 u
B- no u were not i wont tell u can trust me
E- there is nuthin 2 tell
B- I looked up vampire last nite
E- so? wut bout them?
B- pale skin, super powers, piercing eyes.
E- idk wut you are talking bout
B- yes you do
E- stop it bella
B- i kno u r dif trust me
E- i cant trust ne1
B- why
E- bc i am different
B- youre not a........human
E- of course i am
B- edward i wont let this go tell me
E- no
B- i will find out i gtg ttyl byeeee

B- I know you held back the car
E-Bella, I was right next to you
B- No, you were not. I will not tell you can trust me
E- There is nothing to tell.
B- I looked up vampire last night.
E-So? What about them?
B- Pale skin, super powers, piercing eyes.
E- I do not not what you are talking about
B- Yes you do.
E- Stop it Bella
B- Why?
E- Because I am different.
B- You are not a human?
E- Of course I am.
B- I will not let this go, tell me.
E- No.
B- I will find out. I got to go talk to you late. Bye

Figure 9.2 Kate adores texting about reading.

From:
Subject: **Re: Cn you do this?**
Date:
   To:

Hey Laura,
Sorry to get back to you so late. I read a book for english class a month ago that I think could be turned into texts. The book is called Marked, and the two main characters' names are Zoey and Damien. It is a fantasy book and Zoey and Damien are trying to take down the leader of the dark daughters clique named Aphrodite:

Damien: Yo Zo... meet me by the fencing room tonight after dinner... I have a plan.

Zoey: Sry Dam. I have a Dark Daughters meeting @ 7

Damien: Kayy... well Holloween is the Dark Daughters ritual when they release the spirits into the outside world.

Zoey: Yer point Dam?

Damien: We show up with our own spirit circle.

Zoey: Uhmm... idk if i can
(idk = i dont know)

Damien: Scared Zo? You will STILL be a part of the dark daughters even if we get caught.

Zoey: Idts Damien.. Aphrodite has nvr liked me. She will take advantage of any chance she gets to remove me from the Dark Daughters.
(idts = i dont think so) (nvr = never)

Damien: But she cant. She doesnt have the power to decide whos in the clique and who isnt. The Dark Daughters has the most powerful grls in the House Of Night. If you lead your own spirit circle it'll show you are as powerful as Aphrodite.

Zoey: Idk if I AM as powerful as her though

Damien: You are Zo. I believe in you. Holloween @3 be there.

Hope that helped...

Amanda

-----Original Message-----
From:
To:
Sent:
Subject: Cn you do this?

Dear Amanda,

I hope this note finds you well and having a great time in ninth grade. All of your work has helped with the book so much.

I have one more favor. I would love you to take a book (could be a short story) you really enjoyed and have two characters from the book write several text messages to each other. The texts should grow out of an event, conflict, something that happened in the book.

If you could do several exchanges, send me the text format and translate each one, that would be great.

Is two weeks enough time?

Thanks so much for your help.

Best,

Figure 9.3 Amanda uses texting to hold a conversation between two characters.

Kristen Cast. Both girls show us the thoughtful side of the texting process as they dig into each character's personality, which is revealed within specific conflicts and problems.

Texting and letter writing foster the interactive communication that adolescents treasure. Pairs can complete and transcribe these texting suggestions:

- Text between characters about the central conflict.
- Text from protagonist to friend while the protagonist struggles with a problem.
- Text from a minor character to the protagonist about a problem.
- Text about an issue as two readers who've completed the same book.

Perin (2009) points out that when middle school writers collaborate on aspects of writing, their work improves. Partner work is an important aspect of collaboration and one of the Six Fundamental Needs for Middle School Writers. Now I want to show you how extending collaboration to the entire class working together can help students build a mental model of what composing in a specific genre looks like.

Collaboration in Action: Build Students' Mental Models of Genre, Craft, and Technique

Let's look at how students in my eighth-grade writing workshop work together. Three students who have completed *Under a War Torn Sky* by Laura Elliott plan and com-
 pose a Readers Theater script that they'll rehearse and present to the class (see DVD for guidelines). Two groups of five help one another choose a poem from their writing folders and plan a multimedia performance that integrates music, art, and/or dance. Nick, the class musician, plays drums or guitar for some readings; he rehearses with classmates in the hall outside of our classroom. Several students bring CD players and earphones to class. They listen to and select music by rock, rhythm-and-blues, or hip-hop groups to serve as a background while they read their original poems. Liz creates and practices a modern dance to Hattie's poem. Four students gather around a computer, choosing images they'll flash onto a SMART Board during their performance of a play based on Nicholasa Mohr's short story "Shoes for Hector." This is one aspect of collaborating that encourages the exchange of ideas while dipping deeply into each student's well of creativity, including writing and the fine arts. Mei, an eighth grader, showed the benefits of teamwork in her self-evaluation of her project:

Figure 9.4 Eighth graders collaborate on a multimedia presentation of a poem.

> My group worked hard to write a play based on "Shoes for Hector." We had to read the story four or five times to really know it. Sometimes we didn't agree about the writing, but we learned to listen to each other and work things out. I think the play turned out so good because we used the best ideas. We had to divide jobs up like who would write on the computer when others gave ideas for the play. We had to learn about writing a play and giving directions in it. The most fun was finding images to show during our performance. And definitely performing the play for our class and a sixth grade class.

So what are these middle school students learning by working together? First, they're working hard on projects they want to do. They're learning to exchange ideas, listen, compromise, problem solve, write, perform, and tap into their creativity. According to Daniel Pink (2005) and Howard Gardner (2007), tapping into students' creativity, validating their enjoyment of group performance, and designing lessons that foster collaboration can develop the problem solvers and thinkers needed for the twenty-first century and beyond. In addition, performance builds poise and self-confidence, two real-world traits that students can rely on during interviews for jobs, for schools, and for special academic and fine arts programs.

A Mentor Text Lesson that Prepares for Writing

Collaboration for middle school writers also includes planning and drafting a piece with their teacher. When teachers work together with students by sharing the pen, we help them build a mental model of the process of writing in an unfamiliar genre or learning more about craft or technique. The material becomes accessible to students because they observed and helped write. If several students, especially those who struggle with writing, don't contribute to the collaborative writing, then they are learning only by watching. Most will likely need one-on-one support.

I am preparing students in Ms. Malone's seventh-grade class at Johnson Williams Middle School for collaborative writing of a dialogue with me (see pages 267–69). We use the last chapter, "Funeral," from the memoir *Marshfield Dreams* by Ralph Fletcher to study how dialogue reaches far beyond illustrating personality traits (Coker and Lewis 2008; Graham and Perin 2007a; Perin 2009). At our first meeting, I read "Funeral" out loud. Then students read the short chapter silently. It's an absolutely wonderful piece about how Ralph's friends bring him into the woods to say good-bye, an hour before he and his family are leaving the town for good. They make Ralph lie down in the woods and then eulogize him in a mock funeral that is both funny and a tearjerker.

On the chalkboard I write the question groups will discuss: "Show Ralph's personality traits and support your conclusions with text details." In a Think Aloud, I model how I figure out a trait and support it. Here's what I say:

> I believe that Ralph is determined. I know this because he really wants to see his friends for the last time so he "pleads" with his dad and promises to abide by the time limit his dad sets.

Next, I ask students to pair-share and tell me what they notice about my Think Aloud. "You named a trait—determined," one says.

"You explain how you figured it out from the story," says another.

"Yeah," a third pipes in. "It didn't say in the story that he was determined. You figured it out. I think that's an inference."

"That's just what I want you to do in your groups," I say. "Make inferences by using the details in the text. Take about ten minutes, discuss personality traits you see, and find support in the story for each one." As students work, I circulate. I bend down at desk level to listen to their conversations, and I invite them to reread a passage and use it to infer Ralph's personality.

Groups identify obvious traits such as *friendly, sad, popular,* and *helpful.* I want more. But I know that the students have to do the thinking for the lesson to be meaningful. "Let's act out the funeral scene," I suggest and call for volunteers. Only girls volunteer; the boys hunker down in their seats trying to disappear. After we reenact the funeral, I ask students to tell me what they learned about Ralph.

- He was cooperative; he did what his friends asked.
- He was supportive like when he took the punches from John Berkowitz.
- He was popular 'cause he had a lot of friends.

Some boys raise their hands, frantically trying to get my attention. Here's what they say:

- Obedient 'cause he went right back to the car at the end.
- Fun-loving, when he remembers staying up late, eating corn, going to the fair.
- Funny—a member of the Four Stooges.
- Trusting—he went along with the funeral.

The ideas flowed like water cascading down a rocky gorge. "What's happening?" I asked.

"Watching the girls saying the lines helped us understand more." The drama has led the audience and the actors on a journey into this text, a journey that has deepened their comprehension (Wilhelm 2002). Students linger a bit after the bell rings, not their usual behavior pattern, teasing the girls about portraying boys and wanting to know if they can act out more stories.

Day Two and Beyond: A Series of Lessons Based on Fletcher's Piece

Ultimately, I want students to use dialogue in their writing for two or three of these purposes: to create settings and mood; to provide background information; to show personality traits; to show the passing of time; and to move the plot forward. To build students' knowledge of how authors use dialogue, I plan a series of lessons.

Study "Funeral" as a Mentor Text

Revisit "Funeral" as a mentor text to discover how Fletcher's use of dialogue goes beyond understanding personality traits. Since this is a first-time experience reading a text from a writer's perspective, I decide to scaffold students' thinking, inviting them to look for examples of how dialogue:

See DVD for this mentor text lesson.

- Helps them learn about the passing of time;
- Creates a mood and showcases the boys' feelings; and
- Provides information and history.

Use Independent Reading as Mentor Texts

Each group member shares a page or two they feel is rich in dialogue from the book; this takes about thirty to forty minutes. Students discuss whether the dialogue advances time, reveals setting, provides history and information, shows personality traits, and creates a mood. Watch and listen to your students, for you might have to repeat this lesson with other mentor texts.

> Work one-on-one or in small groups with writers who struggle and can benefit from that extra support to understand how authors use dialogue.

Share the Pen with Me

Collaborative writing asks students to share the pen as you and students work together to plan and compose. Doing this builds students' mental model of what the planning and composing process is like for writing dialogue. It also provides the background knowledge that builds the self-confidence students need to risk applying lessons to their own work.

Apply to Their Own Writing

Invite students to take what they've learned and to apply it to a narrative they've written or one they plan to write. In this step, peers will support one another and you will confer with students. Continually support writers who struggle as they work on dialogue in their own writing.

> Writing dialogue can cover so much terrain in terms of craft that it's a lesson worth repeating

This type of collaborative writing, where you share the pen with middle school students, is especially helpful for writers who struggle since these students don't have clear pictures in their minds.

Collaborative Dialogue in Action: Eighth Grade

Sharing the pen and working together to write dialogue is an opportunity to involve students in the planning and composing process as well as to think aloud and illustrate punctuating dialogue. I find that students can parrot these rules, but their writing runs different speakers together, misuses punctuation, or eliminates it.

To plan the dialogue that eighth-grade students will help me write, I explain that I need a situation and two characters, each with a short list of physical and personality traits. In a Think Aloud, I make my planning visible to students so they can experience the value of thinking prior to writing. As I talk, I write on large chart paper (see box on page 268).

I ask students to try to create dialogue that quickly sets up the problem, gives some history about each character, shows time passing, and reveals different personality traits

Writing Plan for a Dialogue

<u>Situation</u>: Morning bus ride to school. Rose has to sit next to Tony—the only empty seat. Tony hasn't done his math homework. He'll try to get Rose to let him copy her work.

<u>Rose</u>: Shy, quiet, great math student, long black hair, pale skin, unathletic, known as a loner and nerd. [Now I ask students to give me descriptors for Tony.]

<u>Tony</u>: Star quarterback, tall, muscular, deep blue eyes, struggles with math and science, every girl in tenth grade wants his attention.

for Rose and Tony. Having these details in the plan, I know, will support students' writing because the big points are in the forefront of their minds. I compose the first two sentences. Students add the title at the end. Here's the revised draft.

No Easy Answer

Rose boarded the school bus at 7:15 AM. She scanned the rows and noticed that there was one empty seat next to Tony, the quarterback every tenth grade girl wanted to date.

As Rose slipped into the seat next to Tony, she wiggled to the edge and buried herself in a book.

"Hi," Tony said. "Good book?" Rose nodded, keeping her head down.

"Say, Rose, did you get that geometry homework last night? Everyone says you're a math whiz ."

"Yeah. It was easy," Rose whispered. She pushed her long black hair close to her face to hide the red blush she could not stop.

"Can I see it?" asked Tony.

"Why?"asked Rose.

"Last night practice ran late, then I had to help my dad stack wood against the side of the house. Didn't have time to do it." Rose did not answer.

"Look, I'll meet you at the soda shoppe after school. Buy you a soda. We can talk. It'll be cool. C'mon."

Anger turned Rose's blush redder. A bribe, she thought. More like he didn't do it.

The bus stopped. Rose looked at her watch. It was 7:30 AM. First bell was in fifteen minutes. She stood up and moved a few seats ahead of Tony; she aimed to get off quickly. Not interested, she told herself, as she walked into school.

Debriefing the Collaborative Process

The writing and revising take part of two consecutive classes, which allows students to write and me to confer with a few. During the second class, electricity fills the room as I reread the revised dialogue. Students express pride in their work with comments like "cool" and "rad." Smiles are everywhere. I explain that it would be beneficial to pair-share about the process, considering three questions, which I write on the chalkboard: *How did the writing plan help? How much did you use the plan? How did the collaborative process feel?*

Here are observations students made:

- We came back to the plan before trying to write a part.
- The plan made us think about what the dialogue should do.
- Showing time was easy.
- We could add to the plans for future pieces things we wanted the dialogue to show.
- Working together, watching, and participating in the writing showed we could do it on our own.

I recommend using collaborative writing whenever you introduce a new craft, technique, or genre. Reserve time to dip into the list (pages 269–71) of some share-the-pen writing you can do with students.

Collaborative Writing Possibilities

You can share the pen with individuals, small groups, and/or the whole class to show and have students experience the craft and technique that professional writers use and students need to absorb. Involving middle school students in the process provides them with a reason to listen and participate. You might have to repeat and review lessons with struggling writers when they have not absorbed specific genre, craft, and technique demonstrations. Here are suggestions for collaborative writing that have worked for me.

Genre
- Poetry
- Short narrative
- Planning an essay
- Composing a journal response

Craft

- Show, don't tell
- Setting the scene
- Sensory imagery
- Leads and endings
- Introductions and conclusions
- Specific nouns
- Strong verbs

Technique

- Writing dialogue
- Character description
- Figurative language

Stanford University Study on New Literacies

Andrea Lunsford, a professor of writing and rhetoric at Stanford University in California, has organized a project called The Stanford Study of Writing. Lunsford's purpose was to study students' prose. From 2001–2006, Lunsford collected 14,672 writing samples, from in-class assignments, formal essays, and journal entries to emails, blog posts, and chat sessions. Lunsford's findings led her to conclude that technology isn't destroying our ability to write—it's reviving it. Here are some results from her study:

- Young people today write more than any other generation.
- Students today write online for an audience. Stanford students were less excited about writing in class because the professor was their only audience and the purpose of the writing was to get a grade.
- Students can assess their audience and adapt their tone and writing style to it.
- First-year students did not include texting language in academic papers.

Lunsford pointed out that good teaching of writing is crucial to students' development as writers, whether for school, online, or while composing stories for themselves and peers. She believes that new forms of online writing have become a new literacy frontier with endless possibilities.

Revision

- Combining short, choppy sentences
- Paragraph transitions
- Organizing supporting details
- Adding details
- Repairing run-ons

The collaborations that I've described emerge from more traditional ways of teaching and learning. As you continue to read, you'll immerse yourself in bringing in twenty-first-century literacies such as blogging and wikis to explore ideas, share book reviews, and teach writing through email. Just as with texting, students' outside-of-school writing lives include social networking on Facebook and MySpace as well as blogging and emailing. Both blogging and emailing have sound applications for middle school students and their studies.

Blogging: Collaboration that Develops Thinking and Writing Fluency

"I love blogging," Thomas exclaimed while reading a response from a classmate. Then he continued to read and write, read and write.

Later, I asked Thomas, "Why do you love blogging at school?"

"I love that feedback to my posts is instant. I enjoy the continuous stream of ideas from classmates. Some are funny; some make me angry. But I enjoy the rush of feelings changing minute-by-minute." Thomas' comments ring true for middle school writers who blog in and outside of school and illustrate the kinds of on-the-spot thinking blogging invites when students engage in running conversations about an issue or a topic (see pages 277–79). Even reluctant writers enjoy these back-and-forth exchanges. The instant feedback that results when a class blogs together brings a dynamic dimension to your instruction and to peer work. It teaches students to think and react quickly, and it can improve reading as students, with practice, learn to process information quickly. If accuracy of information is ever sacrificed, a peer blogger will quickly set that student on the right track.

> **Start a Class Blog**
>
> Go to www.blogspot.com or blogger.com and follow the directions. Have students use their first names or pseudonyms for confidentiality and safety.

According to the survey discussed in Chapter 1, seventh and eighth graders respond to blogs outside of school more than students in grades 5 and 6. Teachers I've worked with, even in grades 5 and 6, use blogging at school to have students discuss issues such as relationships, to respond to a compelling question, or to post book reviews.

When I spoke to Andrew Frye, eighth-grade English teacher at Shelburne Middle School in Staunton, Virginia, about blogging, he pointed out that he experienced many pitfalls his first year, when he used blogs with book groups. In response, he created the following guidelines, which he has kindly allowed me to share:

Blogging About Books: The Teacher's Responsibilities

- Model the standard of citing details and inferences from the text to support points. [Andrew pointed out that text support increased the more he modeled.]
- Encourage and help students question each other and go beyond responding to the teacher's queries. These interactions can build relationships among students and pique their interest in books peers enjoyed.
- Make sure the topics you offer students are "bigger or meatier," such as blogging about theme, how and why a character changed, how settings or other characters affected the main character, etc.
- Show students, after they post entries, how you pose questions about a student's post, then use questions as springboards for responding.
- Model that a response can be a series of questions a specific post raised.
- Demonstrate how referring to earlier blog posts you made can enrich a new post or show how you revised your thinking about a book or topic.

Andrew emphasized that teachers need to model writing expectations many times. "It's like what we do before asking our students to write in journals, try a genre, or writing technique. I found that just saying *blog* and thinking that students would reclaim their experiences from journaling wasn't enough. I had to show them what I wanted in the new medium."

Guidelines for Tweaking Blogging over Time

Here are suggestions I recommend that you try once you and your students are comfortable writing on the class blog and responding to one another's posts in meaningful ways.

- Encourage students to reflect on the uses of technology in their learning at school. Such self-evaluations can lead you to students who need extra support from a peer or you; they can also give you ideas you might not have considered. For example, one student wrote, "I think we should use graphics from the Internet for photo essays as an alternative to taking photographs."
- Ask students to create a podcast of a play, poem, or book review to share with students in other classes. Go to userwww.sfsu.edu/~nshelley/ for information on podcasting in the classroom.

• Become email pen pals (e-pals) with students in other countries. To learn more, go to www.epals.com/; this is a global community of classrooms for teachers and students.

In addition to the guidelines on page 272, Andrew shared a letter that he sends to parents explaining the goals of his blog, safety issues, and the students' audience. Andrew's students also signed a contract asking them to be respectful of others and accountable for information. You'll find a Letter to Parents About Blogging and a Sample Blogger's Contract on the DVD.

Andrew and I agreed that it doesn't matter where we ask students to write—on a blog or in a journal. In either medium, the process should be thoughtful, and students will benefit from having a mental model, supplied by their teacher and peers, of what a great response contains. On his blog's home page, Andrew offers his eighth-grade students ground rules, procedures, and instructions on what to do when they have completed posts about their book (see Figure 9.5).

A "Language Arts Journal" is another aspect of Andrew's class blog. In Figure 9.6, notice how Andrew clearly spells out his expectations and the choices students have on this site. On a second page of the site, Andrew includes a place his students can visit to find weekly homework assignments as well as a way for students to view and read each other's book reviews.

Class blogs are easy to set up, and they are user friendly. Even if you're not a tech guru, you can organize a blog by asking students to help with the process. Remember, startup sites have user-friendly directions. If your school has technology personnel on staff, they will walk you through the process.

Avoid Personal Attacks and Profanity

Ann Kiernan-Robb and I learned a lesson about personal attacks while eighth graders were blogging about this question: "Is there such a thing as a just war? Explain why or why not." Even though Ann and I were observing students' posts, negative comments appeared. That's the moment that Ann and I realized that the teacher needs to be the only person to have access to the *entire* site. If middle school students have free access, they can add personal attacks, use improper language, and even change classmates' postings. Outside of class, students can access the blog only to add posts. Reading other students' posts must occur during class.

AUTHORS

There are many Shelburne authors on this blog. Thank you for your insights.

GROUND RULES FOR POSTING COMMENTS:

No profanity or personal attacks.

No innapropriate remarks

Please comment on the subject of the blog post itself.

If you do not follow these rules, we will remove you from the blog and/or you will lose computer priveleges.

PROCEDURE FOR BLOGGING

1. Click on your book title
2. Read the questions for the day
3. Post your answer to the questions
4. Read comments and questions made by other group members
5. Ask a question relating to your book
6. Make at least one comment in response to someone else's comment or answer a group member's question

THINGS TO DO WHEN YOU ARE DONE BLOGGING

Pass a topic on Study Island

Play Rooting Out Words on Fun Brain

Play Grammar Gorillas on Fun Brain

Read the News Leader Online

MISSION STATEMENT

In this space, Mr. Frye's Language

Figure 9.5 Want to build a class blog? These rules will help.

SEARCH BLOG | FLAG BLOG | Next Blog»   Create Blog | Sign In

LANGUAGE ARTS JOURNAL

A PLACE WHERE READING, WRITING AND THINKING COLLIDE.

What piece of writing are you most proud of creating this year?

105 responses at 5/22/2008

Go into your drive or your hardcopy folder (in the classroom) and find the piece of writing you are most proud of and would like to share. After reading, revising and editing it, post it to the blog. Once you are done, read and make comments on at least two other people's writing.

Blog Title Contest

39 responses at 5/20/2008

I need a new name for this blog. Shelburnebookjournal is not all that cool, hip, or even really interesting. So, I need suggestions. Please submit as many as you'd like as often as you'd like until Thursday. We'll take a vote Friday as to which name you think I should use next year and the winner will get a prize.

Free Verse Discussion Board

48 responses at 4/24/2008

Find a **classmate's poem** that you like and explain why you like it. Possible things you could discuss:

it's *theme, use of imagery, symbolism, use of figurative language, or poetic sound elements.*

Free Verse Poetry

52 responses at 4/21/2008

Share your poem by posting it. Remember to use stanzas, break the lines like you've done in your draft, and include a title.

THINGS TO DO:

Venn Diagram Creator

Study Island

Shelburne Library Home Page

Free Rice Vocabulary

Root Game

Poem Hunter

Poem in Your Pocket

Literary Elements Map

The New Analogy Game

One on One Analogy Action

Analogy Game

WEEKLY ASSIGNMENTS

Click on the composition book to view this week's homework.

GREAT BOOKS PAGE

Click on the pile of books to view reviews written by fellow students.

Figure 9.6 Ideas for Journaling Online

In Andrew's classes, students do not exclusively write on blogs. They have notebook journals and writing folders that include handwritten brainstorming, writing plans, early drafts, and revisions. Students complete final drafts on computers. In my classes, blogs are the most effective tool for initiating sustained conversations among students in a class around a compelling question that relates to a unit of study, such as: "How can wars be prevented?" or "What makes relationships thrive? Break up?"

Blogging: A Conversation of Ideas

In my class, I set aside ten minutes of class time over two to four days to engage students in a conversation around a compelling question related to a unit of study. For me, this is ideal as there's time for students to write and me to confer. You can adjust the time to suit your needs and schedule.

Students' posts literally fly onto the blog as students read and respond to one another's thoughts. I find that students' responses are fluid and detailed; they ask one another questions; they offer opinions. In addition, they're building background knowledge about a topic as they read the posts and react to classmates' posts.

I was preparing eighth graders for a two-week mini-unit on war and conflict using picture books (see Picture Books for Exploring Compelling Issues on the DVD for the list). The purpose of this unit was to build students' background knowledge regarding issues surrounding war, because the class was about to begin a larger study using historical fiction and informational texts on the Holocaust. Three times a week, the class opened with students blogging on these compelling questions:

- Is there such a thing as a just war? Explain why or why not.
- How can language promote or deter war?
- Are conflicts healthy? Explain why or why not.
- How can we avoid conflicts and tensions escalating to a war?
- How did war change the main character of your book?

The excerpts of students' posts in Figures 9.7 through 9.9 illustrate the fast pace of these written conversations.

Notice in Figure 9.7 how thoughtful students' responses are and how easy it is for them to disagree. Students wrestle with whether language can cause wars in Figure 9.8. Again, disagreements pop up, and students feel confident in supporting one another. However, when students blog about the protagonist of *Rose Blanche* by Roberto Innocenti (Figure 9.9), notice how judgmental they are about the main character's death. There is

Thursday, May 8, 2008

Is there such a thing as a just war? Explain why or why not.

Posted by Mrs. Robb at 9:34 AM

126 comments:

Spencer said...

A just war is an opinion. So really there is no such thing because there will always be somebody who apposes the current war.

May 8, 2008 9:42 AM

Nathan said...

no because everyone gets hurt in some way or form, and we think we're making the world a better place by helping some country, but at the same time it can't be helping the world by destruction and brutality.

May 8, 2008 9:43 AM

Anonymous said...

yes, i think there is a thing as a just war, but we should be careful as to what wars we go into. it may not be just to kill many people for someone else's war, or for going into a war with no basis or reason.

May 8, 2008 9:43 AM

meagan said...

I think people believe that, when they go to war, it is justified, and I think if they are in danger, perhaps it is. War changes though and I think that by the end it is never just.

May 8, 2008 9:43 AM

Kathryn said...

A war can be just if we have a good reason and do a lot of research about your war. It should not be rushed into and it has to have good intentions.Intentions such as helping a suffering area that wants our help not because we think that they need help.

May 8, 2008 9:44 AM

Anonymous said...

i have to disagree with nathan here. if by going to war you can eventually save many people (ww2, hitler) it is worth it.

Blog Archive

▼ 2008 (4)

  ▼ May (4)

   How can language promote war or deter war?

   Is there such a thing as a just war? Explain why o...

   We are discussing and writing about war and confli...

   Mrs. Robb's Eighth Grade English Class

About Me

MRS. ROBB

View my complete profile

Figure 9.7 Bloggers converse at a fast pace.

Untitled
70 Comments - Show Original Post
                                    Collapse comments

Leave your comment

---

 anonymous said...

yes, i think that words can deter war. Threats can, Insults can, and several other things can.

May 12, 2008 12:38 PM

 scott said...

i think words can start war and conflict.

May 12, 2008 12:38 PM

 livi said...

language cannot promote a complete war because that kind of war cannot be justified. words should not be a reason to kill a lot of people

May 12, 2008 12:38 PM

 kaleigh said...

I think that words can start war, but not big ones. Just wars between families or a few people

May 12, 2008 12:39 PM

 spencer said...

i think words can start war and conflict

May 12, 2008 12:39 PM

 kathryn said...

I think that words can start conflict sometimes more than actions

May 12, 2008 12:39 PM

 kaleigh said...

i also agree with olivia

You can use some HTML tags, such as <b>, <i>, <a>

Choose an identity

  Google/Blogger
    USERNAME
    PASSWORD
         No **Google Account**? Sign up here.
         You can also use your **Blogger** account.
  OpenID
  Name/URL
  Anonymous

PUBLISH YOUR COMMENT

PREVIEW

Figure 9.8 Bloggers react to war.

Untitled

93 Comments - <u>Show Original Post</u>

<u>Collapse comments</u>

Leave your comment

---

livi to ap said...

In this book war changed the protagonist because in the end she was dead

May 14, 2008 8:36 AM

to livi from spencer said...

How did she die

May 14, 2008 8:36 AM

andrew to livi said...

ya cause shes stupid and got herself shot when she wandered into a battlefield

May 14, 2008 8:37 AM

kathryn said...

In my book war changed the main character because she collected a lot of newspapers to help the people of the war. And she learned a lot about bravery and herself.

May 14, 2008 8:37 AM

to spencer from livi said...

she got shot because she was stupid and tried to give food to the refugees from the concentration camp

May 14, 2008 8:37 AM

major said...

How did war change the protagonist of your books? in faithful elephants the elephants changed by being starved to death because the japanese military thought they were dangerous IDIOTS!

You can use some HTML tags, such as <b>, <i>, <a>

Choose an identity

○ **Google/Blogger**

USERNAME

PASSWORD

No **Google Account?** <u>Sign up here.</u>
You can also use your **Blogger** account.

○ **OpenID**

○ **Name/URL**

○ **Anonymous**

PUBLISH YOUR COMMENT

PREVIEW

Figure 9.9 Not all comments show clear thinking.

no admiration for the young girl, who was killed because she saved food from her meals and passed it through the barbed wire to the starving Jews.

Pull small groups to discuss comments like these. Help them evaluate a story's outcome using the lived-through experiences and decisions of each protagonist. Through discussion, you can transform what adults perceive as negative responses and poor word choice and deepen students' understanding. Posing questions returns students to the text to rethink and revise their initial responses. Questions such as "Why did the protagonist wander onto the battlefield?" or "What motivated the protagonist to give food to refugees in concentration camps?" can encourage students to rethink and revise their initial reactions.

I can hear and understand the protesting voices of teachers who might comment on the lack of or erratic punctuation in students' posts. First, content is primary. Second, students' respond within seconds and don't have time to consider punctuation. The postings are like fast writes and brainstorming when students compose in idea chunks. This will not destroy their ability to write in complete sentences, which is an appropriate standard when drafting a piece. (See the research of Dr. Andrea Lunsford in the box on page 270).

The kind of blog Andrew sets up, inviting students to write book reviews and poems, calls for complete sentences and appropriate writing conventions. However, students compose these from notes written in words and phrases. Scott, an eighth grader, points to the benefits of blogging in his self-evaluation:

> Days or weeks after we discuss, most of the details evaporate. I can go back to our blog and reread posts to refresh my memory and also see how some of the ideas we first wrote have changed as we read.

Continue to hold class discussions, but also include blogging. The fast pace of blogging differs from a thoughtful, slower-paced discussion. Not all students participate in small-group or whole-class discussion. I find that all students participate in blogging.

Students Write Narratives that Emerged from Reading and Blogging

During the second week of the mini-unit on war and conflict, I asked eighth graders to suggest writing ideas that emerged from their reading and blogging. The class lobbied for writing short narratives that centered around a conflict that happened in their lives. I read two selections from Bailey White's *Mama Makes Up Her Mind* and asked students to pair-share to discover memories that might become writing topics. Then, based on White's stories, students developed this content and style criteria:

Writing Suggestions by Eighth Grade, Section B

- Need a title
- Be FOCUSED—get to the heart of your memory
- One or two main characters versus an obstacle, conflict, or problem
- Conflict: determine this before writing—stick to it
- Setting: set it quickly
- Plot: beginning, quickly into rising action, climax, resolution (conflict or problem resolves in a believable way)
- Include dialogue
- Handle time effectively—tightly—you might have to skip ahead
- Include descriptive details

The writing extended the unit to a third week, which allowed students time to think, chat about their ideas, brainstorm, plan, and draft. Paired conversations about their memories helped students narrow and focus their topics. Partners questioned one another, discussed what information to include, and figured out ways to immediately set the scene before jotting down a loose writing plan. Students used the writing suggestions to plan, draft, and self-evaluate.

Figures 9.10 and 9.11 show Sorrel's second draft and her self-evaluation. Her self-evaluation illustrates that having guidelines for evaluating a draft enables students to check their work against the criteria. Her second paragraph pinpoints a specific need based on the criteria: include descriptive details. Her last sentence, "I guess when I write I need to remember that not everyone knows how Jake looks or tends to act," spotlights what all writers wrestle with: to make readers aware of what's stored in their minds. What her self-evaluation doesn't but should include is the humor that emerges from the interactions of Jake and Sorrel.

When students blog about compelling questions, relevant writing projects emerge. This class chose short narratives with a central conflict. From the same blogging interactions, students could have negotiated taking notes for a debate, a panel discussion, or an interview, or writing an editorial or a newspaper story or a photo essay. Negotiate options with students, because this supplies them with reasons for additional reading and writing.

Young Champs

First Grade was always a blur to me. One minute I felt ~~eternity~~ invinceable, the next I'd be sobbing over my what seemed unfair losses. First grade seemed like it was just a big contest to be the best at everything. I had to be able to jump to the furthest monkey bar. I had to be able to color my picture the best. I had to be able to push the tire swing the fastest. If I couldn't do any of that, I had to work harder to prove that I was a worthy friend.

With new seats came new friends and new challenges. Mrs. Kelchner put me at the head of a yellow table. My seat was next to a black-haired, athletic, popular boy named Jake Lewin. Jake always seemed to be a little bit better than me in a way. He was better at running, got picked before me on the playground when we played kickball, and read the Goosebumps books (what a daredevil), which I always thought were beyond me.

Jake and I talked, seeing as our seats were next to each other, and in first grade, you could talk to whomever you wanted to. Normally it was just the usual stuff like "Blue is such a better color," or "Have you seen the movie called Mummies? My sister let me stay up till nine watching it last night." It was stuff like that that we talked about. But one day, it was different.

"I bet you can't make me cry," I challenged.

"I probably could. YOU'RE REALLY UGLY! You're the ugliest girl I've ever seen. I never want to see your face again!" Jake retaliated.

"Nope, I'm not crying. That would never make me cry," I said. *"Sticks and stones may brake my bones but words will never hurt me,"* I recited.

"Fine then, I'll hurt you."

"You're not strong enough"

"Yes I am, I made my brother cry when I did it. I can hurt your arm really badly." And with that Jake was pounding his fists into my arm, which was lying across the classroom table. The less pain I expressed on my face, the harder he pounded. If I said it tickled, he'd get angry that his poundings were failing, so again he'd pound harder. I had him pounding harder than I could take. Then I broke down and cried. Feeling triumphant, he backed off with a smirk and a told-ya-so stamped on his face.

But me, ~~I raised my good arm,~~ sobbing "Mrs. Kelchner! Mrs. Kelchner! Jake made me cry!"

She rushed to the scene and told Jake that hitting wasn't the way to solve problems. He insisted that I told him to do it. Which I did, but in the end, I was the winner. I had out-smarted the boy that thought he had me beat. In the end, I was the one with a full recess while Jake sat on the dreaded curb. That day, all the glory was mine.

Figure 9.10 Conflict Through Sorrel's Lens

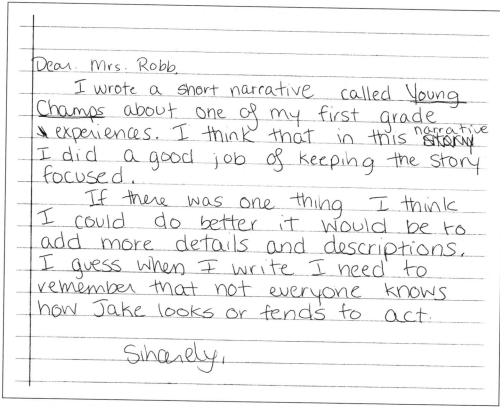

Dear Mrs. Robb,

    I wrote a short narrative called <u>Young</u> <u>Champs</u> about one of my first grade experiences. I think that in this ~~story~~ narrative I did a good job of keeping the story focused.

    If there was one thing I think I could do better it would be to add more details and descriptions. I guess when I write I need to remember that not everyone knows how Jake looks or tends to act.

       Sincerely,

Figure 9.11 Self-evaluate to see what worked and what can be.

Use wikiHow.com to Expand Writing Opportunities

Ann Kiernan-Robb established a wiki for her eighth graders so they could post book reviews and comment on one another's reviews (see her directions on the DVD). She also introduced them to wikiHow, a site that clearly shows students how to write flash fiction, five-hundred-word short, short stories; a graphic novel; or a fully developed short story. The site also contains tips for writing well and completing a specific genre. Excellent student writers can follow the site's directions, freeing you to support those who require scaffolds.

DVD
CLASSROOM
RESOURCES

Reframing a Writing Curriculum for Middle School Students

I'm certainly not advocating transferring all middle school writing onto computers. What I am asking is for us to consider is how new technologies, such as blogs and wikis, can support aspects of writing. The questions to ask yourself are:

- Where will this technology take me and my students?
- How will it support thinking and improve writing?
- Does the blog and/or wiki support my goals and students' needs?
- Do I have the time to work out the kinks of a new literacy take?

Considering these questions will enable you to decide where you want to start and how much time you can give. My advice is to start with a class blog, work out the kinks and pitfalls, enjoy the benefits for a year or two, then consider adding a wiki. I've included a chart of new literacies and how they can support aspects of your writing curriculum on the DVD.

Professional Study Invitation

Invite the technology person at your school or tech-savvy teachers to lead several professional study meetings and help you set up a class blog or wiki. Take the plunge; your students will also help you until you gain confidence and comfort with bringing these new literacies into your writing class.

Conclusion
Making It Your Own

The last big question that I'd like you to consider is how you can use what I've covered in this book so that it works in your unique setting, with the unique learning needs and styles of your students. To help you explore possible answers, I've created a chart that draws on insights from

- The national survey;
- Interviews with students by email, in person, and on the DVD;
- Students' responses to the "Ten Questions About Writing;"
- The Six Conditions for Teaching Middle School Learners;
- New literacies research; and
- Writing instruction: text structure, craft, technique, conventions.

Table C.1 highlights eleven ways to bridge the gap between writing in and outside of school. Remember, teaching students to write well in diverse genres will enable them to score high on standardized state tests. Why? Because they have the writing strength, skill, and technique required to meet the demands of a testing situation.

Transitions: The Support You'll Need to Reframe a Writing Curriculum

"I hate changes. I don't want to move. I'm happy here. Why can't my parents get that?" a seventh grader laments during a conference. We teachers are the same. Significant change in our professional lives is tough because it lifts us up, swirls us around like Dorothy's house, and lands us on unfamiliar terrain. But the camaraderie we establish with colleagues as we take on professional development can lessen the discomfort. Table C.2 lists ten things you and colleagues can do to gather the support, new knowledge, and understandings you'll need on your odyssey of research-based change. I recommend that the first support network you organize is a professional learning community. Think of the additional suggestions as a menu. Start small, remaining within your comfort zone, and add experiences slowly. Find a colleague you can partner with or a small, compatible group. Then let the journey begin!

Table C.1 Eleven Ways to Reach Middle School Writers

Suggestions	Purpose
1. Tap into students' writing lives.	Invite students to complete the "Ten Questions About Writing" questionnaire. Confer with them to discover their attitudes, what motivates them to write, and ways you can support them as writers. Answers can point you to writers who struggle and have negative attitudes toward writing.
2. Offer students choices.	Offering choice of topic and genre provides proficient and struggling writers with powerful reasons to compose. Even with required genres, such as persuasive essay, ask students to discover their topic.
3. Encourage collaboration.	Have students work together to create a piece of writing so they start to understand how a specific genre works. Collaboration makes the learning active and interactive.
4. Teach craft and technique lessons.	Conduct demonstrations that show students the inner workings of writing craft and technique. Help students apply these to their own writing.
5. Show how knowledge of grammar can improve writing.	Teach grammar that gives students the tools for improving style and writing conventions.
6. Study genre, craft, and technique with mentor texts.	Use the finest writing by professionals to illustrate how they effectively integrate writing craft and technique. In addition, explore specific genres by studying professionals' writing.
7. Negotiate writing criteria for each task.	Ask students to reflect on your minilessons and what they have learned about content, style, and writing conventions. Set these criteria before students brainstorm and plan. This supports drafting, revising, and editing. It also provides you with a set of guidelines for responding to the writing and assigning a grade.
8. Encourage paired and small-group discussions about writing.	Learning is social (Vygotsky 1978). Middle school writers are social and adore talking to peers and friends. Harness this gift of gab and focus it on finding topics, revision, and peer and self-editing.
9. Confer with students.	Hold brief, focused conferences that hold the potential for improving students' writing.
10. Introduce compelling questions.	Show students how these questions can create important reasons for writing. In addition, such questions provide the drive to research real-world problems and write about them.
11. Ease into twenty-first-century literacies.	Challenge yourself to choose and try a new literacy, such as establishing a class blog.

Table C.2 Ten Ways to Gather Support as You Grow and Change

Professional Development Experiences	How These Help You
1. Organize a professional learning community.	Meet bimonthly to enlarge your knowledge base of what middle school writers need and how you can support the diverse range of learners in your classes.
2. Mentor with a peer partner.	Create meaningful change together so that you can share lessons, ideas, and offer one another feedback.
DVD CLASSROOM RESOURCES 3. Ask students to complete the "Ten Questions About Writing" questionnaire on the DVD.	Use data from students' responses during conferences, to inform teacher demonstrations, and to identify students who need scaffolding from you.
4. Attend state and national literacy conferences.	Increase your knowledge base by attending sessions on adolescent literacy. Browse through book displays to discover professional materials and adolescent literature.
5. Build your school's professional library.	Invite administrators to set aside funds to purchase several new professional books that support individual efforts and that can be used for conversations when you and colleagues meet.
6. Observe two colleagues in your school.	Explore lessons and teaching practices of colleagues to enlarge your teaching repertoire.
7. Observe two teachers in schools outside of your district.	Gather ideas that work by observing master teachers in other areas. This, along with ongoing learning, can prevent us from sticking to what we're used to instead of discovering what's best for our students.
8. Engage in self-evaluation.	Reflect on your lessons by asking "What worked well? What can I improve?" Self-evaluation enables you to pinpoint areas that benefit from additional study and conversations with your peer partner.
DVD CLASSROOM RESOURCES 9. Interview students.	Based on your observations and students' writing, conduct interviews that help you get to know students, build trust, and discover the kinds of support individuals need. See the DVD for suggested interview questions to choose from.
10. Share materials and lessons with colleagues at meetings.	Bring a lesson that worked, one that flopped, a terrific mentor text, and so forth to professional learning community meetings. The sharing and celebration of what worked can supply others with teaching ideas. Gathering feedback on lessons that didn't work can support change and growth.

Forming a Professional Learning Community

In this last professional study section, I'm turning the spotlight on teachers instead of student writers. Of course, it's beneficial to study and learn from students' writing; I want you to continue this practice. There are, however, five additional professional study practices to integrate into your sessions—practices that can further develop your skill and expertise as a writing teacher.

Additional Professional Study Practices

- Reflecting and taking notes on your teaching and learning year
- Studying and discussing professional articles and books
- Collaborating to develop lessons with mentor texts
- Bringing lessons that did and did not work before the group to gather feedback
- Collaborating to:
  - Find appropriate mentor texts
  - Plan writing units
  - Develop and practice demonstration lessons
  - Explore possible scaffolds and interventions for struggling writers

I suggest that you rotate the task of facilitating two meetings each month. The group facilitator is responsible for finding a professional article or an excerpt from a book. Give colleagues at least one week to read the professional material and prepare for conversations (Routman 1999). Ask your school librarian to suggest journals and/or books.

When teachers and I have conversations about a professional reading, these questions guide our discussions:

- What information have you learned?
- What ideas will you bring to your teaching? Explain why.
- How do you think these ideas will impact students' writing?

The purpose is to cull ideas from the reading that can support your teaching and students' learning. You won't agree with every article, but disagreeing can stimulate reflection and deepen your understanding of why your current practice is more beneficial to your students. Reading and conversations build your bank of background knowledge about writing instruction, cause you to question and mull over current teaching practices, and move you beyond them.

Laura Robb and Gwen Malone enjoy a student's journal entry.

The facilitator, along with teachers, sets the agenda for the next meeting and follows up to make sure that teachers who have volunteered to share a lesson or bring examples of students' writing are prepared so the meeting is productive. When planning units, finding mentor texts, or exploring scaffolds for students, invite teachers to organize themselves into small groups. To collect diverse ideas and perspectives, encourage teachers to learn with different colleagues as the year progresses.

Professional Study Invitation

Now that you've formed a cohesive professional learning community by sharing and discussing students' writing and through conversations about professional articles and books (Routman 1999), I invite you to set aside time near the end of the school year to reflect on your growth as a writing teacher, set goals for summer reading and learning, and establish goals for the upcoming year. The following questions/prompts can help you brainstorm a list of ideas. Respond to questions that apply to your teaching life; add queries not on the list; and share your notes with your colleagues.

- How have I grown as a writing teacher?
- What have students taught me about writing? Explain.
- What challenges have I confronted and worked out? Explain.
- Discuss one success or high point and one struggle or low point you had with teaching.
- Discuss how reading and discussing a professional article has shaped your teaching.
- What new teaching and learning elements did you bring to your students? Explain why you chose these.
- Set one or two goals for the new school year.

In a professional learning community, you'll experience relevant learning because studies emerge from each school's culture and student population. Moreover, a professional learning community builds on Pink's and Gardner's charge to be creative, collaborate to problem solve, foster trust and empathy, and improve middle school writing instruction.

Revisiting the Closing of Jared's Letter

Some things in life are worth repeating—the closing of Jared's letter is one of those (see pages 253–54). The points that Jared makes are points I hope will linger in your mind and nudge you to continually think about teaching writing: writing supported Jared through his parents' divorce; writing enabled Jared to work through his feelings and confusions; writing for a meaningful personal purpose motivated Jared to "become a better writer at school."

> Soon enough I stopped writing in my journal. I was feeling better and didn't have the urge to write anymore. That experience of writing changed my whole view on what writing was. I became much more motivated to become a better writer in school. In 6th grade I loved making crazy stories with my friend Kevin McNally about weird animals. We had such a good time writing them. Mrs. Medina was probably the best teacher I have ever had and she pushed me to become better at not just writing, but also reading.
>
> I would definitely like to start writing again if time allows it. All that I need is a motive to get me going.

Having powerful reasons to write and a teacher who motivates—a teacher who's tuned into the emotional and academic needs of young adolescents—is a tough order. But I believe that you can do it!

A Statistical Analysis
of the National Survey

A primary goal my editor, Wendy Murray, and I had when we decided to launch this student survey was that it would supply school districts and teachers with data that could help them reimagine their writing curricula. The research of NCTE (2008) on the status of writing among middle school students points to a need to reexamine how we teach writing. Today's classrooms emphasize test preparation and grammar and usage drills instead of helping students use inquiry and their interests to find meaningful writing topics. Graham and Perin's *Writing Next* (2007a) and NCTE's "Writing Now" (2008) offer suggestions for teaching writing in an ever-changing world. Along with the *Common Core State Standards Initiative* (2008), there's a call for writing assignments that invite students to analyze texts and personal experiences, and use diverse forms of writing to solve problems and persuade.

To prepare middle school students for the heightened literacy demands of high school, college, and the workplace in our times and beyond, I invite teachers to consider offering more intense writing instruction and use assessments to scaffold all students' needs in a safe and nurturing environment (Coker and Lewis 2008; Graham and Harris 2005; NCTE 2008; Troia et al. 2009). I'm hoping that you will review the information that follows along with the reporting of middle school students about their outside-of-school writing lives in *Teaching Middle School Writers*, because this information can help us reexamine and reimagine the way we teach writing.

The Survey Statistics

Interpreting the Analysis

Statisticians have to study and work with data to ensure that chance, instead of an accurate pattern or conclusion, does *not* cause a specific statistic; it's the data that's primary. When studying data, chance can cause two problems. First, chance can result in seeing patterns that aren't there. Chance can also prevent the statistician from seeing results that are there. The job of the statistician is to help see

My thanks to Dr. Larry Hembroff of Michigan State University, who completed the survey's analysis.

291

through this chance or randomness, and two things enable the statistician to accomplish this.

1. Large numbers—in this case large numbers of students who completed the survey.
2. The large number of items in the survey: in this case, thirty-four.

The analysis of the data included regression studies to control for variations and chance findings among states, gender, and grade levels. I have chosen not to share the few variations among states because the sample from each state was too small to make valid inferences.

Reporting of the analysis of the surveys will focus on data yielded from the statements as well as statistically significant correlations and inferences that can be made from this data. At other times, when it's not possible to make valid inferences from the data, I will use the findings to raise questions for classroom teachers and researchers to consider. Students could select from these options when responding to each question:

1 Strongly disagree
2 Disagree
3 Neither agree or disagree
4 Agree
5 Strongly agree

The "neither agree or disagree" option could mean that students were neutral or that for the most part they did not relate to the survey statement.

Before launching into the information gathered from the surveys, I have included, in the box on page 293, an explanation of terms that I will use when sharing the results.

Survey Findings on Students' Writing Attitudes and Behaviors

Two and three asterisks mean that its highly unlikely that chance had anything to do with the results. Three asterisks are even more unlikely than two.

I will present the findings based on the statistical analysis of responses to the surveys statements by specific categories. Categories contain groups of related survey statements. Each category used 1324 valid cases—those who identified their gender with the exception of Table 1.4 on page 297.

Writing Outside of School

The survey found that nine out of ten students report engaging in some type of writing outside of class. Table 1.1 lists the kinds of writing students indicated they do. The chart shows the percent of students who write outside of school

Terms that Can Support Your Understanding of the Statistical Analysis

If you're like me, you do not have a strong background in statistics. Moreover, since data gathered from the surveys can be used to reimagine middle school writing curricula, an understanding of the statistical terminology is necessary to gain a deeper understanding of the data and inferences that emerge from it.

Variables: In this case, the variables are each one of the thirty-four survey statements.

Correlations: A statistical technique that tells you how much the responses collected from one item relate to another or how strongly pairs of variables (answers to statements) are related.

Correlation Coefficient Reported as "r": This is the main result of a correlation or how closely scores cluster around an expected value. It ranges from −1.0 to 1.0. The closer "r" is to −1 or +1 the more the two variables (statements) are related.

Sometime statisticians square the coefficient "r" because squaring makes it easier to understand. So if r = .2 and we square "r" so that r = .4, meaning that 4 percent of the variation in one variable (statement) is related to the variation in another variable (statement).

Probability Value: Called p values when reporting statistical significance of data. Reported as p < .01. What this p value means is that there is less than 1 percent that chance alone was the cause for the correlation. When probability values are low, research consider them statistically significant. The lower the p value the greater the statistical significance, and the less likely that correlations are simply by chance.

by the type of writing in the survey statements. Percentages are for all students, males and females, and grade levels. It's interesting to note that 89.4 percent of students who responded indicate that they do at least one type of writing on the list. The percentage drops to 47.0 percent for students who do three or more of the types of writing listed. There is a significant difference between males and females who do three or more types of writing (37.2 percentage points), and less of a difference (12.5 percentage points) between males and females who do at least one type of writing.

Writing Outside of School
% of students who write outside of class by type of writing
       (agree or strongly agree to . . .)

	% of All Students	5th	6th	7th	8th	9th		Males	Females	
Writing in a journal (Q1)	30.5%	38.5	28.9	25.6	31.0	25.4	**	16.9	46.3	***
Respond to blogs	24.1%	18.6	21.6	30.7	24.7	22.5	**	22.6	26.5	NS
Write stories	37.3%	45.2	43.0	34.4	27.9	33.8	***	29.2	46.8	***
Write poems	22.4%	19.7	23.0	22.2	23.3	27.1	NS	11.5	33.9	***
Write email to friends	62.1%	45.0	61.2	72.1	69.1	52.1	***	55.3	71.2	***
Text friends	63.2%	43.6	58.1	75.4	71.9	66.2	***	57.5	69.1	***
Write letters	36.2%	39.0	38.6	34.5	35.5	22.5	NS	25.0	49.8	***
Do at least one of the above	**89.4%**	**83.6**	**89.5**	**93.2**	**92.0**	**85.9**	***	**84.1**	**96.6**	***
Do 3 or more of the above	**47.0%**	**44.6**	**47.4**	**46.8**	**50.7**	**40.8**	NS	**29.7**	**66.9**	***

Nine out of ten students engage in some type of writing outside of class.

Table 1.1 Writing Outside of School

Seven out of ten students who do some writing outside of school do not believe that the majority of their teachers know about this. Of the students who do three or more types of writing outside of school, 47.0 percent are more likely to agree that their teachers know about this out-of-school writing.

The survey's results indicate that students are more likely to write outside of school if they have one teacher who encourages them to write. Of the students who engaged in none of the different kinds of writing, 52.6 percent said that they had at least one teacher who encouraged them to write. More than 70 percent of students who do three or more kinds of outside-of-school writing are more likely to agree with the survey statement that there is at least one teacher who encourages them to write; the percentage drops to 62 percent for students who do zero to two kinds of writing.

Writing in Journals

The "Strongly agree" and "Agree" responses to the survey statement "I enjoy writing in a journal outside of school" were used as an indicator that students do write in a journal, and "Neither agree or disagree," "Disagree," and "Strongly disagree" as the indicator that students do NOT write in a journal outside of school. Table 1.2 presents percentages for grade levels, males and females, and students' responses for each statement. The "n" on the chart lists the number of students who answered each statement.

Among students who write in journals 57.6 percent report that they write about their feelings, 71.5 percent report writing about experiences, and 76.2 percent report that journaling helps them think about their lives. Note too that more students above grade 5 write about their feelings in journals.

In Table 1.2, females who write in journals are more likely to report writing about their feelings (67.3 percent) than males (30.3 percent). Males (67.2 percent) and

Writing in a journal (Q1)	% of All Students 30.5%	5th 38.5	6th 28.9	7th 25.6	8th 31.0	9th 25.4 **		Males 16.9	Females 46.3 ***
		SA	A	Neither	D	SD		n	
>Q1< 1. I enjoy writing in a journal outside of school.		9.4%	21.1%	25.3%	20.4%	23.8%		1,493	
>Q2< 2. In my journal, I write about my feelings.		11.1%	18.0%	20.0%	19.7%	31.1%		1,487	
>Q3< 3. In my journal, I write about my experiences.		17.8%	31.0%	20.0%	13.0%	18.2%		1,481	
>Q4< 4. Writing in my journal helps me think about my life.		16.3%	24.3%	21.6%	15.1%	22.8%		1,487	

Table 1.2 Writing in a Journal

females (73.2 percent) are equally likely to write about their experiences in journals. Males and females who report that writing in journals helps them think about their lives are statistically equally likely to agree and strongly agree (70.2 percent vs. 74.9 percent respectively).

Based on the clusters of correlations, there appears to be two groups of students: those who write in journals also tend to write stories, poems, and letters; those who respond to blogs are more likely to text and email friends; and students who email friends are more likely to text.

Teachers and Writing

Table 1.3 shows the percentages of the students' responses to the six statements that relate to teachers and writing for all students, grade levels, and males and females.

Only 8.7 percent of students surveyed agreed that their teachers knew about their outside-of-school writing; 71.0 percent disagreed (see Table 1.3). Responses between males and females to these statements showed no *significant differences*. Females who responded were more likely to agree or strongly agree (67.6 percent) than males (60.0 percent) that they had a trusting relationship with a teacher (p < .01). More than half of

Teachers and Writing.

% of students who . . .
    (agree or strongly agree to . . .)

	% of All Students	5th	6th	7th	8th	9th		Males	Females	
Teachers know about my writing outside school	8.7%	10.7	8.5	7.0	10.4	2.8	*	8.1	10.0	*
At least 1 teacher encourages to write	67.0%	68.4	73.0	68.2	59.3	60.6	***	68.7	67.0	NS
A trusting relationship with at least 1 teacher	62.7%	68.1	63.9	63.5	58.3	49.3	***	59.9	67.6	**
Find writing at school positive experience	48.7%	48.9	55.2	48.0	41.7	49.3	***	43.4	54.3	***
Writing at school is relevant to own life	35.9%	36.5	38.5	35.1	32.6	39.4	N.S.	31.2	40.5	***
Teacher tries to find out what help needed as a writer	61.6%	57.3	63.5	67.8	57.5	56.3	**	61.5	61.8	*

Table 1.3 Teachers and Writing

female students (54.2 percent) compared to 43.4 percent of male students agreed that writing at school was a positive experience (p < .001).

Nearly half of the students surveyed (48.6 percent) agreed that they find writing at school a positive experience. More than half of the females (54.2 percent) compared to 43.4 percent of male students agreed that they find writing at school to be a positive experience (p < .001).

The strength of the agreement or disagreement was correlated with the number of different kinds of writing students do outside of school. Students who more strongly agreed that writing at school is a positive experience also tended to engage in more types of outside-of-school writing. Students' responses raise these questions: Do students enjoy writing at school because they are writing at home? Or, is it the teacher who is making writing at school a positive experience?

Table 1.4 shows the correlations between statements 11, 12, 13, 14, 15, and 22 on the survey. On the table a double asterisk (**) means that the correlation is significant at the .01 level. "N" equals the number of students who responded to both statements. Pearson's represents the correlation coefficient between responses to the two statements. According to the chart, all the correlations are significant but some are stronger than others.

Based on the regression analysis, the most powerful predictor variables regarding the number of different kinds of writing students do outside of school are

> Writing at school is relevant to my life; and
>
> I find writing at school is a positive experience.

So, even though the survey doesn't directly speak to this conclusion, I believe that it's possible to infer that relevance of topic to a student's life is a key factor in engaging and motivating students in writing tasks at school and encouraging students to write outside of school.

Writing at School

Students' responses indicated that there is an association between the kind of writing students do at school and their feelings about writing. Students who said they usually have a choice of topic when they write at school were much more likely to agree that writing at school is relevant to their lives (45.9 percent vs. 29.1 percent) (p < .001).

The correlation table (Table 1.5) shows correlations between statements 19, 22, 23, 24, 27, 12, 14, and 15 on the student survey. Strongly correlated to finding writing at school a positive experience is writing being relevant to students' lives (r = .549). Other

Correlations		Q11 11. My teachers know about the writing I do outside of school.	Q12 12. There's at least one teacher at my school who encourages me to write.	Q13 13. I have a trusting relationship with at least one teacher at my school.	Q14 14. I find writing at school a positive experience.	Q15 15. Writing at school is relevant to my life.	Q22 22. My teacher tries to find out what kind of help I need as a writer.
Q11 11. My teachers know about the writing I do outside of school.	Pearson r	1	.234**	.151**	.233**	.245**	.157**
	Sig. (2-tailed)		.000	.000	.000	.000	.000
	N	1477	1474	1470	1474	1473	1452
Q12 12. There's at least one teacher at my school who encourages me to write.	Pearson r	.234**	1	.358**	.310**	.264**	.307**
	Sig. (2-tailed)	.000		.000	.000	.000	.000
	N	1474	1493	1486	1489	1487	1468
Q13 13. I have a trusting relationship with at least one teacher at my school.	Pearson r	.151**	.358**	1	.340**	.282**	.225**
	Sig. (2-tailed)	.000	.000		.000	.000	.000
	N	1470	1486	1489	1486	1484	1465
Q14 14. I find writing at school a positive experience.	Pearson r	.233**	.310**	.340**	1	.549**	.249**
	Sig. (2-tailed)	.000	.000	.000		.000	.000
	N	1474	1489	1486	1492	1489	1468
Q15 15. Writing at school is relevant to my life.	Pearson r	.245**	.264**	.282**	.549**	1	.224**
	Sig. (2-tailed)	.000	.000	.000	.000		.000
	N	1473	1487	1484	1489	1490	1466
Q22 22. My teacher tries to find out what kind of help I need as a writer.	Pearson r	.157**	.307**	.225**	.249**	.224**	1
	Sig. (2-tailed)	.000	.000	.000	.000	.000	
	N	1452	1468	1465	1468	1466	1471

**. Correlation is significant at the 0.01 level (2-tailed).

Table 1.4 Correlations Between Some Survey Questions

strong correlations are between students' perceptions of themselves as good writers and writing as a positive experience ($r = .416$).

The correlations from Table 1.5 shape my thinking about middle school writing. Look at the correlations for Number 22: "My teacher tries to find out what kind of help I need as a writer." This statement strongly correlates with every other statement on the chart.

Use of Computer or Writing by Hand

Results based on the three statements in the survey that address using a computer for writing or writing by hand have little relationship to whether a student enjoys writing or how students view themselves as writers. Table 1.6, which has the data for using a computer or writing by hand, shows that among students surveyed, 37.6 percent state that

Correlations

	Amount student has control over writing (+ has control, - imposed)	Q19. Our class uses computers for writing projects at school.	Q22. My teacher tries to find out what kind of help I need as a writer.	Q23. I write every day at school.	Q24. I revise writing at school.	Q27. I see myself as a good writer.	Q12. There's at least one teacher at my school who encourages me to write.	Q13. I have a trusting relationship with at least one teacher at my school.	Q14. I find writing at school a positive experience.	Q15. Writing at school is relevant to my life.
Amount student has control over writing (+ has control, - imposed)	1	-.057*	.079**	.008	-.020	-.014	.070**	.030	.076**	.018
Q19. Our class uses computers for writing projects at school.	-.057*	1	.171**	.043	.145**	.081**	.168**	.113**	.119**	.074**
Q22. My teacher tries to find out what kind of help I need as a writer.	.079**	.171**	1	.175**	.290**	.168**	.307**	.225**	.249**	.224**
Q23. I write every day at school.	.008	.043	.175**	1	.218**	.130**	.138**	.080**	.192**	.205**
Q24. I revise writing at school.	-.020	.145**	.290**	.218**	1	.226**	.240**	.233**	.278**	.297**
Q27. I see myself as a good writer.	-.014	.081**	.168**	.130**	.226**	1	.204**	.229**	.416**	.359**
Q12. There's at least one teacher at my school who encourages me to write.	.070**	.168**	.307**	.138**	.240**	.204**	1	.358**	.310**	.264**
Q13. I have a trusting relationship with at least one teacher at my school.	.030	.113**	.225**	.080**	.233**	.229**	.358**	1	.340**	.282**
Q14. I find writing at school a positive experience.	.076**	.119**	.249**	.192**	.278**	.416**	.310**	.340**	1	.549**
Q15. Writing at school is relevant to my life.	.018	.074**	.224**	.205**	.297**	.359**	.264**	.282**	.549**	1

Table 1.5 More Correlations Between Some Survey Questions

The Three Survey Statements

Our class uses computers for writing projects at school.

Our class does all writing by hand.

At home I always write on a computer.

they use computers for at-school writing projects, 39.6 percent of the students reported they do all writing by hand at school, and 41.6 percent state that when writing at home, they always use a computer. Students' reporting about their use of computers at school might be affected by the fact that some schools have a few computers, and others that do have a computer room might not have enough dollars to maintain the computers.

After controlling the data for differences among states, across grade levels, and between males and females, the chart shows that from grades 5 to 8, use of computers tends to increase while writing by hand tends to decrease. In the classroom setting, there are no significant differences between males and females regarding writing on a computer or writing at home (see Table 1.6).

% of students who . . . (agree or strongly agree to . . .)	% of All Students	5th	6th	7th	8th	9th	Males	Females
Our class uses computers for writing projects at school	37.6	26.0	34.0	52.0	37.5	31.4***	37.3	38.8
Our class does all writing by hand	39.6	55.9	37.6	33.1	34.9	38.0***	37.8	41.1
At home I always write on a computer	41.6	35.1	42.0	48.3	40.1	38.6*	40.2	44.0*

Table 1.6 Writing on Computers or By Hand

Four Survey Statements About Blogging

I respond to blogs outside of school.

I blog with classmates about books we read.

I blog with classmates about important questions my classmates write.

I blog with classmates about questions the teacher gives us.

However, girls (44.0 percent) were slightly more likely to use a computer at home for writing than boys (40.2 percent).

Blogging

Four questions about blogging were part of the survey (see box above). The survey data shows that there are no significant gender differences across grade levels as to whether students blog at all. The survey indicates that 51.8 percent of students do no blogging while 48.2 percent engage in at least one kind of blogging.

Blogging is a great teaching and learning tool, as I discussed in Chapter 9. The advantage of having a class blog is that students can read one another's journal work or book reviews. In addition, blogging about a question allows students to have a written conversation with all of their classmates.

Writing About Books

Statements 29 and 30 address writing about reading:

29. I write about the books I read.

30. I write about the books my teacher reads aloud.

Question 29 could mean writing about books in a journal, book review, or essay. The question is too open-ended, so the survey does not reveal which kinds of writing about books students do. However, the survey does reflect that more students write about the books they read themselves (34.7 percent) than books their teacher reads aloud (20.5 percent). There was no significant difference across grade levels for either question. On both items, middle school girls (60 percent) agreed or strongly agreed that they write about books more than boys (49.3 percent).

Writing about reading is another aspect of the writing curriculum. It can include journaling about books, book reviews, and analytical essays. I believe that if the same person teaches reading and writing, it is more likely that writing about books will be integrated into the workshop.

The Role and Influence of the Teacher on Middle School Writers

From the analysis, it's possible to infer that teachers can and do make a difference in their students' writing lives. Having a trusting relationship with at least one teacher at school correlates strongly with questions 12, 14, 15, and 22 (see table on page 297). So what kind of a teacher helps students enjoy writing at school, makes the writing relevant, and tries to help students improve their writing? As I read the survey statistics, I believe that writing teacher is nurturing and emphasizes process; presents craft, technique, revision, and editing lessons; and sets aside time to scaffold writing lessons for those who need them.

Appendix A

Katherine Paterson's Writing Plans for *Bridge to Terabithia*

Invite students to read the novelist's plan and compare the length of pages and chapters on the plan to the published book. Help students understand that a plan is a road map and that often, like drivers, writers take detours and adjust their plans. Ask students, "What do you notice about this plan?" Discuss their observations and how they apply to planning a narrative.

96 pages

Chapter one: introduce Aaron —
Family
School   he can run faster than anyone
loneliness
   only bright light is music teacher
   who comes twice a week.
   special relationship — gives
   his drawings
Father commutes to Washington — no more
wrestling on the floor   too tired —
Chapter two
Leslie moves to next farm —
She can run faster than Aaron
   Bad situation in which he feels
      threatened —
Also Leslie + music teacher
      strike immediate friendship —

Chapter three
   Leslie + Aaron begin to be friends

Chapter four
Leslie + Aaron's friendship deepens —
whole new life for him —

Chapter five —
Their friendship against rural
   society
   family objections
   school — teasing —
Music teacher teaches
   class "Free to be you + me"

Chapter six
   which
   Leslie is killed — goes to Washington to see the gallery with

Hey, Aaron your girlfriend's dead!"

Chapter seven —
   Aaron's grief + disbelief
   taunting at school
   "God's will" at home
Chapter eight

Leslie the Great, Great, Great

There is a green meadow behind the junior high, or at ~~one~~ least the start of one. turns from green to red ~~and on the~~ ~~took~~ side on the far side. And near its The people you ~~Boal~~ use the ~~alley~~ side for come because it is out of sight of the ~~town~~ road. It's the kind of place ~~people~~ bratty citizens are always referring to in casual meetings. as a "municipal disgrace." But if you are ~~right~~ eight and lonely as David was it becomes a "secret place ~~and the~~ ~~just such old~~
David's
Hts family moved to Brenton last in August

Leslie the Great, Great, Great

Characters —
Aaron third child in large
country family — (Lovettsville)
artistic, always drawing or reading
only reason he has any friends
in country school is because
he can run faster than anyone
in the third grade (maybe fourth)
willing to fight —
family worn down by fighting out
living from farm — father commutes
to Wash. in Pick-up truck &
janitorial job — Mother too

Appendix B

Jean Van Leeuwen's Writing Plans for *Cabin on Trouble Creek*

These writing plans illustrate the thinking process that many writers experience. Ask students, "What do you notice?" Then, discuss their observations and help them apply what they've studied to their own planning process.

Sunfish Creek
Logan - Indian - Dooley-Doogan   Dailey
Big Turtle
Soloman
Buckwheat

Daniel - Jacob - Eli - Will

Tell Bible stories as remember them
     Make up variations - Indian
D. learns story about Mad Mary at mill

Daniel - older one - 12-13. He is serious, tall, strong,
     quiet, thoughtful, reliable. Thinks like father.
Will - younger - 10-11 Talkative, impulsive, scared,
     sometimes does foolish things. Wants to show how
     capable, brave, etc. he is.
Father - quiet, religious man. Reliable, capable. Doesn't
     compliment sons, but expects a lot from them.
Mother - (in memory of D.) warm, good cook, somewhat
     sickly. Has 4 more younger kids - baby
Indian - straight & tall, mysterious, comes & goes, like a
     phantom or animal of frost. Wise, gives advice in
     mysterious ways. Leaves D. to figure it out.

Chap. 14

Big snow goes on for 2 days. Snow comes into cabin, cold wind. D. feels alone, scared. Trapped. Tells stories 2nd night, around fire.

Chap. 15.

Next morning bright sky. Deep snow. Can't go out. Have to stay in for 3 days. Work on hat, carving, snow shoes (mits) Tell more stories.

Ch. 16   February

D. realizes he is 12. Snares empty, reset. Don't catch anything. Think about fishing – Night. Wolves, deer.

Ch. 17

(Holidays?)   deer hide, Snow

Ch. 18 – March

Turkey trap. Warming weather. Snow melts. India appears.

Ch. 19

Solomon stays few days. Shows them where to find edible plants, medicine, make fish trap, arrowhead for spear. Leaves again.

20 – April – spring (D. thinks cold arrives if left at first spring doesn't tell Will)
Look for Pa again, still doesn't come. Tell about clearing + planting. Start learning to use axe. leave I don't know more

Begin – overnight – all green trees spring

21 – Go out to look for plants, encounter bear. (Will doesn't stay w. D. wanders off – calls to D.) Spear. W. saves D. but again

22. - D's recuperation. W. tells stories. Gets back that Sloan told them about to reduce infection. Make things of bark. W. does everything. Cooks green. (Bear - not dead but gone)

23. - Gradually D. able to get around. Start chopping trees again. Make clearing. Bee tree? Ready to go to horse mill for seed corn. count down # of trees to go. 5.4.3 -- If only Pa were here to help - D. calculates time

24. -

Prepare to go to horse mill. They are about to set off when hear a shout outside. Look out + see little brother, followed by rest of family. Pa doesn't look the same. Shrunk. Ma looks ok. Rest are bigger. (Dog.) Tell story of why delayed. Took Ma to Bedtime, family. Then Pa got sick (or injured?).

Outline

Chap. 1 — August

① Boys + Father arrive, carrying tools, few cooking implements on horse. ② Build lean-to + live in it while building cabin. ③

Get it to a point where can live in it, but not finished.

Chap. 2 - September

④ Father leaves to go back to PA to bring rest of family. Will return in about a month. Boys start working on cabin — daubing for winter, etc. ⑤ 5 gns of free in air. Nuts + berries. Daily routine. Nervous about wolves, Indians, etc. Anxiously watch for father's return w. family. ⑥ Fishing, bear

(margin left: Cut small trees for ?)
(talk about chin, floor.)
(Fish, mal)

Chap. 3 - October

⑦ Begin rustle of falling leaves

More anxiety. Food running low, cold night. Boys chop wood, gather nuts, get lost in woods. but unsuccessful.

(Finish chinking. Father won't come.)
(Fell walnuts)
(When gets back, fire is out. Have to use threads of shirt to get started again.)
(go to gather nuts fodder)
(w. gets father—D)

Chap. 4 - November

⑨ ⑩ Meet Indian. He teaches them about trapping, using materials of woods. Also to keep warm. (Will's shoes are nearly gone. ⑪ ⑫ Winter preparations — coats

(margin left: No Pa the Feel wolves gift of moccasins)
(from the trees)

Chap. 5 - December

Afraid that Father not coming. Have to be on their own.

⑫ Daniel makes trip to mill to get cornmeal. Follows Indian path. Talks to miller. Hears stories. Returns w. enough meal for winter. gift for ...

(Mal'nvry, hawk in tree)
(Snow beginning)
(moccasins)

(margin left: Thomas Cabron John Hutchin Sam Cook)

Chap. 6 - January

⑬ Snow. Hard to catch game. Try to keep warm as storms continue. D. learns to make things of wood. Tell stories to each other to pass time. ⑮ W — Snow shoes

(chinking falls out)
(rabbit skins)
(big storm-18")
(stop rabbit mouse ???)
(trap turkey birthday)

(margin left: ⑭ hunter Daughter)

Chap. 7 - February

⑯ Harsher weather continues. One night hear ruckus outside.

In morning discover part of deer killed by wolves. Drag to cabin +
skin it (17) Save hide, door? Prepare for clothing. Now can get
through winter on food they have.

Chap. 8 - March

(18) Signs of spring. Can trap again as snow melts. Indian

(19) appears again. Shows them where edible greens grow. Teaches
them to make trap finish. Disappears ag—. arrowhead for spear

Chap. 9 - April   leaves on trees again

(20) Looking for father still doesn't come. But now boys
are confident. D. makes table, canoe whittle. Talk about clearing + planting. Go out
(21) to check traps + encounter bear. Narrow escape. Dying? W. takes use spear
look for plants   care of —. D. injured —

Chap. 10 - May

(22) Learn to use axe, cut down small trees + girdle
(23) larger ones. Gradually make a clearing in which to
plant.

Chap. 11 - June

(24) D. is about to go to mill again when family arrives.

Ohio Story

Start w. journey w. father from Philadelphia

Then building of camp

Cutting trees to build cabin — not finished but will finish later

+ father leaves to get rest of family -- leaving enough food for boys

They wait for his return - 1 month

He does 't come

Run out of food, getting cold, no warm clothing, shoes

Fear — wolves, bear, Indians

No gun, just axe + knives

  Tries to catch animals — not successful
    Tries to daub cabin — falls out
Encounter w. Indian — moccasins, talk of hunting

  Lost in woods ~~Finds~~
  wolf — deer
Trip to get meal —

  getting through winter — surely F. will come in Spring
He doesn't. Learn to trap rabbits
Encounter w. bear
Boys stronger. Decide to clear for planting
Learn to cut trees
Indian teaches th to get food (fish? nuts? ~~track to make snares~~)
  June — family arrives

jack-knife - make tools
Winter nights - read or tell stories - Bible?

          Daniel
Boys' names - Josiah, Will

Chaps - 11 months? Aug, Sept. Oct. Nov. Dec. Jan. Feb. March, April, May, June

     summer —
Food - fall - berries
     late fall - nuts, fish
     winter - deer meat (when desperate), rabbits
     spring - more animals to hunt, trap

Works Cited

Professional Materials

Allington, R. L. 2002. "What I've Learned About Effective Reading Instruction." *Phi Delta Kappan* 83 (10): 740–47.

Allington, R. L., and P. M. Cunningham. 2002. *Schools that Work: Where All Children Read and Write.* 2d ed. Boston: Allyn and Bacon.

Allison, B. N., and M. L. Rehm. 2007. "Effective Teaching Strategies for Middle School Learners in Multicultural, Multilingual Classrooms." *Middle School Journal* 39 (2): 12–18.

Allison, N. 2009. *Middle School Readers: Helping Them Read Widely, Helping Them Read Well.* Portsmouth, NH: Heinemann.

Anderson, C. 2000. *How's It Going? A Practical Guide to Conferring with Student Writers.* Portsmouth, NH: Heinemann.

———. 2009. *Strategic Writing Conferences.* Portsmouth, NH: firsthand.

Alphonso, C. 2006. Texting helps teens grammar. At http://theglober and mail.com/servet/story/LAC.20060801.TEST01/TPStory/TPNationalOntario.

Barth, R. 1991. "Restructuring Schools: Some Questions for Teachers and Principals." *Phi Delta Kappan* 73 (2): 123–29.

Baumann, J. F., and J. J. Bason. 2004. "Survey Research." In *Literacy Research*, edited by N. K. Duke and M. H. Mallette, 287–307. New York: Guilford.

Boscolo, P., and C. Gelati. 2007. "Best Practices in Promoting Motivation to Write." In *Best Practices in Writing Instruction*, edited by S. Graham, C. A. MacArthur, and J. Fitzgerald. New York: Guilford Press.

Buckner, A. 2005. *Notebook Know-How: Strategies for the Writer's Notebook.* York, ME: Stenhouse.

Calkins, L. M. 1994. *The Art of Teaching Writing.* Portsmouth, NH: Heinemann.

Coker, D., and W. L. Lewis. 2008. "Beyond Writing Next: A Discussion of Writing Research and Instructional Uncertainty." *Harvard Educational Review,* 231–51.

Cramer, R. L. 2004. *The Language Arts: A Balanced Approach to Teaching Reading, Writing, Listening, Talking, and Thinking.* Boston: Allyn and Bacon.

Deshler, D. D., A. S. Palinscar, G. Biancarosa, and M. Nair. 2007. *Informed Choices for Struggling Adolescent Readers: A Research-Based Guide to Instructional Programs and Practices.* Newark, DE and New York: International Reading Association and The Carnegie Corporation.

Dillon, D. R., and E. B. Moje. 1997. "Listening to the Talk of Adolescent Girls: Lessons About Literacy, School, and Lives." In *Reconceptualizing the Literacies in Adolescents' Lives,* edited by D. E. Alvermann, K. A. Hinchman, S. F. Phelps, and D. R. Waff, 193–224. Mahwah, NJ: Erlbaum.

Dufour, R., and R. Eaker. 1998. *Professional Learning Communities at Work: Best Practices for Enhancing Student Achievement.* Bloomington, IN: National Education Service.

Dyson, A. H. 1989. *Multiple Worlds of Child Writers: Friends Learning to Write.* New York: Teachers College Press.

Eaker, R., R. Dufour, and R. Burnette. 2002. *Getting Started: Reculturing Schools to Become Professional Learning Communities.* Bloomington, IN: National Educational Service.

Elbow, P. 1981.*Writing with Power: Techniques for Mastering the Writing Process.* New York: Oxford University Press.

Ehrenriech, B. 2001. *Nickel and Dimed: On (Not) Getting By in America.* New York: Metropolitan Books.

Elementary and Secondary Education Act. 2008. *Common Core State Standards Initiative,* Washington, DC.

Fisher, D., and N. Frey. 2007. "A Tale of Two Middle Schools: The Difference in Structure and Instruction." *Journal of Adolescent and Adult Literacy* 51 (3): 204–13.

Flanagan, A. 2008. "The Role of Research in Improving Adolescent Literacy." *NCTE's Council Chronicle* 17 (3): 6–9.

Fletcher, R. 1996. *A Writer's Notebook: Unlocking the Writer Within You.* New York: HarperCollins.

Gainer, J. 2008. "Who Is Deandre? Tapping the Power of Popular Culture in Literacy Learning." *Voices from the Middle.* Urbana, IL: National Council of Teachers of English.

Gardner, H. 2007. *Five Minds for the Future.* Boston: Harvard Business School Press.

Graham. S., and K. R. Harris. 2005. *Writing Better: Effective Strategies for Teaching Students with Learning Difficulties.* Baltimore, MD: Brookes Publishing.

———. 2007. "Best Practices in Teaching Planning." In *Best Practices in Writing Instruction,* edited by S. Graham, C. A. MacArthur, and J. Fitzgerald. New York: Guilford Press.

Graham, S., and D. Perin. 2007a. *Writing Next: Effective Strategies to Improve the Writing of Adolescents in Middle and High Schools.* Washington, DC: Alliance for Excellent Education.

———. 2007b. "What We Know, What We Still Need to Know: Teaching Adolescents to Write." *Scientific Studies of Reading* 11: 313–35.

Graves, D. H. 2003. *Writing: Teachers and Children at Work.* 20th Anniversary ed. Portsmouth, NH: Heinemann.

Hansen, J. 2008. "'The Way They Act Around a Bunch of People': Seventh-Grade Writers Learn About Themselves in the Midst of Others." *Voices from the Middle.* Urbana, IL: National Council of Teachers of English.

Jackson, A. W., and G. A. Davis. 2000. *Turning Points 2000: Educating Adolescents in the 21st Century.* New York and Westerville, OH: Teachers College Press and National Middle School Association.

Klassen, R. M., and C. Welton. 2009. "Self-Efficacy and Procrastination in the Writing of Students with Learning Disabilities." In *Instruction and Assessment for Struggling Writers: Evidence-Based Practices*, edited by G. A. Troia. New York: Guilford.

Lamott, A. 1994. *Bird by Bird.* New York: Anchor Books.

Lawrence, M. 2007. "Students as Scientists: Synthesizing Standards-Based with Student-Appropriate Instruction." *Middle School Journal* 38 (4): 30–37.

Lieberman, A., and L. Miller. 2008. *Teachers in Professional Communities: Improving Teaching and Learning.* New York: Teachers College Press.

Marzano, R. 2003. *What Works in Schools: Translating Research into Action.* Alexandria, VA: ASCD.

McTighe, J., E. Seif, and G. Wiggins. 2004. "You Can Teach for Meaning." *Phi Delta Kappan* 62 (1): 26–31.

Michener, J. 1993. *Literary Reflections: Michener on Michener, Hemingway, Capote and Others.* New York: State House Press.

Moffett, J., and B. J. Wagner. 1983. *Student-Centered Language Arts and Reading, K–13: A Handbook for Teachers.* Boston: Houghton Mifflin.

Moje, E. B. 2000. *All The Stories that We Have: Adolescents' Insights About Literacy and Learning in Secondary Schools.* Newark, DE: International Reading Association.

Murray, D. 1982. *Learning by Teaching.* Portsmouth, NH: Boynton Cook.

———. 1984. *Write to Learn.* New York: Holt, Rinehart and Winston.

———. 2009. *Holding on to Good Ideas in a Time of Bad Ones: Six Literacy Principals Worth Fighting For.* Portsmouth, NH: Heinemann.

National Commission on Writing. 2004. "Writing: A Ticket to Work . . . or a Ticket Out: A Survey of Business Leaders." Retrieved from www.writingcommission.org/report.html.

———. 2005. Writing: A Powerful Message from State Government. Retrieved from www.writingcommission.org/report.html.

National Council of Teachers of English. 2008. "Writing Now: What Is Writing in the 21st Century?" *Council Chronicle* 18 (1): 15–22.

National Middle School Association. 2003. *This We Believe: Successful Schools for Young Adolescents.* Westerville, OH: National Middle School Association.

Newkirk, T. 2002. *Misreading Masculinity: Boys, Literacy, and Popular Culture.* Portsmouth, NH: Heinemann.

Noden, H. R. 1999. *Image Grammar.* Portsmouth, NH: Heinemann.

Perin, D. 2009. "Best Practices in Teaching Writing to Adolescents." In *Best Practices in Writing Instruction,* edited by S. Graham, C. A. MacArthur, and J. Fitzgerald, 242–64. New York: Guilford Press.

Persky, H. R., M. C. Daane, and Y. Jin. 2003. *The Nation's Report Card: Writing 2002, MCES 2003.* Washington, DC: Center for Educational Statistics.

Pink, D. H. 2005. *A Whole New Mind: Why Right-Brainers Will Rule the Future.* New York: Riverhead Press.

Pinker, S. 1994. *The Language Instinct: How the Mind Creates Language*. New York: William Morrow and Co.

Plester, B. 2006. Research on textisms presented at the British Psychological Society's Developmental Section Annual Conference at the Royal Holloway, University of London. See http://www.coventry.ac.uk/latestnewsandevents/a/2341.

Rief, L. 2003. *100 Quickwrites*. New York: Scholastic.

————. 2007. "Wiring: Common Sense Matters." In *Adolescent Literacy: Turning Promise into Practice*, edited by K. Beers, R. F. Probst, and L. Rief. Portsmouth, NH: Heinemann.

Robb, L. 2001. *Grammar Lessons and Strategies that Strengthen Students' Writing*. New York: Scholastic.

————. 2004. *Nonfiction Writing from the Inside Out*. New York: Scholastic.

————. 2008. *Differentiating Reading Instruction: How to Teach Reading to Meet the Needs of Each Student*. New York: Scholastic.

Rosenblatt, L. 1938. *Literature as Exploration*. 4th ed. New York: The Modern Language Association of America.

————. 1978. *The Reader, the Text, the Poem: The Transactional Theory of the Literary Work*. Carbondale, IL: Southern Illinois University.

Routman, R. 1999. *Conversations: Strategies for Teaching, Learning, and Evaluating*. Portsmouth, NH: Heinemann.

Schunk, D. H., and B. J. Zimmermann. 1997. "Developing Self-Efficacious Readers and Writers: The Role of Social and Self-Regulatory Processes." In *Reading Engagement: Motivating Readers Through Integrated Instruction*, edited by J. T. Guthrie and A. Wigfield, 34–47. Newark, DE: International Reading Association.

Shanahan, T. 2009. "Connecting Reading and Writing Instruction for Struggling Learners." In *Instruction and Assessment for Struggling Writers: Evidence-Based Practices*, edited by G. A. Troia. New York: Guilford.

Tomlinson, C. A. 1999. *The Differentiated Classroom: Responding to the Needs of All Learners*. Alexandria, VA: ASCD.

————. 2008. "The Goals of Differentiation." *Educational Leadership* 66 (3): 26–30.

Troia, G. A., and S. Graham. 2002. "The Effectiveness of a Highly Explicit, Teacher-Directed Strategy Instruction Routine: Changing the Writing Performance of Students with Learning Disabilities." *Journal of Learning Disabilities* 35: 290–305.

Troia, G. A., S. C. Lin, B. W. Monroe, and S. Cohen. 2009. "The Effects of Writing Workshop Instruction on Performance and Motivations of Good and Poor Writers." In *Instruction and Assessment for Struggling Writers: Evidence-Based Practices*, edited by G. A. Troia, 77–112. New York: Guilford.

Van Hoose, J., and D. Strahan. 1988. *Young Adolescent Development and School Practices: Promoting Harmony*. Columbus, OH: National Middle School Association.

Vokoun, M. J., and T. P. Bigelow. 2008. "Dude, What Choice Do I Have?" *Educational Leadership* 66 (3): 70–74.

Vygotsky, L. S. 1978. *Mind in Society: The Development of Higher Psychological Processes.* Cambridge, MA: Harvard University Press.

Weaver, C. 1998. *Teaching Grammar in the Context of Writing.* Portsmouth, NH: Boynton/Cook.

Wilhelm, J. D. 2002. *Action Strategies for Deepening Comprehension: Role Plays, Text Structure Tableaus, Talking Statues, and Other Enrichment Techniques that Engage Students with Text.* New York: Scholastic.

———. 2007. *Engaging Readers and Writers with Inquiry: Promoting Deep Understandings in Language Arts and the Content Areas with Guiding Questions.* New York: Scholastic.

Wilhelm, J. D., and M. W. Smith. 2007a. "Making It Matter Through the Power of Inquiry." In *Adolescent Literacy: Turning Promise into Practice*, edited by K. Beers, R. F. Probst, and L. Rief, 231–42. Portsmouth, NH: Heinemann.

Willis, J. 2007. "Cooperative Learning Is a Brain Turn-On." *Middle School Journal* 38 (4): 4–13.

Wormeli, R. 2007. *Differentiation: From Planning to Practices, Grades 6–12.* York, ME: Stenhouse.

Zinsser, W. 1988. *Writing to Learn.* New York: Harper & Row.

———. 1998. *Writing About Your Life: A Journey into the Past.* New York, Marlowe & Co.

———. 2001. *On Writing Well: The Classic Guide to Writing Nonfiction.* New York: Quill.

Literature Cited

Adler, D. A. 2007. *Satchel Paige, Don't Look Back.* Illus. Terry Widener. New York: Harcourt.

Anderson, L. H. 1999. *Speak.* New York: Penguin/Putnam.

———. 2009. *Wintergirls.* New York: Viking.

Avi. 2010. *Nothing but the Truth.* New York: Scholastic.

Barron, T. A. 2007. *The Day the Stones Walked.* Illus. by William Low. New York: Philomel.

Baum, F. L. 2000. *The Wonderful Wizard of Oz.* New York: HarperCollins.

Blake, R. 2007. *Swift.* New York: Philomel.

Bloor, E. 1997. *Tangerine.* New York: Harcourt.

Bocarro, J. "A Long Walk Home." 2007. In *Chicken Soup for the Teenage Soul*, edited by Jack Canfield, Mark Victor Hansen, and Kimberly Kirberger. New York: Scholastic.

Brashares, A. 2003. *Sisterhood of the Traveling Pants.* Book 1. New York: Random House.

Bridges, S. Y. 2008. *The Umbrella Queen.* Illus. by Taeeun Yoo. New York: Greenwillow.

Bruchac, J. 2006. *Jim Thorpe: Original All-American.* New York: Dial.

Carbone, E. 2008. *Night Running, How James Escaped with the Help of His Faithful Dog.* Illus. by E. B. Lewis. New York: Knopf.

Cast, P. C., and K. Cast. 2007. *Marked: House of Night.* Book 1. New York: St. Martins Griffin.

Collins, S. 2008. *The Underland Chronicles.* Series. New York: Scholastic.

Cooper, F. 2008. *Willie and the All-Stars.* New York: Philomel.

Cunxin, L. 2007. *Dancing to Freedom.* Illus. by Anne Spudvilas. New York: Walker.

Cutler, J. 2009. *Guttersnipe.* Pictures by Emily Arnold McCully. New York: Farrar, Straus & Giroux.

D'Aulaire, I. 1992. "Apollo," "Pandora," "King Midas," "Sisyphus," and "Orpheus." In *D'Aulaire's Book of Greek Myths.* New York: Delacorte Books for Young Readers.

Deedy, C. A. 2000. *The Yellow Star: The Legend of King Christian X of Denmark.* Illus. by Henri Sorensen. Atlanta, GA: Peachtree.

Dessen, S. 2006. *The Truth About Forever.* New York: Speak.

Dickinson, E. 2000. "I started early, took my dog," "I'll tell you how the sun rose," "A narrow fellow in the grass," and "I never saw the moor." In *Poetry for Young People: Emily Dickinson.* New York: Scholastic.

Dygard, T. J. 1998. *Running Wild.* New York: Puffin.

Elliott, L. M. 2003. *Under a War Torn Sky.* New York: Hyperion.

Flake, S. 2004. *Begging for Change.* New York: Hyperion.

Fletcher, R. 2005. *Marshfield Dreams: When I Was a Kid.* New York: Henry Holt.

Fradin, D. B. 2008. *Duel! Burr and Hamilton's Deadly War of Words.* Illus. by Larry Day. New York: Walker.

Frank, A. 1997. *Diary of a Young Girl.* New York: Bantam.

George, J. C. 2008. *The Wolves Are Back.* Illus. by Wendell Minor. New York: Dutton.

Grimes, N. 2002. *Bronx Masquerade.* New York: Dial.

Harper, S. 2008. *The Juliet Club.* New York: Greenwillow.

Harrison, D. 2004. *Connecting the Dots: Poems of My Journey.* Honesdale, PA: Boyds Mills Press.

Horowitz, A. 2008. *Raven's Gate.* New York: Scholastic.

Hughes, L. 1974. "Merry-Go-Round." *Selected Poems: Langston Hughes.* New York: Vintage.

———. 1974. "Tell Me." *Selected Poems: Langston Hughes.* New York: Vintage.

———. 2006. "The Negro Speaks of Rivers," "Mother to Son," "Dream Variations," "The Dream keeper," "Merry-Go-Round," and "I dream a word." In *Poetry for Young People: Langston Hughes,* edited by D. Roessle and A. Rampersad. New York: Scholastic.

Innocenti, R. 1985. *Rose Blanche.* New York: Creative Paperbacks.

Kellogg, S. 1973. *The Island of the Skog.* New York: Dial Books.

Kerley, B. 2008. *What to Do About Alice?* Illus. by Edwin Fotheringham. New York: Scholastic.

Klass, D. 1994. *California Blue.* New York: Scholastic.

Kneece, M. 2009. *Rod Serliings' Twilight Zone: The Big Tall Wish,* illustrated by C. Lie. New York: Walker.

Krull, K. 1996. *Wilma Unlimited: How Wilma Rudolph Became the World's Fastest Woman.* Illus. by David Diaz. New York: Harcourt Voyager Book.

Larson, K., and M. Nethery. 2008. *Two Bobbies.* Illus. by Jean Cassels. New York: Walker.

Lasky, K. 2006. *A Voice of Her Own.* Illus. by Paul Lee. Cambridge, MA: Candlewick Press.

———. 2009. *Georgia Rises: A Day in the Life of Georgia O'Keeffe.* New York: Farrar, Strauss & Giroux.

Lee, M. 1997. *Nim and the War Effort.* Pictures by Yangsook Choi. New York: Farrar, Straus and Giroux.

———. 2006. *Landed.* Illus. by Yanksook Choi. New York: Farrar, Straus and Giroux.

McCarty, S. 2008. *Running Wild.* New York: Berkley Trade.

McCully, E. A. 2007. *The Escape of Oney Judge.* New York: Farrar, Straus & Giroux.

McGill, A. 1999. *Molly Bannaky.* Pictures by Chris K. Soentpiet. New York: Houghton Mifflin.

Medina, T. 2002. *Love to Langston.* Illus. by R. Gregory Christie. New York: Lee and Low.

Mercer, P. 2007. *There Come a Soldier.* Illus. by Ron Mazellan. New York: Handprint.

Meyer, S. 2005. *Twilight.* Boston: Little Brown.

———. 2006. *Twilight.* Boston: Little Brown Young Readers.

Miller, W. 1997. *Richard Wright and the Library Card.* Illus. by Gregory Christie. New York: Scholastic.

———. 2000. *The Piano.* Illus. by Susan Keeter. New York: Lee & Low Books.

Mochizuki, K. 1997. *Passage to Freedom: The Sugihara Story.* Illus. by Dom Lee. New York: Lee & Low Books.

Mohr, N. 1993. "Shoes for Hector." In *El Bronx Remembered.* New York: Harperteen.

Moss, M. 2001. *Rachel's Journal: The Story of a Pioneer Girl.* New York: Harcourt.

———. 2002. *Galen: My Life in Imperial Rome.* New York: Silver Whistle Books.

———. 2003. *Max's Logbook.* New York: Scholastic.

Myers, W. D. 1993. "History of My People." In *Soul Looks Back in Wonder*, collected by T. Feeling. New York: Dial.

———. 2000. *Malcolm X, A Fire Burning Brightly.* Illus. by Leonard Jenkins. New York: HarperCollins.

———. 2002. *Bad Boy: A Memoir.* New York: Amistad.

———. 2004. *I've Seen the Promised Land: The Life of Dr. Martin Luther King, Jr.* Illus. by Leonard Jenkins. New York: HarperCollins.

Myracle, L. 2004. *ttyl.* New York: Abrams Books.

Nivola, C. A. 2008. *Planting the Trees of Kenya.* New York: Farrar, Straus and Giroux.

Noble, T. H. 2006. *The Last Brother.* Illus. by Robert Papp. Ann Arbor, MI: Sleeping Bear Press.

Nolen, J. 2007. *Pitching in for Eubie.* Illus. by E. B. Lewis. New York: Amistad.

Paterson, K. 2004. *Bridge to Terabithia.* New York: HarperTeen.

Paulson, G. 1987. *Hatchet.* New York: Viking.

Pennypacker, S. 2009. *Sparrow Girl.* Illus. by Yoko Tanaka. New York: Hyperion Books.

Rappaport, D. 2004. *John's Secret Dreams.* Illus. by Bryan Collier. New York: Hyperion.

Roessle, D., and A. Rampersad, eds. 2006. *Poetry for Young People: Langston Hughes.* Illus. by Benny Andrews. New York: Scholastic.

Serling, R. 2008. *Twilight Zone.* Series. New York: Walker Books.

Shihab-Nye, N. 2000. "Secrets." In *Come with Me: Poems for a Journey.* New York: Greenwillow.

Skármeta, A. 2000. *The Composition.* Pictures by Alfonso Ruano. Toronto, ON: Groundwood.

Spinelli, J. 2003. *Milkweed.* New York: Random House.

Stanley, D. 2009. *Mozart, The Wonder Child.* New York: HarperCollins.

Stine, R. L. 1999. "Alien Candy," Nightmare Inn," "I'm Not Martin," and "The Black Mask." In *Nightmare Hour.* New York: HarperCollins.

Van Leeuwen, J. 2004. *Cabin on Trouble Creek.* New York: Penguin.

Watkins, Y. K. 1994. *So Far from the Bamboo Grove.* New York: HarperCollins.

Weatheford, C. B. 2007. *Birmingham, 1963.* Honesdale, PA: Wordsong.

———. 2007. *Jesse Owens, Fastest Man Alive.* Illus. by Eric Velasquez. New York: Walker.

———. 2008. *Becoming Billie Holiday.* Honesdale, PA, Wordsong.

———. 2008. *I, Matthew Henson, Polar Explorer.* Illus. by Eric Velasquez. New York: Walker.

Whelan, G. 2004. *Chu Ju's House.* New York: Scholastic.

White, B. 1993. "Porsche," "Instant Care," "Dead on the Road," "The Monkeys not Seen," and "Scary Moves." In *Mama Makes Up Her Mind and Other Dangers of Southern Living.* New York: Vintage.

Whitehead, K. 2008. *Art from Her Heart: Folk Artist Clementine Hunter.* Illus. by Shane W. Evans. New York: Putnam.

Williams, M. 2005. *Brothers in Hope.* Illus. by R. Gregory Christie. New York: Lee & Low Books.

Winter, J. 2005. *The Librarian of Basra.* New York: Harcourt.

Woodson, J. 2009. *Peace, Locomotion.* New York: Putnam.

Yezerski, T. F. 1988. *Together in Pinecone Patch.* New York: Farrar, Straus and Giroux.

Yoo, P. 2005. *Sixteen Years in Sixteen Seconds.* Illus. by Dom Lee. New York: Lee & Low Books.

Index

accountability, era of, 40
"Alien Candy" (Stine), 118
Allington, Richard, 15
aloud, reading writing, 179–81
Alphonso, Caroline, 259
"A narrow fellow in the grass" (Dickinson), 118
Anderson, Carl, 239
Anderson, Laurie H., 146, 212–13
Anne Frank (Frank), 35, 39
"Apollo" (d'Aulaire), 118
Armstrong, Sarah, 108
Art of Teaching Writing, The (Calkins), 56
artwork, stirring writing ideas with, 118
assessment. See evaluation
assignments
    writing at school for, 48
    writing outside of school for, 49
attitudes, teachers'
    in national survey on student writing, 8, 14–16
    in survey highlights, 15
    using survey results to affect teaching, 15–16
Atwell, Nancie, 239
Avi, 2

Bad Boy (Myers), 235
"Bam, Bam, Bam" (Merriam), 125
Bason, James J., 5
Baumann, James F., 5

BBC News Channel, 259
Becoming Billie Holiday (Boston), 146
Begging for Change (Flake), 150
behavior support interventions, conferring over, 242, 246–49
"Ben's Logbook," 210
"Best Practices in Teaching Planning" (Graham and Harris), 24, 25
"Best Practices in Teaching Writing to Adolescents" (Perin)
    on activities that gather and organize ideas, 131
    on benefits of collaboration, 168, 170, 177, 216, 263
    on importance of good writing models, 71
Best Practices in Writing Instruction (Graham, MacArthur, and Fitzgerald), 24, 25
"Beyond Writing Next" (Coker and Lewis), 93, 106–7, 185
Big Ten Revision Strategies, 176–83
Bird by Bird (Lamott), 162
Birmingham (Weatherford), 150
"Black Mask, The" (Stine), 118
blogging, 271–83
    anecdotal evidence about students', 2
    avoiding personal attacks and profanity, 273
    benefits of, 271–72
    as conversation of ideas, 276–80
    guidelines for use, 272, 273, 276
    in national survey on student writing, 8, 11–12

blogging (*continued*)
    survey results, 12, 299
    in "Ten Questions About Writing," 3
    tweaking, 272–76
    using survey results to affect teaching, 12
    writing of narratives that emerged from,
        280–83
Bloor, Edward, 150
Bocarro, Jason, 150
Bolin, Frances S., 72–73, 116–17, 118
books, writing about
    in national survey on student writing, 8,
        17–18
    survey results, 17–18, 299–300
    using survey results to affect teaching, 18
Boston, Carole, 146
brainstorming, 132–35
    allowing conversations, 132–33
    having partners pose questions in, 133, 134
    interventions and scaffolds for, 246
    posing questions yourself in, 133, 135,
        136–37
    with revision, 181
Bridge to Terabithia (Paterson), 121, 123,
    301–5
Bronx Masquerade (Grimes), 18, 62–66, 68
Bruchac, Joseph, 146
Buckner, Aimee, 119
Build self-confidence with a conference, form,
    217
"Bullseye Operation, The," 228, 229

Cabin on Trouble Creek (Van Leeuwen), 93, 96,
    121, 123, 306–12
California Blue (Klass), 235
Calkins, Lucy, 41, 56, 113
Cassel-Bonilla, Leslee, 175
Cast, Kristen, 260, 263
Cast, P.C., 260, 263
challenges, as issue for writing, 77

change and loss, as issue for writing, 77
Chin, Jared, 32
Chin, Ting, 32, 254
choice
    as condition for writing, 105
    free, value of, 57–58
    as issue for writing, 77
    in revision, 170–74
    in setting writing criteria, 161–62
    in writing instruction, value of, 26, 32–33
Coker, David, 93, 106–7, 185
collaboration, 263–71
    on a mentor text lesson, 265–67
    on writing dialogue, 267–69
    writing possibilities, collaborative, 269–71
Collins, Suzanne, 2
Common Core State Standards Initiative, 291
compelling questions, 79–93, 94, 95
    about obstacles, 83
    demonstrating the process, 79–81
    for fifth grade biography unit, 81–84
    leading to fiction, 89, 90, 93
    as leading to plans and drafts, 84–89
    leading to poetry, 89, 90, 91–92
    personal experiences, students' views on
        writing about, 85, 88–89
    reading-writing units, questions about,
        83–84
    value of, 81
"Computer," 132–33
computers, use of
    in national survey on student writing, 8,
        16–17
    survey results, 16–17, 297–99
    using survey results to affect teaching, 17
Conceptual Age, 43
conferring, 198–252
    to add details, 220–21, 222, 223
    as assessment, 199
    benefits of, 199–201

to check notes, 235–37
to discuss grading, 228, 229–34
to discuss self-evaluation, 228, 229–34, 237–39
empathy, exercising, 200–201
with evaluations of writing stages and behavior support interventions, 242, 246–49
guidelines for teacher-student conferences, 202, 203–6
and guiding writing process through email, 239–42, 243, 244–45
improving writing conventions by, 226–28, 229
learning from students' writing, 219, 249–52
to listen and follow students' leads, 221, 222, 223–24
"making the rounds" conferring (see "making the rounds" conferring)
pair conferences, 216, 218
to revise genre structure, 225–26
in revision, 182
scheduled conferences (see scheduled conferences)
students collaborating, 202
students seeing themselves reflected back, 200
student-to-student conferring, benefits of, 201–2
teachers seeing teaching reflected back, 199
using feedback to confer with students, 54–55
writing conference, form, 215, 217
"Confessions of a Broken Soul," 30
conflict, as issue for writing, 78
conformity, as issue for writing, 79
Connecting the Dots (Harrison), 89, 129, 160
content
    asking questions with, 185
    as attention grabber, 53

conventions, writing, 53–54
coping with fears, as issue for writing, 77
craft, collaborative possibilities with, 270
Cramer, Ronald L., 201
criteria
    attributes common in all genres, naming, 161–62
    for autobiographical poems, sample, 160
    deciding what students revise, 170–74
    for eighth-grade memoir or personal essay, 163
    fiction and nonfiction, 162–64
    for fifth-grade journal entries, 163
    as more valuable than rubrics, 159–61
    negotiating, 158–59, 161–62
    responding and grading fairly with, 165
    revision, 174–75
    setting, 157–74
    for seventh-grade persuasive essay, 164
    turning in all phases, benefits of, 165–74
    value of, 158–60
curriculum
    conditions for teaching middle school writers, 104–7
    development of writing, 40–41
    problem-solving approach, embracing, 58
    reframing a writing curriculum for middle school students, 284, 285–87
    revisiting, 56–58
    writing process approach, using a, 56–57

Daane, Mary C., 41
D'Aulaire, Ingri, 118
D'Aulaires' Book of Greek Myths (d'Aulaire), 118
"Dead on the Road" (White), 118
decisions, as issue for writing, 77
demonstrations, presenting explicit, 114–15
details, using conferences to add, 220–21, 222, 223
dialogue, collaboration on writing, 267–69

Dickinson, Emily, 72–73, 116–17, 118, 143

discussions, procedure for, 83

"Distant Snow Dropping," 221, 224–25

drafting, interventions and scaffolds for, 247

"Dream Keeper, The" (Hughes), 118

dreams, as issue for writing, 78

"Dream Variations" (Hughes), 118

Duke, Nell, 4, 5

ease of writing in the writing plan, 193, 194

editing
    interventions and scaffolds for, 248
    learning from students' writing, 193–97
    lessons, sample, 187–92
    paragraphing, lesson on, 187–88
    procedures for, 175
    purpose of, 182–83
    questions and prompts for positive confer-
        ring, 204–5
    run-on sentences, lesson on, 188–90
    sentence fragments, lesson on, 190–91
    sentence openings, lesson on, 191–92
    separating revision from, 176
    using questions to edit, 181

educational philosophy, need to name,
    127–28

Elbow, Peter, 41, 162

Eleven Ways to Reach Middle School Writers,
    286–87

Elliot, Laura, 263

email
    conferring and guiding writing process
        through, 239–42, 243, 244–45
    in "Ten Questions About Writing," 3

endings
    analyzing, 152–53
    satisfying, 152

essays
    criteria for eighth-grade memoir or personal
        essay, 163

criteria for seventh-grade persuasive essay,
    164

planning analytical, 211

questions and prompts for positive confer-
    ring, 204–5

writing at school, 48

writing outside of school, 49

evaluation
    conferring as, 199
    conferring to discuss grading, 228, 229–34
    criteria, responding and grading fairly with,
        165
    grades, discouraging students with, 161
    research on writing, 40–41
    self-evaluation, using criteria for (see
        self-evaluation)
    tests (see tests)
    two grades, use of, 165–74

"Everything Happens for a Reason," 225

Facebook, 253

fan fiction, 2
    anecdotal evidence about students' writing,
        2
    in "Ten Questions About Writing," 3

"Fantasy," 168, 171–72, 173

fast writes
    as leading to fiction, 89, 90
    on sharing your life with an audience, 85,
        86–87, 88

Faulkner, William, 129

Feeling, Tom, 146

fiction
    compelling questions leading to, 89, 90, 93
    criteria, 162–64

"First Friendships," 177, 178–79

"First Grade" (Medina), 37

Fitzgerald, Jill, 24, 25

Five Minds for the Future (Gardner), 44–45,
    106, 264–65

Flake, Sharon G., 150

Fletcher, Ralph, 119, 163, 265–67

focusing ideas, interventions and scaffolds for, 246

folksongs used as mentor texts, 125–26

formulaic, writing instruction as, 40

Frank, Anne, 35, 38–39

Frye, Andrew, 175, 272, 273, 276, 280

Galen (Moss), 146, 163

Gardner, Howard, 41, 44–45, 58, 106, 264–65

gender

    differences in writing, 2–3, 9

    issues in "Ten Questions About Writing," questions about, 21

    treatment of, in national survey, 6–7

genres

    collaborative possibilities with, 269

    structure, using conferences to revise, 225–26

    writing in different, 83–84

Georgia Rises (Lasky), 146

goal setting

    interventions and scaffolds for, 249

    by students, 237

Goethe, Johann, 52

Graham, Steve

    "Best Practices in Teaching Planning," 24, 25

    "What We Know, What We Still Need to Know," 107

    Writing Better, 131, 168, 170

    Writing Next (see *Writing Next* (Graham and Perin))

Graves, Donald, 14, 41, 56, 113, 114

Grimes, Nikki, 18, 62–66, 68

Guidelines for Teacher-Student Conferences, 203–4

Harper, Suzanne, 149

Harris, Karen R., 24, 25, 131, 168, 170

Harrison, David, 89, 129, 130, 160

Hatchet (Paulsen), 190

"Heartbreak Phonecall, The," 241, 244–45

Hembroff, Larry, 4, 7, 291

"History of My People" (Myers), 146

hope, as condition for writing, 106

hopes and dreams, as issue for writing, 78

Hughes, Langston, 35, 36, 37–38, 118, 143

"I, Too" (Hughes), 37

identity shaping, as issue for writing, 78

"I Dream a World" (Hughes), 118

"I had to" writing, 255

"I'll tell you how the sun rose" (Dickinson), 118

"I'm Not Martin" (Stine), 118

"In Between Faces," 68, 70

independent reading as mentor text, using, 267

Individual Educational Plan (IEP), 166–70

"I never saw the moor" (Dickinson), 118

Information Age, 43

Ingredients for Reshaping a Writing Curriculum, 56, 57

"In High School" (Medina), 37

inner and outer influences, as issue for writing, 77–78

Innocenti, Roberto, 276, 280

inquiry

    as condition for writing, 105

    with mentor texts, 66–74

insights into self, as issue for writing, 77

"Instant Care" (White), 118

Instant Message (IM), in adolescent lives, 253–55, 290

Instruction and Assessment for Struggling Writers (Troia), 242

Instructor, 107

"Invisible Me," 30

"I started early, took my dog" (Dickinson), 118

"Jim Crow Row" (Medina), 37

Jim Thorpe (Bruchac), 146

Jin, Ying, 41

journals

    anecdotal evidence about students' writing, 2

    criteria for fifth-grade journal entries, 163

    in national survey on student writing, 8, 10–11

    survey findings, 11, 294–95

    in "Ten Questions About Writing," 3

    using survey results to affect teaching, 11

"Juba Dance," 125

Juliet Club, The (Harper), 149

Kesler, Cheri, 81–84, 120–21, 133, 135, 147–48, 154, 207

Kiernan-Robb, Ann, 24, 89, 90, 93, 273, 283

"King Midas" (d'Aulaire), 118

Kittle, Penny, 14

Klass, David, 235

Kneece, Mark, 2

Krull, Kathleen, 82, 153

Lamott, Anne, 162

Landed (Lee), 153

Language Arts Journal, online, 273, 275

Lasky, Kathryn, 146, 183–84

"Last Leaf on the Tree, The," 30

Lawrence, D.H., 26

leads

    enticing readers with, 149–51

    structure of lessons on writing, 148–49

    studying essence of, 147–49

Learning by Teaching (Murray), 162

learning communities, forming professional, 288–90

Lee, Milly, 153

Lessing, Doris, 56

lessons, 124–56

    allowing conversations, 132–33

    brainstorming, 132–35

    changing telling to showing, 144

    craft and technique, 130–42

    endings, crafting satisfying (see endings)

    finding topics, 131–32

    having partners pose questions, 133, 134

    leads (see leads)

    pair practice, 144

    philosophy, need to name, 127–28

    planning, 135, 137–38, 139

    posing questions yourself, 133, 135, 136–37

    prewriting stage, 131–42

    professional writers, starting with, 147–48

    reading lessons as informing writing lessons, 128–30

    student writing, learning from, 154–56

    teacher demonstration, 143–44

    writing craft lessons, 142–44

    written plans, use of, 138–39, 141–42

Lewis, William L., 93, 106–7, 185

Linguistics Association of Canada and the United States, 259

Literature as Exploration (Rosenblatt), 68

"Long Walk Home, A" (Bocarro), 150

loss, as issue for writing, 77

Love to Langston (Medina), 35, 37

Lowry, Lois, 107–8

Lunsford, Andrea, 259, 270, 280

MacArthur, Charles A., 24, 25

"making the rounds" conferring, 202, 206–13

with eighth grade, 209–13

with fifth grade, 207–9

Mama Makes Up Her Mind (White), 129, 280–81

Marked (Cast and Cast), 260, 263

Marshfield Dreams (Fletcher), 163, 265–67

Max's Logbook (Moss), 209, 212

McKissack, Patricia, 147

Medina, Tony, 35, 37

memoirs, criteria for eighth-grade, 163

mentor texts, 63–102

    analyzing, 72–75

    collaboration on lesson, 265–67

    compelling questions (see compelling questions)

    defined, 51

    guidelines for using, 68, 70–71

    inquiry with, 66–74

    issues that connect to students' lives, 75–79

    leads (see leads)

    organizing instruction, 66–68, 69, 70

    planning reading and writing units together, 74–75

    questioning techniques, 73–74

    reading-writing units, questions about, 83–84

    sources of, 71

    student writing, learning from, 93, 96–101

    turning process over to students, importance of, 73–75

    use of folksongs as, 125–26

    using independent reading as, 267

    value of, 63

Merriam, Eve, 125

"Merry-Go-Round" (Hughes), 37, 38, 118

Meyer, Stephenie, 260, 261

Miami Herald, 165

Michener, James, 26

Milkweed (Spinelli), 149

Mochizuki, Ken, 149

modeling

    in "Ten Questions About Writing," teacher, 22

    with thinking and talking about a poem, 36–37

Mohr, Nicholas, 263–64

"Monkeys Not Seen, The" (White), 118

"Moonlight Sonata," 30

Moss, Marissa, 146, 163, 209, 212

"Mother to Son" (Hughes), 118

motivation, use of high-interest questions for, 36

Murray, Donald, 14, 41, 162

Murray, Wendy, 4, 291

"Music of the Night," 30

Myers, Walter Dean, 128, 146, 235

"My Secret," 68, 69

narrative

    questions and prompts for positive conferring, 204

    that emerged from blogs, writing of, 280–83

National Assessment of Educational Progress (NAEP), 106–7

National Commission on Writing, 106–7

National Council of Teachers of English (NCTM), 41, 43, 107, 291

national survey

    administration, 6–7

    categories, 7, 8

    designing, 5–6

    questions generated by, 19

    results, 7, 9

    statistical analysis of, 291–300

National Writing Project, 40

Nation's Report Card, The (Persky, Daane and Yin), 41

"Needs Help," 216

negotiating

    criteria, 158–59, 161–62

    with mentor texts, 67–68

    with students, 120–21

"Negro Speaks of Rivers, The" (Hughes), 118, 143

Newbery Award, 93

Newkirk, Bob, 14

"Night, The" (Selzer), 155

Nightmare Hour (Stine), 118

"Nightmare Inn" (Stine), 118

nonconformity, as issue for writing, 79

nonfiction criteria, 162–64

Northrup, Thomas, 30, 31

"Not a Statistic," 93, 94–95

Notebook Know-How (Buckner), 119

note taking, in conferences, 214

Nothing but the Truth (Avi), 2

nouns

    best, developing lists of, 146

    specific, 145, 146

numbering strategy, 181

obstacles

    compelling questions about, 83

    to selfhood, as issue for writing, 78

100 Quickwrites (Rief), 119

On Writing Well (Zinsser), 162

opinions, writing outside of school to express, 49

orally reading writing, 179–81

"Orpheus" (d'Aulaire), 118

out loud, reading writing, 179–81

Paint Pictures with Stong Verbs and Specific Nouns lesson, 145–46

pair practice, 144

"Pandora" (d'Aulaire), 118

paragraphing, editing lesson on, 187–88

Passage to Freedom (Mochizuki), 149

Paterson, Katherine, 93, 106, 121, 123

    plans by, 135, 301–5

Paulsen, Gary, 105, 190

Peace, Locomotion (Woodson), 150

Peer Evaluation, form, 181

peer readers, 168–70

Perin, Dolores

    "Best Practices in Teaching Writing to Adolescents" (see "Best Practices in Teaching Writing to Adolescents" (Perin))

    "What We Know, What We Still Need to Know," 107

    Writing Next (see *Writing Next* (Graham and Perin))

Persky, Hillary R., 41

personal experiences, students' views on writing about, 85, 88–89

personal study

    early and recent pieces of students' writing, comparing, 52–54

    guidelines for, 52–56

    professional study, invitations for, 55–56

    using feedback to confer with students, 54–55

    of writing instruction, 40–41, 50–56

Phi Delta Kappan, 15

philosophy, need to name, 127–28

Pink, Daniel, 41, 43, 58, 216, 264–65

Pitts, Leonard, 164, 165

planning

    interventions and scaffolds for, 247

    lessons, 135, 137–38, 139

    with mentor texts, planning reading and writing units together, 74–75

    a reading and writing unit, sample, 129–30

    rereading plans with revision, 181

    student writing, learning from, 93, 96–101

    writing before drafting, importance of planning, 93, 96

    writing plan for a dialogue, 268

    written plans, use of, 138–39, 141–42

Planning an Analytical Essay, 211

Planning Your Writing, form, 122

Plester, Beverly, 259

poetry

compelling questions leading to, 89, 90, 91–92

criteria for autobiographical poems, sample, 160

questions and prompts for positive conferring, 204

for students, list of, 37

in "Ten Questions About Writing," 3

thinking and talking about a poem, Think Aloud on, 36–38

writing outside of school, 30–31

Poetry for Young People: Emily Dickinson (Bolin), 72–73, 116–17, 118

Poetry for Young People: Langston Hughes (Roessel and Rampersad), 37, 118

"Porche" (White), 118

pressures, as issue for writing, 77

prewriting questions and prompts for positive conferring, 204

process approach, 106–7

revising writing curriculum through, 56–57

routines for keeping track of process, 119–20

scaffold and intervention chart for, 243, 246–49

stages, negotiating, 120–21

profanity while blogging, avoiding, 273

professional development workshops, 109

professional learning communities (PLCs), 40, 288–90

professional study

among teachers, 109

improving students' writing through, 55–56

prompts, in writing at school, 48

publishing students' work, 176

Pulitzer Prize, 26

questions

motivation, use of high-interest questions for, 36

as revision strategy, 181, 183–86

techniques, questioning, 73–74

using, to edit, 181

writing outside of school to answer, 49

Questions and Prompts for Positive Conferring, 204–6

quick consults, with scheduled conferences, 216

Rampersad, Arnold, 37, 118

Read Alouds, used with mentor texts, 65

Reader, the Text, the Poem, The (Rosenblatt), 68

reader response theory, 68, 70–71

reading

introducing texting into curriculum, 259–63

with mentor texts, planning reading and writing units together, 74–75

Reasons Adolescents Write Outside of School, The, 47, 49

Reasons and Purposes for Writing at School, The, 47, 48

"Rebel Angels," 30

rebellions, as issue for writing, 79

relationships, as issue for writing, 77

relevance, as condition for writing, 105

Rella, Kate, 244

Renzi, Lauie, 212

research, on improving instruction, 40–45

Research on textisms presented at the British Psychological Society's Developmental Section Annual Conference, 259

responsibility as condition for writing, 106

rest, letting writing, 179

restrictions, as issue for writing, 79

revision

asking questions as strategy for, 181, 183–86

revision (*continued*)

    choice in, 170–74

    collaborative possibilities with, 271

    content and style, questions for, 185

    criteria, 174–75

    deciding what students revise, 170–74

    interventions and scaffolds for, 248

    learning from students' writing, 193–97

    procedures for, 175

    questions and prompts for positive confer-ring, 204–5

    revising genre structure in conferences, 225–26

    separating editing from, 176

    strategies, 176–83

    teacher feedback for, 177

    using numbering strategy, 181

    using questions to revise, 181

    writing convention, questions for, 185

rewriting

    parts related to criteria, 181–82

    sentences to rewrite, 144

Rief, Linda, 119, 239

Robb, Laura, 147

Rodriguez, Michael, 85

Roessel, David, 37, 118

Rose Blanche (Innocenti), 276, 280

Rosenblatt, Louise, 68

Rose's Journal (Moss), 163

routines, 103–23

    conditions for teaching middle school writers, 104–7

    demonstrations, presenting explicit, 114–15

    for keeping track of process, 119–20

    for managing time, 113–21

    for negotiating with students, 120–21

    process approach to writing, 106–7

    professional writers, learning from, 121–23

    schedule, posting and reviewing, 114

    for stirring writing ideas, 118–19

    test prep, writing as being, 107–11

    truths about successful writing instruction, 111–12

    what teachers do while students write, 119–20

    writer's notebooks, using, 116–19

    writing time, reserving, 115–16

    writing workshop, adjusting routines with, 112–13

Routman, Regie, 239

rubrics

    disadvantages of, 160–61

    use of, 159–60

rules, as issue for writing, 79

run-on sentences, editing lesson on, 188–90

Scaffold And Intervention Chart for Process Writing Stages, 243, 246–49

scaffolding

    scaffold and intervention chart for process writing, 243, 246–49

    by writing and thinking aloud, 183–84

Scars, 60

"Scary Movies" (White), 118

Schain, Katy, 52

scheduled conferences, 213–16

    keeping other students engaged, 214

    note taking, 214

    opening, 214

    preparation, 213–14

    quick consults, 216

"Scream," 28

self-discovery by adolescents, 103–4

self-evaluation

    conferring to discuss, 228, 229–34, 237–39

    interventions and scaffolds for, 249

    using criteria for, 181

Self Evaluation of Choice Writing, 168, 173

self-regulation by students, 237, 249

Selzer, Ned, 155, 156

sentence fragments, editing lesson on, 190–91

sentence openings, editing lesson on, 191–92

Serling, Rod, 2

"Shoes for Hector" (Mohr), 263–64

short texts, stirring writing ideas with, 118

Show, Don't Tell lesson, 142–44

Sisterhood of the Traveling Pants (Brashares), 2

"Sisyphus" (d'Aulaire), 118

Smith, Jenny, 45, 85, 89

Social Responsibility Club, 44

So Far from the Bamboo Grove (Watkins), 193

Soul Looks Back in Wonder (Feeling), 146

Speak (Anderson), 212–13

Spinelli, Jerry, 149

Stanford Study on Writing, 270

statistical terms, 293

Stine, R.L., 118

stories

    anecdotal evidence about students' writing, 2

    in national survey, student writing of, 8–9

    in "Ten Questions About Writing," 3

    writing outside of school, 28

strategies, Big Ten Revision Strategies, 176–83

struggling writers, supporting, 24–25

students

    collaboration by, 202

    improving writing by talking to, 40–41, 45–50

    issues that connect to students' lives, 75–79

    in National Survey, student writing (see national survey)

    needs of middle school students, honoring, 57–58

    in "Ten Questions About Writing," student writing (see "Ten Questions About Writing")

style

    asking questions with, 185

    as attention grabber, 53

"Summer Night," 230, 231–33

"Survey Research" (Baumann and Bason), 5

Tagliamonte, Sali, 259

Talbot, Hudson, 152

Tangerine (Bloor), 150

teamwork, as condition for writing, 105

technique, collaborative possibilities with, 270

Tedesco, Carolyn, 45

"Tell Me" (Hughes), 36

"Ten Questions About Writing," 2–5, 7–8

    administration, 20–22

    development, 19–20

    gender issues, questions about, 21

    instruction, questions about, 20

    stepping into students' writing lives, questions about, 20

    student responses, 21–24

Ten Ways to Gather Support as You Grow and Change, 287

tests

    focusing on, 40

    test prep, writing as being, 107–11

    writing at school for, 48

    writing outside of school for, 49

texting, 257–63

    anecdotal evidence about students' use of, 2

    benefits of, 263

    introducing, into curriculum, 259–63

    research on, 259

    students interviewed about, 257–59

    in "Ten Questions About Writing," 3

    as writing, 258–59

Texting helps teens' grammar (Alphonso), 259

"The Good, the Bad, and the Beating," 212

Think Alouds

    on thinking and talking about a poem, 36–38

    writing endings with, 152–53

time, routines for managing, 113–21

topics
  finding, 131–32
  interventions and scaffolds for, 243
  value of powerful, 53
Translating part of a book to a news story,
      193, 195
Troia, Gary A., 242
Twilight (Meyer), 260, 261
Twilight Zone, The (Serling), 2

Under a War-Torn Sky (Elliot), 263
Underland Chronicles (Collins), 2
United States Board on Books for Young
      People (USBBY), 106

Van Leeuwen, Jan, 93, 96, 121, 123
  plans by, 135, 306–12
verbs
  best, developing lists of, 146
  strong, 145, 146
Volpicella, Douglas, 85
Vonnegut, Kurt, 135

war, as issue for writing, 78
Watkins, Yoko K., 193
Weatherford, Carole B., 150
websites, stirring writing ideas with, 118
"What has happened to my beloved earth?", 30
"What I've Learned About Effective Reading
      Instruction" (Allington), 15
"What We Know, What We Still Need to
      Know" (Graham and Perin), 107
White, Bailey, 118, 129, 130, 280–81
Whole New Mind, A (Pink), 43, 216, 264–65
Williams, Brian, 85
Wilma Unlimited (Krull), 82, 153
Wintergirls (Anderson), 146
"Wishing for Death," 255
Woodson, Jacqueline, 150

workshop model
  adjusting routines, 112–13
  for reading and writing connections, 106
writers
  professional, learning from, 121–23
  struggling, supporting, 24–25
Writer's Notebook, A (Fletcher), 119
writer's notebooks
  books about, 119
  using, 116–19
Write to Learn (Murray), 162
writing
  conferences (see conferring)
  criteria (see criteria)
  current teaching practice, 40–41
  endings, crafting satisfying (see endings)
  gender differences in, 2–3
  improving students' (see writing, improving
      students')
  introducing texting into curriculum,
      259–63
  issues that connect to students' lives, 75–79
  with mentor texts, planning reading and
      writing units together, 74–75
  national survey of student (see national
      survey)
  as need, 4
  out-of-class, by students (see writing out-
      side of school)
  process approach to, 106–7
  reframing writing curriculum for middle
      school students, 284, 285–87
  at school (see writing at school)
  in "Ten Questions About Writing" (see "Ten
      Questions About Writing")
  truths about successful writing instruction,
      111–12
  what teachers do while students write,
      119–20

Writing (Graves), 56, 114
writing, improving students', 34–61
  debriefing demonstration lesson, 38–39
  demonstration lesson, 36–38
  learning from students' writing, 59–61
  needs of middle school students, honoring,
    57–58
  personal study (see personal study)
  problem-solving approach, embracing, 58
  research on, 40–45
  students, improving writing by talking to,
    40–41, 45–50
  teaching craft and technique for, 50
Writing About Your Life (Zinsser), 162
"Writing: A Powerful Message from State
    Government" (National Commission on
    Writing), 107
"Writing: A Ticket to Work . . . or a Ticket Out"
    (National Commission on Writing), 107
writing at school
  from adolescent student's perspective,
    254–57, 290
  in national survey on student writing, 8,
    12–14
  reasons and purposes for, 47–48
  survey results, 13–14, 296–97
  using survey results to affect teaching, 14
Writing Better (Graham and Harris), 24, 25,
    131, 168, 170
Writing Conference, form, 214, 215, 217
writing conferences. See conferring
writing conventions
  editing for, 182–83

improving, by conferring, 226–28, 229
writing criteria. See criteria
Writing Next (Graham and Perin), 58, 107,
    291
  on benefits of collaboration, 216
  goal setting by students, effectiveness of,
    159
  in improving writing achievement, 56
  on improving writing achievement, 41–42,
    43
  teachers' growth, facilitating, 52
  on value of knowing how to write effec-
    tively, 174
Writing Now (National Council of Teachers of
    English), 41, 43, 107, 291
writing outside of school
  anecdotal evidence about, 11–12
  in national survey on student writing, 7–10
  reasons and purposes for, 48–49
  students who write outside of school, snap-
    shots of, 26–32
  survey findings, 9, 292–94
  using survey results to affect teaching, 9–10
writing stages, conferring over assessments of,
    242, 246–49
Writing With Power (Elbow), 162
writing workshop
  adjusting routines, 112–13
  value of, 106

"Young Champs," 281, 282

Zinsser, William, 162